THE VETRI CUCINA BREAD PROGRAM began over a decade ago and has been part of the American movement to reclaim high-quality bread as a cornerstone of our food culture. In *Mastering Bread*, Marc Vetri and his former head baker, Claire Kopp McWilliams, show home cooks how to create simple breads with unique flavors in a home oven.

Included are more than seventy recipes for their bestselling sourdough and yeast loaves as well as accompaniments to serve with the breads. Their process of bread-making is broken down into three easy-to-digest chapters: Mix, Shape, and Bake. Another chapter includes recipes for enjoying bread in dishes such as Bruschetta, Panzanella, and Ribollita. There's even a bonus chapter revealing the secrets of Vetri's coveted Panettone. This book shares everything that Vetri and McWilliams have learned over the years about the art and science of making incredible bread. They explain how to use fresh milled and whole-grain flours as well as local and regional wheat varieties, with easy instructions for adapting bread recipes for success with whatever flour is available in your market. Included throughout are bios and interviews with grain farmers, millers, and bread bakers from around the nation.

MASTERING BREAD

THE ART AND PRACTICE OF
HANDMADE SOURDOUGH, YEAST BREAD, AND PASTRY

———

MASTERING BREAD

———

MARC VETRI and CLAIRE KOPP McWILLIAMS

with David Joachim

Photography by Ed Anderson

TEN SPEED PRESS
California | New York

To our grain chain around Philadelphia and around the country, including the farmers, millers, and bakers who are making better grains, flours, and breads available, as well as the people who are seeking out, baking, and eating more wholesome loaves.

CONTENTS

RECIPE LIST

OUR DAILY BREAD MATTERS

"Without imperfection, you or I would not exist."
—STEPHEN HAWKING, THEORETICAL PHYSICIST

WHEN I OPENED VETRI IN 1998, I spent a lot of time shopping. Once a week, I went down to the vegetable market near the Philly sports stadiums, picked up fresh fish from Samuels and Sons, and stopped by the Italian market on 9th Street. Emilio Mignucci was always there, and he'd fill me up with the best cheeses from Italy. I usually got parking tickets, but it was so worth it to see and taste what I was buying.

I always got my 00 flour at Di Brunos. They had the blue bag of Gran Mugnaio that I recognized, the one that I had used in New York when I was the chef at Bella Blu. I didn't know much about flour then. I just knew that my pasta was good, and this was the stuff that I used. Nothing else really mattered.

I didn't know that much of the wheat in that bag was probably imported from America, ground into 00 flour in Italy, and sold back to us. I didn't know that "00" really only means that it's ground super-fine; it has nothing to do with protein content or how fresh it is. That flour had probably been ground and bagged up months if not a year before I bought it. But it didn't matter. That was the flour I knew, the flour I was used to.

Around the same time, I started buying produce from Green Meadow Farm. The farmer, Glen Brendle, was a big, burly man. He would gather local vegetables, fruits, dairy, and meat from the Amish farmers around Lancaster and truck it to the city. Thursdays became my favorite day of the week, when Glen's truck rolled up with some of the best food from southeastern Pennsylvania. He had a list of everything that he had faxed—yes, faxed—to us on Mondays. We had to fax back our requests by Monday night for Thursday delivery. He always had freshly milled flour on the list, but it wasn't my 00 flour in the blue bag from Italy, so I never ordered it.

For the next ten to fifteen years, restaurants evolved, and a new term, "farm to table," became code for a serious chef who was truly in tune with the landscape of his or her area. Better and better products were becoming available. Farmers were raising more animals on pasture, and fisheries were fishing more sustainably. Since then, understanding the impact of our food choices on the environment and being champions of a sustainable ecosystem have been of the utmost importance to chefs. I am willing to spend more on a pig that's raised on mother's milk or fed apples and acorns. Give me that beautiful line-caught fish. Take my money. Hand over that grass-fed beef and that axis venison that roamed free on a ranch.

In the past two decades, and especially during the pandemic of 2020, the whole world's awareness of food has grown tremendously. If you care about where your food comes from, what's in it, and the consequences of what you cook and eat, you pay attention to your choices. And there are so many great choices available today. From heirloom tomatoes to organic milk, it has become easier than ever to buy food that is more flavorful, better for the environment, and better for our health. Everything has evolved. Except for one thing . . . flour.

The truth is, most American flour is still stuck in the 1950s. At home, most people reach for a bag of refined all-purpose flour. At restaurants, some very talented chefs go to great lengths to source premium vegetables, fish, and meats, but they make breads, desserts, and pastas with flour that is so old and processed that it has lost almost all its flavor. Not to mention the impact of massive commodity wheat crops on our soils. And our health.

But all that is changing. Better flour is becoming more available. By changing this one basic ingredient—flour—the flavor and quality of pastas, breads, and pastries improves dramatically. Boom! Just like that.

That's why we wrote this book. It seems that now, more than ever, people are rediscovering the joys of baking bread, and we are so excited to share these incredible breads with you! We show you everything we've learned about baking bread with fresh flour. . . . the recipes, the techniques, the little tricks . . . everything. It's not hard. These days, lots of farmers and millers are selling fresh flour (see page 284 for a regional directory). Or you could buy whole grains at your local grocery store and grind them in your own kitchen. It's like grinding whole beans for coffee. Anyone can do it. There are all kinds of affordable stone mills available today, and some even attach to your average stand mixer.

There's nothing like freshly baked bread and pastries made with fresh flour. They taste so good! The best part is that at Vetri, all our breads are baked in a regular home oven. No fancy equipment. So, if you're new to baking,

please don't be intimidated. All you need is an oven. Start with an easy dough and bake a simple pan loaf, like Potato Bread (page 110). If you have a baking stone and a little experience, try a bread like Artichoke Fougasse (page 87) or Olive Oil Durum Rolls (page 121). If you're already in the sourdough habit, dig in to Omni Bread (page 169) or Chocolate Rye Sourdough (page 189). There's a lot to explore here.

We organized the bread chapters from easiest to hardest, starting with simple yeast breads, moving on to enriched yeast breads, then sourdough breads, and finally enriched sourdough breads that tend to be a little trickier. We also use freshly milled and whole-grain flours in quick pastries like Hazelbutter Cookies (page 224) and Lemon Durum Cake (page 215). And we didn't limit the book to bread alone. The Eat chapter includes recipes for foods made with leftover bread, like Panzanella (page 246), and foods that go well with bread, like Cultured Butter (page 264). Ever try making your own butter? It's not hard and it's the best thing on freshly baked bread. And finally, if you're already a serious baker, try our recipe for Panettone alla Vetri (page 275). This is by far the most challenging and rewarding bread you'll ever make. That's why we devote an entire chapter to it.

In *Mastering Bread*, there are chapters detailing each step of the bread-making process: mix, shape, and bake. We also explain the science of fermentation in its own chapter, so you get a sense of what's going on inside bread dough from the moment you start mixing. But bread science is only useful if it helps you make a better loaf. Honestly, the best way to understand all that invisible alchemy is to get in there and do it. That's why we included a huge variety of breads—more than fifty-five recipes that demonstrate all the basic principles. Some quick and easy breads use dry yeast and are ready the same day. Some use sourdough starter and develop deep flavor over a long, cool fermentation period of one to two days. We included an "active time" estimate in every recipe so you get a sense of how long things will take. Most of the breads don't require much actual hands-on work; they just take time to ferment while you can do other things. Best of all, none of these breads requires traditional kneading. You can mix our doughs in a machine or by hand, and when you're hand-mixing, a few folds are usually all it takes for the dough to come together. Whether you're new to bread making or a seasoned baker, don't worry too much about things being perfect. Mastering bread is not about perfection. Imperfection can be beautiful! It's about paying attention and being open to constant improvement. Maybe read a little about the principles, then bake some loaves. Read, bake, and then repeat. The bread you make will be worth it. Fresh bread can be so incredibly satisfying to make and eat, especially when you share it.

Sharing has been one of the best things about writing this book. Our focus on better flour has connected us to an entire community of farmers, millers, and bakers in our region and around the country. There's a whole world of people out there improving the quality of American wheat and trying to make better bread. Look for their stories throughout the book. These relationships and people have been life-changing for us, and we want to share them with you.

There's no doubt that the pandemic of 2020 caused all kinds of changes all over the globe. But during the many disruptions, there was another seismic shift quietly taking place, one that began many years ago. In America, at least, we are living through a big change in one of our most fundamental American foods—our amber waves of grain. Better, healthier, more flavorful, more nutritious wheat is becoming more available to everyone. Wheat was the first food that our country centralized, industrialized, and produced on a massive scale. Mass-produced bread soon followed. But, as we've learned with tomatoes and countless other foods, industrialization isn't always the best thing for our soil, our water, our food, and our bodies. Growing food is different from manufacturing cars—because we eat food. Flavor matters. Less processing matters. Nutrition matters. Entire civilizations were founded on wholesome grains and breads. Our daily bread is worth caring more about—especially now. It's comforting to know that even during tough times, when you might not be able to find dry yeast or bread flour in stores, you can always bake nourishing loaves with sourdough starter and freshly milled grains.

All these years later, I still buy produce from Glen Brendle. And sometimes I buy his wheat! If you truly care about "farm to table" cooking and all its upsides, add fresh flour to your shopping list. It's available. Look around. Buy a bag and start making some of the breads in this book with it, or try fresh flour in your go-to recipes for pancakes and cookies. And even when you're not baking from scratch, consider picking up bread from a local bakery that uses fresh flour. This one simple choice could change your world.

Final note: Claire Kopp McWilliams, David Joachim, and I wrote this book together, but sometimes one of us has a personal story to share about a recipe or about baking in general, which is why you'll see our initials throughout the book. —MV

Why We Measure by Weight Instead of Volume

Most serious bakers measure ingredients by weight instead of volume. Bread recipes rely on a specific ratio of flour to water, and weights give you more accurate and reliable measurements. Metric weights are the most precise, so most of the ingredients in our recipes are measured in grams. For reference, we also list measurements in volume (cups and tablespoons), but we strongly encourage you to measure by weight.

Weights are more precise than volumes because they remain constant. Believe it or not, volumes change. With flour, for instance, factors like the fineness of the grind and how the flour is measured can change the actual amount of flour you use in a recipe. Dipping a cup measure into a bag of flour compacts the flour in the measuring cup, while spooning the flour into the cup leaves the flour looser. Sifting flour also loosens it, expanding its overall volume. Depending on how you measure your flour—dipping, spooning, or sifting—you will get slightly different amounts of flour in the cup. But the weight of flour remains constant.

What's more, cups and tablespoons are limited to relatively large measurements. For example, how do you measure a volume of flour that is between ¾ cup and 1 cup? Most manufacturers don't make odd-size measures such as ⅞ cup. Rounding to the nearest available cup measure could mean a difference of as much as 3 tablespoons of flour in your bread dough. This imprecision is the reason that ingredient measurements converted from weight to volume are not always 100% accurate. The available volumes are simply not precise enough to equal the exact weight measurement you may be trying to achieve. For instance, our Honey Durum Batard (page 132) and Pain Normand (page 162) recipes call for 700 grams and 712 grams of flour, respectively. But both recipes list the same volume conversion at 5⅔ cups of flour. That is not an error; 5⅔ cups is simply the nearest available volume measurement to which those weights can be rounded. Yet, the difference between 700 and 712 grams of flour can be as much as 1½ tablespoons. Suffice it to say, the volume measurements given in our recipes are as precise as they can possibly be.

For the recipes in this book, weight is the primary and only reliable measurement. We measured by weight when creating and testing all of the recipes, and we encourage you to do the same. Digital scales are inexpensive and widely available (see page 33 for recommendations). Remember that successful yeast and sourdough bread baking is largely a matter of guiding biological interactions based on the ratio of ingredients. Changing that ratio, even slightly, alters the result. Plus, if you plan to scale up the recipe to make more loaves, what may have been a minor difference in the volume-to-weight conversion could balloon into a major discrepancy between what the recipe calls for and what you actually end up using in the dough.

1

GRAIN

I HAD MY FIRST FLOUR EPIPHANY IN 2014 WHEN I WENT TO A CONFERENCE ON SEEDS AND GRAINS THAT WAS ORGANIZED BY CHEF DAN BARBER. A wheat breeder named Dr. Stephen Jones gave a speech on the history of flour, heritage wheats, and the flavor of freshly milled flour. I was mesmerized. How did I never realize that flour can have flavor? I might not have believed it if I hadn't tasted it for myself. We sampled a few breads made with lesser-known wheat varieties, and the flavors were simply amazing. You could taste things like tobacco, hazelnuts, and vanilla. Right there in the flour. That day, I became a believer in paying more attention to this ingredient.

That experience was the catalyst for the Vetri Grain Project. I bought a grain mill, got in some heritage wheat varieties, milled them, and started experimenting with fresh flour in my pasta. That changed everything. My pastas taste even better now. We decided to take the Vetri Grain Project to the next level and hired Claire Kopp McWilliams as head baker at Vetri. Claire is a talented Philadelphia baker who was also exploring heirloom grains and milling around the same time we were. She was baking amazing breads with freshly milled and whole-grain flours at restaurants all over the city. Claire converted most of our breads, desserts, and other flour-based menu items over to freshly milled flour, and we started serving serious breads like Farro Miche with Whey (page 164) and Ciabatta Grano Arso with Einkorn (page 173). Our breads are now better than ever, and we've reduced the amount of white flour we buy down to almost nothing. By improving the one ingredient that we'd been overlooking—flour—we also got connected to the heritage grain movement happening all around the country. Back in 2014, that first taste of bread made with freshly milled flour catapulted us into a community that is now doing some of the most interesting things in the food world. —MV

GOOD FLOUR MAKES GOOD BREAD

Any good chef will tell you that good cooking starts with good ingredients. It's the same with baking. The main ingredient is flour, and the first thing you can do to improve the taste of your bread or baked goods is to use better-tasting flour.

Fortunately, better flour is becoming more and more available. Remember twenty years ago when farmers' markets started getting amazing heirloom tomatoes with flavors that blew away the pale, stiff tomatoes at the grocery store? That's what's happening now with grains and flours. Farmers are growing better-tasting grains like heirloom varieties of wheat, getting them milled locally, and selling fresh flour at farmers' markets, local bakeries, regional mills, and online. This kind of flour is light-years ahead of the all-purpose and common white bread flours that have usually been sitting around for weeks or months getting stale. Both of these types of white flours have had the most flavorful parts of the grain—the germ and bran—removed so the flour can withstand long storage.

But why bake bread with old, stale, less-nourishing ingredients when you can get fresh flour full of amazing flavor?

Don't get us wrong. We don't hate white flour. It is ultra-consistent, and that's why we use it in one of the most difficult breads in the book, Panettone alla Vetri (page 275). But for all the other recipes, we use whole-grain flour or bolted hard wheat flour, which is simply hard wheat that has been milled and sifted to remove some of the bigger bran flakes. (See page 10 for more about hard wheat.)

We buy our grains mostly from Castle Valley Mill just outside Philadelphia, where Mark and Fran Fischer (see page 30) put a lot of care into sourcing, storing, and cleaning the grain before they even mill it. The recipes in this book have been tested with several common wheat varieties, like Redeemer, Warthog, and Turkey Red, all of which can be found around the country and online at places like Breadtopia. For our recipes, we recommend you buy whatever bolted hard wheat flour you can get locally, regionally, or online (see page 284 for sources).

It helps to keep in mind that, like every other food, grain is variable. Weather conditions change. The exact percentage of protein in the grain may change a little, and the flour may be less predictable from year to year than your typical bags of white flour. But that's what you want! You want those nuances of flavor and texture that you can't get with white flour. Taste the bolted wheat flour you buy. Work with it on an easy, familiar loaf, like Potato Bread (page 110) or Simple Sourdough Table Bread (page 149), to see how it performs. Or use your own favorite tried-and-true bread recipe if you want. Then stick with that same flour to get used to working with it. You may notice that doughs made with freshly milled flour tend to be softer and stickier; that's fine. It's just something to be aware of. Baking with freshly milled flour will help you advance tremendously as a baker. And it will make your breads taste so much better.

SOME KEY THINGS TO KNOW ABOUT WHEAT

Cereal grains are the seeds of grasses. Wheat is a cereal grain, and what makes it so special—and an enormous staple for more than half of the world's population for thousands of

Flour Has Flavor

If you don't believe flour has flavor, do a side-by-side taste test. Buy a little bag of whole-wheat flour from the grocery store. Pick up some all-purpose flour, too, if you don't already have some. Those are both commercial flours that were milled weeks if not months before you bought them. Now, for the other side of the test, get some fresh flour that's been milled within the past few days (see the sources for fresh flour on page 284). Better yet, mill some flour at home from whole grains of wheat, using an inexpensive mill for home use (see page 17 for more on home mills and milling).

Now, taste the commodity whole-wheat flour. At first, it will probably taste just sort of "earthy." Then, after a few seconds, you will notice an off-taste, not quite bitterness but not very pleasant either. That is the taste of rancid oil. You see, the oils from the bran in commodity whole-wheat flour have been sitting around for so long that they have gone rancid, making the flour taste off.

Now, taste the commercial all-purpose flour. It probably won't taste rancid because all-purpose flour has had the bran and germ removed. In fact, the all-purpose flour probably won't taste like much at all except a powder. That's because most of the subtle flavors and aromas in grains, which are volatile and fleeting, reside in the bran and germ.

Now, taste the fresh flour. Notice any difference? Getting any more flavor? You'll probably notice right away that fresh flour tastes not only earthy but also somewhat grassy, nutty, almost buttery, slightly sweet, and slightly minerally with aromas of warm spices. Only a few days after grinding grains, these flavors dissipate from the flour, but when flour is fresh, you can taste its natural flavors, particularly when the flour is whole or has been only lightly sifted, so there's still some germ and bran left. That's why we call for bolted hard wheat flour throughout this book whereas typical recipes would use refined white flour. Fresh flour tastes so much better than commercial wheat flours. No rancid taste! Now, rancid oils—in flour or otherwise—won't make you sick. They just taste bad.

We prefer to bake with the freshest, most flavorful ingredients possible. Flour is the primary ingredient in most baked goods, and using better flour will make your baked goods taste better. You can also change the taste of your baked goods in subtle or even dramatic ways by using various fresh flours. Different grains have different flavors, even within the wheat family. For instance, spelt flour has sweet notes of cinnamon. Sonora wheat flour has aromas of pine nuts, probably because it grows well in the same arid regions in which pine nuts grow. Farro flour tastes more like pecans. Rye flour tastes more like walnuts. We use all of these freshly milled flours and more to get different flavors in the breads throughout this book.

years—is that it's a pretty nutritionally balanced food. It's also relatively easy to grow in different environmental conditions, and it's easy to store the grain for months or even years.

Gluten. Grains are like the eggs of the plant world. A grain of wheat consists of a small oil-rich germ, a plant embryo, surrounded by a blend of starch and protein that provides food for the baby plant, all of which is encapsulated in a shell of bran. What makes wheat a culinary gem is a special protein, gluten, that's unlike all others. Gluten only forms when flour is mixed with water. Then, gluten can be worked and stretched and molded into almost any shape you can imagine. Wheat contains various proteins, but the two that are functionally important for bread are glutenin and gliadin, two components of the bigger gluten molecule. Each variety of wheat has its own balance of glutenin and gliadin; this is partly what gives wheat varieties their baking characteristics. Glutenin tends to lend elastic strength to dough, while gliadin lends extensibility. Elasticity is what

Red/White. The color of the bran dictates the color of the flour. Red wheat is more common. White wheat is like an albino: it's missing the genetic trait for red pigmentation. White wheats also tend to have a more low-key, oaty flavor. Red wheats have more complex sweetness and bitterness with flavor notes such as apple. Keep in mind that not every last wheat variety is red or white. Durum, kamut, and spelt are in the wheat family but are neither red nor white.

Winter/Spring. This refers to when the wheat is planted. Certain varieties grow better in the winter or spring in certain regions of the country and the world. Spring wheats tend to be higher in protein and are usually favored for bread baking. Winter wheats tend to be a little lower in protein, but we like them for bread baking, too. You may just need to make some adjustments in the mixing or fermentation. If you know what you are working with, you can better predict how it will behave, which we'll discuss in greater detail later on.

Know that when you buy a bag of flour or wheat berries, you may not have all the information about it, such as protein content, red/white, and winter/spring. It's not always printed on the bag, even for commercial flours. The first thing new bakers should practice is observing the dough, especially how it feels and looks. By making different doughs and observing how different flours behave, you learn what kinds of adjustments to make to create the loaves you're going for. To play it safe, your best bet for most breads in this book is to use a hard red winter wheat or hard red spring wheat. If that info isn't printed on the bag, ask the farmer or miller for it, or get the name of the wheat variety and then search online. We often use Redeemer and Warthog varieties because they grow well in the Northeast. But you can just buy whatever hard wheat that grows well in your region and stick with it.

Commercial Wheat Flours. We hardly ever use commercial refined white flour anymore, but you should know some terms for reference. Most commercial flours are bleached and/or bromated. Bleaching is a process of chemically oxidizing the flour, which whitens it, and it's usually done with benzoyl peroxide. Unbleached flour has a natural tan or yellowish cast, which many artisan bakers prefer. Bromated flour is treated with potassium bromate to speed up the "aging" of commercial white flour. Normally, flour ages

you see when bread dough stretches but also springs back, like a rubber band. Extensibility is what you see when dough continues to stretch without breaking and without snapping back, sort of like taffy. Different ratios of glutenin and gliadin create doughs with different characteristics, from stretchy to bouncy to moldable.

Hard/Soft. When you buy regional wheats and flours, you may see references to hard, soft, red, white, winter, and spring wheat varieties. Hardness or softness refers to protein content. Generally, hard wheats have more protein and are better for bread baking, where you rely on the weblike structure of gluten to hold the shape of the loaf. Soft wheats tend to have less protein and tend to be better suited to flatter breads and baked goods, like cookies, cakes, and pastries, that don't need as much gluten structure. But you can bake well-risen breads with soft wheats, too.

Inside the Whole Grain

Bran refers to the hard, fibrous outer layer of a grain—whether it's wheat, rye, or barley. Deep inside, the germ contains vitamins, minerals, and fatty acids that allow the grain to germinate and grow into a plant. But the bran and germ are small parts of the whole grain. The rest of the grain, about 80% of it, is the endosperm. It's mostly starch, which contains 9 to 17% protein, depending on the grain. This is the part that's mechanically separated out and ground to make refined white flour. Whole-grain flour, on the other hand, is the entire grain—bran, germ, and endosperm—ground into flour. "Bolted" refers to whole grains that have been milled into flour, then sifted to remove some of the bigger bran flakes.

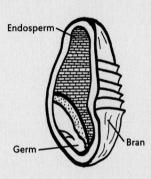

Endosperm

Germ

Bran

Both Ancient and Modern Wheats Have Their Merits

In our breads, we use lots of heritage and ancient grains like einkorn, emmer, durum, and spelt. Einkorn is the oldest cultivated variety of wheat: it was used more than fourteen thousand years ago, ground to make bread that nourished some of the earliest civilizations in Mesopotamia or the "Fertile Crescent." But we also use modern varieties of wheat. For instance, our favorite type of spelt is a more recent cultivar called Maverick. It grows well in the Northeast and is fantastic for milling and baking. Many bakers like ancient and heritage wheat varieties because they taste better, and some people find them easier to digest. But it's a mistake to vilify modern wheat varieties just because they're new. There is no GMO wheat approved for commercial agriculture in the United States, so you don't have to worry about that—yet.

What's more important than how long ago a wheat variety was bred is how well it grows in a particular place. Skagit 1109 is a good example. This new wheat variety was named for the Skagit Valley in Washington, where it was developed and bred to grow in wet, non-grain-belt areas. It's now being grown in Vermont, New York, and other northeastern states. Bakers love it because it tastes amazing yet slightly different from region to region, and it makes beautiful bread. Of course, the way that any flour behaves in bread dough matters, and this is where the baker's skill comes in: you make subtle adjustments to the mixing or fermentation as you work with the dough to make sure the bread will produce the loaf that you want. We'll discuss those adjustments in more depth in the next few chapters.

Top row, left to right: Emmer, Spelt

Middle row, left to right: Soft White Wheat, Blue Beard Durum, Sonora

Bottom row, left to right: Redeemer, Rye, Einkorn

Commercial Flour Types

A bag of flour with the generic label "bread flour" contains commercial flour milled from a blend of hard red spring and hard red winter wheat with 11 to 13% protein. It may be bleached or unbleached. Pastry flour is usually milled from soft red winter wheat and has 7 to 9% protein. Cake flour is also milled from soft red winter wheat, but it's often blended with cornstarch, has 6 to 8% protein, and is usually bleached pure white with chlorine gas, which weakens the gluten and totally flattens the flavor. All-purpose flour is typically a mix of hard and soft wheats that may be bleached or unbleached and usually has 9 to 11% protein.

naturally as it is exposed to air. During that time, the flour oxidizes; this restructures and strengthens the gluten protein, making it easier to work with in bread making. Potassium bromate also ages the flour, but it does the job faster. The problem is that potassium bromate is a carcinogen. It's outright banned in Canada and Europe. Yet, in the United States, potassium bromate is still allowed. Some American companies sell "unbromated" flour that is aged with ascorbic acid instead. We prefer to go the natural route and use unbleached, unbromated flour. If you want to buy freshly milled flour but use aged flour in your baking, you can age the flour naturally by storing it in an oversized container for a few weeks before using it. A large container with plenty of airspace exposes the flour to more oxygen, so the flour ages faster. Just know that much of the flour's flavor nuance will have dissipated when you use it.

DON'T GET TOO HUNG UP ON PROTEIN CONTENT

Flours with 11 to 13% protein tend to work best for bread baking. But more or less than that might be fine. A flour's protein level isn't the only factor to consider. Other factors such as enzymatic activity can completely negate the protein level.

We're about to venture into some extra-credit know-how, so if you're just getting started with bread baking, perhaps skip ahead to the Mix chapter now. You don't want to get bogged down in the granular details of flour until you've actually played around with some dough. Once you wrap your head and hands around the basics, then what follows will be of more use to you. Maybe bookmark this section, alternate between study and practice, and refer back here as you go.

To get a handle on enzymatic activity, remember that a cereal grain is a seed. Inside the seed, the germ is the baby plant, and the endosperm is a store of food for the beginning of the baby's growth. While intact, the endosperm is all large molecules of complex carbohydrates and protein, which is a good format for long-term storage, but not so good for the baby. When conditions are right for the baby plant to grow (warmth, moisture, and light usually do the trick), and germination or sprouting happens,

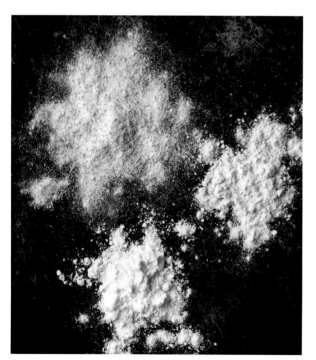

Clockwise from top left: Redeemer Whole Grain, Redeemer Bolted (High Extraction), Bread Flour (Low Extraction)

DR. STEPHEN JONES
The Bread Lab | Burlington, Washington

Dr. Stephen Jones is a grain breeder and director of the Washington State University Bread Lab in Burlington, Washington. He has a PhD in genetics and raised his first wheat crop as a student back in 1977. Today, he breeds varieties of wheat and other grains to be grown on small farms in various regions of the United States. The Bread Lab is a combination think tank and baking laboratory, where scientists, bakers, chefs, farmers, maltsters, brewers, distillers, and millers experiment with regional varieties of wheat, barley, and other grains and beans to improve flavor, nutrition, and functionality.

"

After talking with local farmers and the community at large, we realized that there was a huge interest in a local grain chain. As grain breeders, our part is to develop and introduce diversity into the system and help form connections between farmers, millers, bakers, and consumers.

The growers are individuals and families who proudly live and work in a place they treasure. And they put forth a product that is delicious and nutritious. This is only possible on a regional scale. A national, industrial commodity system has no room for sense of place and community.

Our version of the grain movement is defined by food value in terms of flavor, nutrition, and price. For thousands of years, wheat and grains have been affordable, and we embrace the effort required to make regional grains available for all. This is radical for a crop as centralized as wheat.

"

enzymes stored within the seed begin to break the large complex molecules of starch and protein down into simpler sugars, amino acids, and peptides. These are smaller molecules that the plant embryo can actually use to grow. That breakdown of starch and protein into smaller sugars, amino acids, and peptides is called enzymatic activity. It's measured in grains and flours by something known as the falling number test. A low falling number indicates high enzymatic activity.

Now, let's think about agriculture for a minute. When a crop of wheat is nearly ready to harvest, those grains are fully mature and have the potential to sprout. A farmer has to judge how long to let the grain continue to grow and ripen, while keeping in mind that a rainstorm may blow through, creating ideal conditions for those little seeds to spring to life. Not so ideal for the farmer. Do you pick before a pending storm or wait and risk it? Harvesting too early or too late will reduce both the quality and yield of a grain crop. And you thought farming was easy.

Now let's connect these concepts to the bread you bake. Every crop of harvested grain is tested for its protein level and enzymatic activity. The information is out there. But consumers are not often given those details. Why? Most likely because industrial mills blend several different crops of flour along with malted grain to hit precise enzyme and protein levels year after year. That's why most bakers don't think much about protein level and enzymatic activity. And once you have a flour you like, you won't either.

When you're working with an unfamiliar flour, maybe one you sourced locally and ground yourself (go you!), just keep in mind that fresh milled flour tends to make *all* bread doughs feel silkier and a bit stickier than doughs made with refined white flour. And high enzymatic activity in the flour pushes those traits even further. If the enzymes are working overtime, your dough will be weak and sticky, and it will ferment extremely quickly. Your breads won't necessarily be bad. In fact, the flavors will most likely be bigger and brighter than normal. On the other hand, if the enzymes are

Use that Leftover Bran

When you mill flour and bolt or sift it, you get a fair amount of leftover bran flakes. Don't throw them away! You can use bran flakes to dust the bottoms of your loaves, as in Spelt Sourdough Boule (page 157). Or mix the bran into muffins and quick breads. Raisin bran muffins are always a good choice. You can also add the flakes to your favorite granola, cereal, oatmeal, or yogurt in the morning. If you have more bran than you can use, you can always compost it. The owners of Castle Valley Mill in Doylestown, Pennsylvania, compress their sifted bran into pellets and use it to heat their home. Kevin Fink, the chef at Emmer and Rye in Austin, Texas, uses bran a number of ways: to make bran graham crackers, malted bran and red fife vinegar, black butter and toasted bran oil, and toasted bran soap. *Nukazuke*, a Japanese type of vegetable pickling done in fermented rice bran, is another good use for bran; it works just as well with wheat bran. Here's a recipe: Mix the bran with 10% salt by weight. Then mix in water with an ungloved hand until it feels like wet sand. Jump-start the fermentation by burying vegetable scraps (turnip peels, ginger skins, whatever) in the bran and leaving the mixture out for three to four days. It should continue to feel like wet sand and begin to smell like sourdough. Then pick out the veg scraps and bury your whole small vegetables (cucumbers, carrots, whatever) to be pickled in the mixture. Leave them to ferment for at least twenty-four hours or up to four days. Remove the vegetables, rinse and refrigerate them, and your pickles are done. They will keep refrigerated in an airtight container for about five days.

not as active (which happens less frequently), the doughs will form a nice gluten structure but will ferment more slowly than you might expect and have a flatter flavor. In that case, mixing in a little malted flour will correct the issue. What if you wind up with one of each: a flour with a high enzymatic activity *and* a flour with low activity? Yahtzee! You can just blend the two flours.

The moral of the story is that when you're buying grains and flour, if you can get the falling number, it's helpful to know (low falling number = high enzyme activity). At least it tips you off about what to expect from your flour. For more details on enzymes and fermentation, see chapter 3.

As you can see, the baking qualities of flour can't be reduced to protein content alone. The enzymatic activity, the protein quality (the balance of glutenin and gliadin), the starch quality, and even a gum called pentosan all contribute structure to bread. Some flours may be relatively high in protein yet make dough that's more extensible, while others may be lower in protein and make dough that's more plastic.

Plus, the flour itself isn't the only thing that leads to good gluten development and structure in bread. Looser doughs can be strengthened by using more preferments, folding the dough, or simply allowing more time for the available gluten to develop (see the Mix and Fermentation chapters for more details).

Yes, you won't always have access to flour specs, especially when you buy from local farmers, mills, and bakeries, or when you mill the flour yourself. Don't worry about it. It's not crucial to know the exact numbers. The majority of our recipes just call for "bolted hard wheat flour" and that's what matters most. Find one you like and stick with it. When we prefer a mix of flours, we specify which type. For instance, the dough for Cornetti (page 137) is rolled out several times, so it's best to include a flour like spelt that makes a highly extensible dough. But the dough also needs a hard wheat for structure, so that recipe calls for a mix of bolted hard wheat and whole-grain spelt flours.

FRESHLY STONE-MILLED FLOUR TASTES BEST

When choosing flour for great-tasting breads, the highest priority should be its flavor. Whether you buy it or mill it yourself, freshly stone-milled whole-grain or bolted flour has the best flavor. Most commercial flours on store shelves are not made that way. They are roller milled, a process that mechanically separates the different parts of the grain first, so they can be ground separately. That's how you get refined white flour, but it has none of the flavorful and nutritious bran and germ.

Stone mills, on the other hand, grind the whole grain, retaining all the flavor and nutrition. They are simple machines consisting of two stones, a motor, and a dial to adjust how closely the stones come together. Bigger models also include a sifter so you can sift the flour to varying degrees. The easiest way to bake with freshly stone-milled flour is to buy flour from a local mill or bakery (see page 284 for sources). But the most flavorful way is to mill it yourself. Just buy a mill and start milling your own flour!

At home, you can use a Mockmill attachment for a KitchenAid, Kenmore, or a few other stand mixers. This small stone-mill attachment is reasonably priced at less than $200. For just a little more, you can get their countertop version or another countertop model, like the KoMo mill, which can handle a bit more volume if you bake often. Hand-cranked mills like the WonderMill and GrainMaker are also popular. Professional bakeries will want a larger commercial mill. At Vetri, our main mill is a Meadows mill with 8-inch stones that can handle up to 50 pounds of flour per hour.

Picking a mill is like choosing a knife. Some are more expensive, some are cheaper, some are more utilitarian, and some are drop-dead gorgeous. Shop around for the one you like best.

Big professional mills often come with sifters, so the bakery can sift the flour as finely or coarsely as necessary. At home, all you need is a fine-mesh sifter, nothing fancy, just one of those mesh sifters with a handle that you can buy at supermarkets and online. Simply mill the grains, then pass the flour through the sifter. If you want to get really precise, buy a flour sifter with a mesh rating that specifies the size of

the mesh. For our recipes, a 40-mesh sifter is sufficient and creates our basic bolted hard wheat flour. If you want superfine flour for more delicate pastries, pass the flour through a 50- or 60-mesh sifter.

Millers use the term "bolted flour" and "high-extraction flour" interchangeably. These terms just mean that some of the bran has been sifted out and removed, leaving 75 to 90% of the flour after removing the chunkier bits. In the recipes in this book, we use the term "bolted hard wheat flour" to mean the same thing. This kind of flour is quite a bit closer to whole grain than what you get in bagged white flour, but it handles more easily in bread dough than 100% whole-grain flour. If you're making fresh milled flour, you can easily check the extraction. Weigh the flour before you sift it, then weigh it after. Divide the sifted weight by the total weight to find your extraction. Don't confuse the term "bolted flour" with wheat that has "sprouted" or "gone to seed." In milling and in this book, "bolted" simply means "sifted."

When milling flour for bread, you're trying to get pretty fine particles. That means setting the millstones somewhat close together. Look for a balance between a too-tight setting, which can heat up the mill and the flour (potentially damaging both), and a too-loose setting, which makes the flour too coarse. Feel the flour. It should be a powder with larger flakes of bran that feel stiff but flat. If it's milled too coarsely, the bigger bits will feel gritty or pebbly. If the flour starts feeling clumpy or is hot to the touch, you're getting too much friction and need to loosen the stones. Adjust the mill to find a good balance. Try to keep your milling area cool.

Here's another reason to feel the flour before mixing it into dough: a sandier-feeling flour indicates higher protein. That flour will need either a longer rest or longer mixing to hydrate the flour and develop the gluten. Try giving the flour a longer autolyse (see page 23). A more silky, powdery-feeling flour indicates starchier or more oily grain and will probably come together more readily and develop gluten sooner but will likely have less gluten overall. Be prepared for a stickier dough and be careful not to overhydrate it with too much water, which could make handling the dough more challenging.

For the most vibrant flavor, use freshly milled flour right away. Just know that freshly milled grains are a little more enzymatically active, which tends to give you a weaker gluten structure in bread. That can make it harder to get a super-open, airy, and irregular crumb (the size and pattern of the holes inside a loaf of bread). But a gigantic open crumb structure isn't the only objective in bread baking. If your doughs are consistently sticky and soft, and make unpleasantly dense bread, let the flour age in a bowl or bag in the open air for a few days. After about three days, you will have lost only a little flavor, but the first big push of enzymatic activity will have mellowed out, giving you a more reliable, predictable flour for developing structure in your bread. For even more

structure, age the flour for a week or two. Of course, then you're trading flavor for functionality, and we prefer flavor.

We typically use freshly milled flours within seventy-two hours of milling. If you want to store your flour for a couple months, we recommend freezing it. Just pull the flour from the freezer before baking to bring it back to room temp. You can store whole grains long term, too. Just keep them somewhere cool and dry. It's best to mill grains somewhat cold to keep the flour from heating up too much as you mill. During milling, once the flour temperature starts to go above 110°F or so, its structure and flavor start to degrade.

GO WHOLE-GRAIN WHEN YOU CAN

By now, you're seeing that the main point of this book is to bake with freshly milled bolted flours and whole-grain flours. The breads taste so much better than if you just use plain white flour!

We think whole-grain flour is the gold standard for both flavor and nutrition. But it's also the trickiest flour to work with structure-wise. That has everything to do with the presence of so much bran in the flour. People talk about bran flakes as little knives that cut through the gluten structure in bread dough. But, depending on the grain, bran can be super hard or somewhat soft, and the bran gets softer as it hydrates. The truth is that bran is an interruption in the dough, similar to nuts, seeds, and other inclusions that are simply in the way of the gluten structure without contributing to it. Bran makes it harder for gluten to form in a continuous and interconnected way, but if you let the dough sit, the gluten network will form around the bran. Sometimes with whole-grain breads, the dough just needs more time and less mixing to develop a stronger structure and come together.

Whole-grain flours also tend to be thirstier than white flour, so you may be adding more water than you're used to. It's important to recognize that you will not get an insanely open crumb with whole-grain flour. But if you use a mix of whole-grain and bolted flours, you can achieve a fairly open crumb while maintaining a good balance of flavor and structure in the bread. Ciabatta Grano Arso with Einkorn (page 173) is a good example: it uses a fifty-fifty mix of bolted hard wheat flour and whole-grain einkorn flour.

Many of our breads mix bolted and whole-grain flours. The English Muffins (page 125) use a fifty-fifty mix of bolted and whole-grain hard wheat flour. The Ursa Challah (page 119) and Brioche (page 115) both use an eighty-twenty mix of bolted and whole-grain hard wheat flour. And lots of our breads are 100% whole-grain, like our Grissini (page 113), which is made entirely with whole spelt flour for its silky texture and extensibility. The Einkorn Pan Loaf (page 160) uses 100% whole-grain einkorn flour, and the 100% Sonora Slab (page 161) uses 100% whole-grain Sonora, a beautiful white wheat with a delicate, sweet flavor. The All Rye (page 186) uses 100% whole-grain rye flour, and even the Lemon Durum Cake (page 215) uses whole-grain durum flour. Pastry dough actually takes very well to whole-grain flour. Our 100% Whole-Grain Pâte à Choux (page 226) and Whole-Grain Rough Puff Pastry (page 229) are fine examples.

THE CIRCLE OF WHEAT

A farmer plants seeds
The seeds grow into wheat
The farmer harvests the wheat
The farmer ships the wheat to the mill to sell
The miller grinds the wheat into flour
The miller sells the flour to a baker
The baker makes bread
The baker sells the bread at the market
The baker buys more flour from the miller
The miller buys more wheat from the farmer

2

MIX

WHEN I STARTED URSA BAKERY, A TINY LOCAL-GRAIN BAKERY, I DID
NOT MAKE A FRUIT-AND-NUT BREAD. But after selling breads at various
Philadelphia farmers' markets for a year, I added one. People love fruit-and-
nut breads, and if the bread is good, there's nothing wrong with them. I set
about developing an apricot pecan bread with a fifty-fifty mix of whole
grain and bolted hard wheat flour. For the whole grain, I used a Pennsylvania
red spring wheat I wasn't familiar with. When I milled it, the flour was really
sandy, which told me there was good protein in there. But when I mixed
the dough, I wasn't seeing any gluten development. So, I kept mixing.
It still wasn't coming together. I did a bulk retard (see page 39), hoping that
would do the trick. Halfway through shaping some test loaves, I thought,
"Oh God, this isn't working. I shouldn't waste my time."

But I had already milled 50 pounds! I started another batch and did a long autolyse (see facing page) with just the whole-grain wheat flour and water. I let it sit for eight hours. When I mixed in the rest of the ingredients and stretched the dough, it felt firmer, and I could see the gluten strands. It was finally working. It turned out that the protein in this whole-grain spring wheat flour just needed a longer autolyse to develop into a bread dough with good gluten structure.

The Apricot Pecan Couronne (page 191) came out great. It makes people happy, and that's reason enough to bake it. The best part for me is that, since I see the same customers week after week, I can tell them everything that goes into making the bread, from the grain varietals to the mixing, shaping, and baking. I love that personal connection. It's one reason why, after nine years of baking in Philadelphia restaurants, including Vetri, I left the restaurant world and started Ursa Bakery. —CKM

MIXING HYDRATES FLOUR AND DEVELOPS GLUTEN

Even though flour brings its own flavors and textures to bread (see the previous chapter for more on that), a skilled baker finds ways to make the flavor and texture shine through the mixing, fermentation, and baking. That's what we'll explain in the next couple of chapters. Bread baking can get complicated, so please know that you don't need to get bogged down in all the scientific info. People have been baking bread by touch and feel for millennia, and we highly recommend that you learn by doing, not just by reading.

That said, the ultimate goal of mixing or folding the dough is to build its strength. Then you want to maintain that strength throughout the shaping and baking so that the dough structure is strong enough to hold up the bread. The first mixing step is to combine the flour with water to hydrate it. As this happens, the dough gradually goes from separate ingredients to a cohesive, single thing. The dough begins to cling less to the bowl or the countertop or your hands, and more to itself. When that occurs, you know that gluten is developing.

On a molecular level, gluten consists of interconnected chains of two smaller proteins, glutenin and gliadin. Chains of glutenin are often shaped like long ropes, while gliadin chains usually fold around themselves in a sort of 3-D sphere. Mixing and folding help the glutenin and gliadin proteins link up with each other more thoroughly. It's as if you had groups of people arranged randomly in a room, and you told them to hold hands and form a chain. If the people don't move, some will be out of reach, cut off from each other, or arranged at weird angles. When you mix and fold bread dough, you walk everyone through the room, rearranging the chains and forming more connections that reinforce and strengthen the entire gluten network.

During mixing, fermentation, and even shaping, the whole structure becomes this stretchy, flexible, doughy web in which starches, yeasts, and bacteria undergo fermentation (see chapter 3). As gases are created during fermentation, the web of gluten traps them, and the dough expands like a honeycombed balloon holding air. With mixing, your job is to develop a structure that's strong and stretchy enough to accommodate the expanding fermentation gases, then to bake the inflated dough at the right moment to make a well-risen loaf of bread (see "Is the Dough Ready to Bake?" on page 42). This is, in a nutshell, the challenge and the magic of bread making.

Here's the thing that eternally fascinates us: some doughs can be fully mixed and developed with just a few gentle stirs. Other doughs get knocked around like crazy for a good fifteen to twenty minutes. And they're both perfectly good methods! Some of our breads, like Omni Bread (page 169) and Farro Miche with Whey (page 164), are simply hand-mixed, rested, and folded; while others, like Grissini (page 113) and Pane alla Zucca (page 130), are more intensively mixed by machine. Then there is Panettone alla Vetri (page 275). The dough for that bread mixes forever and gets big fermentation bubbles!

WATER IS WHAT MAKES DOUGH

Generally, we like to add water or other liquids like milk to the mixing bowl first, then add the leavening, flour and dry ingredients, salt, any enrichments like oil or sugar, and finally any inclusions like fruit and nuts. Some bakers get fussy about water temperature, but we don't. Typically, we use room temperature water, about 75°F. If you use cold water (about 50°F), it can make the dough feel tighter and less extensible. It also doesn't trigger fermentation as rapidly. That might be an advantage on a hot summer day if you want to slow down the entire fermentation process. Or on a chilly winter day, you might want to use warm water (about 90°F) to kick-start fermentation before the dough inevitably cools down. In that case, you can expect the dough to feel a little looser and more extensible. There's only one recipe in this book that calls for warm water, Panettone alla Vetri (page 275), because we do want to get the fermentation going early in that dough. For most breads, room temperature water will be ideal. When you make bread, use whatever water you would drink. If your tap water is good for drinking, use that. If it's not, you might want to use distilled water.

AUTOLYSE IMPROVES FLAVOR, TEXTURE, AND COLOR

Here's another great example of how time improves bread dough. French baking teacher Raymond Calvel promoted the "autolyse" technique in the 1970s, and it has some advantages. Basically, you mix only the flour and water together, then let the dough rest for anywhere from fifteen minutes to ten hours. During that time, "autolysis," or self-digestion, occurs: the flour's own enzymes start decomposing the flour. Protease enzymes break down some of the proteins, and amylase enzymes convert some of the starch into sugars. The protease activity makes the dough more extensible and easier to shape, and the amylase activity makes more food available for the yeast, so fermentation proceeds more swiftly. During autolyse, gluten is also forming passively; this means you don't need to mix as much for the dough to come together. That's good because mixing oxidizes the flavorful, colorful carotenoids in flour; therefore, less mixing preserves more flavor and color in the bread. Autolyse is particularly helpful for high-protein flours that take a little longer to hydrate.

Traditionally, autolyse was done with flour and water only: no leavening, no salt. But these days, the more common autolyse, and what we call for a ton in this book, is

a fifteen- to thirty-minute rest after the leavening goes in but before the salt is added. This type of autolyse also helps to soften the bran in high-extraction and whole-grain flours, making it easier for them to form a strong gluten network. We hold the salt to keep it from inhibiting the yeast activity.

Autolyse is usually not a do-or-die step, but it does tend to make a nicer dough that comes together a little faster and easier once mixing resumes. Dough that isn't autolysed may be more difficult to shape, and if it doesn't have enough extensibility, your loaf may look more ripped, rather than nicely stretched, as the bread springs in the oven.

Baking has all kinds of weird little tweak decisions like this: you could do it or not! The Ursa Challah (page 119) does not have an autolyse, and that dough can be shaped into ropes and braids just fine, in part because it's enriched with eggs, sugar, and oil (see page 26 for more on enrichments). The Ursa Baguette (page 81), on the other hand, does have an autolyse because it's a lean dough (no enrichments), and you're trying to take a small lump of it and stretch it out to a long, smooth shape. Autolyse helps you do that.

YEAST ACTIVITY INFLATES THE DOUGH

Yeast is what blows all those bubbles into bread dough. This little single-celled fungus exists everywhere, and in dough, we cultivate an environment that it likes. Yeast's temperature comfort zone is similar to ours, 60° to 90°F. It starts dying at around 110°F and is killed entirely at 140°F, so you want to keep the yeast moderately warm and moist and give it food in the form of flour. Then you just let it transform that flour into really flavorful, nourishing bread.

When yeast is active and happy, it feeds on the broken-down carbohydrates (sugar) from the flour, then gives off carbon dioxide (CO_2) and alcohol as by-products. The CO_2 gas is what inflates the dough. Yeast fermentation is a big part of what makes finished bread taste radically different from a simple mixture of flour and water. (Check out the next chapter for more details on fermentation flavors.)

Thousands of species of yeast live all around us, but in the mid-1800s, scientists recognized that one species, *Saccharomyces cerevisiae*, stood out as particularly good

Leavening Terms

Yeast breads, quick breads, cakes, cookies . . . they all get their lift from different types of leaveners. A leavener is basically anything that lightens dough by introducing air bubbles. It could even be plain ol' butter or eggs that have been beaten to aerate them. That's how you get light and airy cakes. Quick breads, like muffins, rely on chemical leaveners such as baking powder. Yeast breads rely on various forms of yeast. Here's a quick glossary of terms. (For more details on specific preferments, see page 38.)

ACTIVE DRY YEAST: Dry dormant commercial yeast formulated in somewhat large particles that take slightly longer to hydrate than instant yeast. Formerly required an additional hydration or "proofing" step, but modern versions have eliminated this. Not very perishable but must be refrigerated after opening.

BAKING POWDER: Chemical leavening that works by releasing carbon dioxide when hydrated and heated in an acid-base reaction. Contains acidic and basic ingredients.

BAKING SODA: Chemical leavening that works by releasing carbon dioxide when hydrated with an acid. Contains only basic ingredients.

BIGA: A preferment, typically at lower hydration, credited to the Italian baking tradition.

COMMERCIAL YEAST: Isolated yeast (species Saccharomyces cerevisiae) that is sold commercially in fresh or dry form. See also active dry yeast, fresh yeast, and instant yeast.

FRESH YEAST: Commercial yeast that comes fully active and mixed with barley to subsist on before use. Also known as cake yeast. Highly perishable. (Note: In recipes translated from Italian, fresh yeast is sometimes called brewer's yeast. But in America, the term "brewer's yeast" often refers to something else entirely—nutritional yeast—which is not relevant to baking.)

INSTANT YEAST: Dry dormant commercial yeast that comes in very small particles that hydrate quickly. Least perishable.

LACTIC ACID BACTERIA: An enormous category of bacteria that are found all over the world and throughout the human body. Helpful in fermentation and digestion.

LEAVENER: A substance that makes a batter or dough rise.

LEVAIN: A mixture of flour, water, yeast, and bacteria that leavens bread. Often, but not always, measured out for a particular batch of dough.

POOLISH: A preferment, typically at 100% hydration, credited to the French baking tradition.

PREFERMENT: A portion of a recipe's ingredients that are fermented before the main mix.

SPONGE: A preferment using all of a recipe's liquid, some of its flour, and some or all of its leavening, typically fermented for a shorter period than other preferments.

STARTER: Any mixture of flour, water, yeast, and lactic acid bacteria that leavens bread but does not contain commercial yeast. Also known as levain, mother, lievito madre, pasta madre, and many other names.

YEAST: A single-celled organism in the fungus family that leavens dough by digesting sugars and giving off carbon dioxide gas and ethyl alcohol. The species of primary concern in fermentation is Saccharomyces cerevisiae.

for bread making. Louis Pasteur (the pasteurization guy!) figured out how to cultivate it on its favorite food, malted barley, and then he dried it. This became what we now know as commercial yeast, and it created a major split in baking traditions. Before that, all bread was naturally leavened. Now, dried yeast is used to make most commercial breads, which we mimic with recipes like Pita (page 77), Bagels (page 97), and English Muffins (page 125).

For the recipes in this book, you can use either instant dry yeast or active dry yeast. The recipes were tested with both, and we prefer instant dry yeast because it is less expensive. You might notice that in our recipes, we mix dry yeast, even if it's active dry, right into the dough without dissolving it in warm water first. In the past, you had to dissolve active dry yeast in warm water before mixing it into dough. But today's active dry yeast is made with a gentler drying process, and the granules are a bit smaller, so you can mix it right in with the other ingredients.

The main difference between instant dry yeast and active dry yeast is that instant dry yeast works faster. Active dry yeast does catch up over time, however. As professionals, we use instant dry yeast more often than active dry because it's more concentrated and shelf stable. We typically buy SAF instant yeast (red label). It keeps for months at room temperature. Sometimes we use SAF Gold label instant yeast, which is osmotolerant, meaning that the yeast is better adapted to sugar in the dough. Osmotolerant yeast tends to work better in sugary doughs such as Brioche (page 115), Ursa Challah (page 119), and Pane alla Zucca (page 130), but it's not crucial. You can make these breads with any dry yeast.

Labels can be confusing, though. Bread machine yeast from store brands, like Fleischmann's, may be labeled as instant yeast. Bread machine yeasts often contain dough conditioners like ascorbic acid, and they work best in the environment of a bread machine and not as well in the environments of a mixer and a home oven. For the best results, choose one type of instant yeast or active dry yeast and stick with it so you can at least keep that variable constant in your bread making.

Now, whereas all dried yeast is predictable and consistent, a sourdough starter (see "Leavening Terms" on the facing page) captures wild yeast from the flour, your hands, and the air. When you mix together flour and water and let it ferment naturally, you are starting a sourdough. You're cultivating a variety of natural yeasts and bacteria that already exist in your environment. Once your starter is established, those yeasts and bacteria will have altered the starter itself to create the ideal colony for themselves and to defend it from intrusion by other bacteria that may ruin the starter. To maintain a sourdough starter (sometimes called a culture), your job is simply to feed the starter often enough that the yeast and bacteria have a continual food supply. Check out the Sourdough Starter recipe on page 147 as well as the next chapter for a lot more detail on the flavors that sourdough brings to bread.

SALT FLAVORS BREAD, TIGHTENS GLUTEN, AND SLOWS YEAST

In most bread doughs, the common range of salt is 1.8 to 2.2% of the flour weight. If you see 2.4% salt in a sourdough bread, that's because we are also salting the portion of flour that's in the starter. When adding inclusions, we like to add even a bit more to season the inclusions. And in simpler yeast breads, like Pita (page 77) and Grissini (page 113), it sometimes helps to goose up the salt just to make the bread taste better.

Salt plays a few important roles in dough: it flavors the bread, it tightens the gluten by causing the gliadin and glutenin protein chains to contract, it limits the gluten-weakening effect of acids in sourdough, and it moderates the activity of yeast, giving you a slower and steadier rate of fermentation. Without salt, your yeast will take off fast after mixing, and it will also expire fast, leaving your dough with a flatter taste due to a lack of fermentation flavors. Without salt, your loaves will also come out looking pale and dull.

The volume measurements in our recipes were calculated with fine salt (sea salt or table salt) because that is what most bakers have at home. For bread recipes, the volume of salt is so small that the kind of salt you use shouldn't be a big worry. If you measure by weight, you can use whatever salt you want (maybe grind it first if the crystals are really big).

ENRICHMENTS MAKE BREADS MORE TENDER

Dough goes from lean to enriched when you mix in butter or oil (or another fat), eggs, and/or sugar. Think Brioche (page 115). Enrichments tend to sacrifice volume and airiness in bread, but they give it a more tender crumb, a softer crust, and make it taste richer and sweeter. Enrichments also cause bread crusts to darken sooner, so heavily enriched breads are often baked at lower temperatures of 325° to 400°F.

Fat. Adding any kind of fat tenderizes bread dough. You might want that in something like Hoagie Rolls (page 94), where a firm bread would squish out all the filling. Fat also creates a finer, more even crumb and helps extend a bread's shelf life. Fats (oil or butter, for example) behave a lot like liquids in dough. If you're using just a bit of fat, you can mix it in with the other liquids. But for highly enriched doughs, like Brioche, Olive Oil Durum Rolls (page 121), and Panettone alla Vetri (page 275), you need to hold the fat out until the end of mixing. Think of the term "shortening." That is literally what fat does in dough: it shortens the gluten strands, interrupting the whole gluten network. That's super helpful for something like piecrust, which you want as tender as possible. But for bread, you need good gluten structure, so it helps to establish the structure first. If you mix the flour with fat early, the gluten strands get coated with fat and aren't able to link up. By holding the fat until later in the mix, you can develop the gluten structure first. Our go-to olive oil is a mild-flavored extra-virgin olive oil (EVOO) that's slightly fruity but not very peppery. Save your super-expensive EVOO for salads or serving with the bread. We use a local, non-GMO, expeller-pressed canola oil, too. When we call for canola oil in the recipes, that's what we mean. When using butter, we recommend unsalted butter, and usually soften it by taking it out of the fridge first, then scaling and mixing the remaining ingredients. By the time everything else is mixed, the butter is softened enough to easily mix into the dough.

Eggs. Eggs add both protein and fat to bread dough. The protein makes the dough firm, and the fat makes it tender, giving the dough a nice spongy feel. Ursa Challah (page 119) is a good example. It's a soft dough, but the egg proteins give it enough integrity to hold its shape when soaking up beaten eggs and milk for French toast. We typically use medium eggs, each weighing about 50 grams, with a volume of about 3 tablespoons. If you measure by weight, it won't matter which size eggs you use. If necessary to get the correct weight, scramble an egg, then weigh the amount you need.

Sugar. Surprisingly, sugar behaves like a liquid in dough. It also makes breads sweeter and more tender and helps extend shelf life. We use granulated cane sugar in most doughs. Large amounts of both sugars and fats will slow down the fermentation process, something to keep in mind.

INCLUSIONS ARE USUALLY MIXED IN LAST

Inclusions are things added to dough that do not become dough themselves. Think of the dried fruit and nuts in Apricot Pecan Couronne (page 191). The inclusions are normally added later in the mix because, otherwise, they're in the way when you're trying to develop the dough's gluten structure. That said, if your mix is very passive and your inclusions aren't very obstructive to the mix, you can toss them in from the get-go. For example, the Malted Grain Sourdough (page 204) is hand-mixed very gently, and the malted grain pieces are small, hydrated, and fermentable, so you can add them early in the mix without them getting in the way.

OUR HAND-MIXING METHOD

Professional bakers don't use the term "knead." We call it "mixing," which helps you understand this stage of bread making better.

Mixing can be short and intensive (usually by machine) or long and gentle (usually by hand). Here's how we like to hand-mix.

1. Put the liquids, leavening, and dry ingredients into a bowl, then stir them with stiff fingers until everything is hydrated.

2. Make your hand like a paddle (you could also use a dough scraper or paddle). and scrape the sides of the bowl, folding everything together a few times.

3. Once the dough comes together and tension is building, squeeze the dough into pieces to break down the tension. For one round of hand mixing, go through the pinch-apart-and-fold-back-together process about three times.

4. After the initial hand mix, we usually give the dough a series of rests with one or more gentle four-folds (see page 28) in between. Early in hand mixing, you can be more aggressive because you are creating structure. Later on, after the dough is more developed, use a lighter hand to avoid overly de-gassing and weakening the structure.

THE FOUR-FOLD

Bulk fermentation is the period when the dough is rising (see page 39 for details) before being divided into loaves. During this time, it is often helpful to give the dough a little stretch and fold. That's because protease enzymes are breaking down the gluten during fermentation, and folding helps to build new gluten connections. If the dough is getting active too early, folding also helps de-gas the dough. And it redistributes and evens out the dough temperature.

1. To do a four-fold, think of the dough as having a middle and four sides. If the dough is sticky, wet your hand to prevent sticking, then make your hand like a paddle (or just use a dough scraper) and dig it down one side of the container. Scoop up the dough, stretching just a little to create some tension.

2. Then flop that section onto the center of the dough.

3. Give the container a quarter turn and repeat the stretch-and-fold action.

4. Repeat until all four sides are folded. The dough should now appear less slack and have some more height. At this point, we like to flip the dough over, so the folds are on the bottom and the smooth side is on top. This helps to hold more tension in the bulk shape, a good thing for overall structure.

TIPS ON MACHINE MIXING

When we are machine mixing, we generally add the liquids first, then the leavening—flour and dry ingredients—and salt, and finally any enrichments and inclusions. To avoid undermixing the dough, you may need to stop and scrape the bottom of the mixing bowl to make sure all the flour is incorporated. On many stand mixers, you can raise the bowl height by turning a screw on the stand so that the dough hook reaches the bottom of the bowl.

Commercial dough mixers often have only two speeds, but KitchenAid mixers can have as many as ten for whipping things, like cream or egg whites, on high speed. Generally, you want to use low- or medium-low speed for the initial mix, then switch to medium speed for the final mix. With machine mixing, you're generally forcing all the gluten formation into the beginning of the bread-making process, so you want to make sure the gluten is fully developed at the end of the mix.

Know that pretty much any of our doughs can be hand-mixed or machine-mixed. The methods were somewhat randomly assigned in the recipes to show you the options. We recommend trying both mixing methods. Once you get a sense of how mixing develops the dough structure, you can switch back and forth. Bread is very forgiving: there's a huge range of ways to do it right.

WHAT TO LOOK FOR IN THE MIXED DOUGH

In most doughs, the gluten structure develops within eight to fifteen minutes in a mixer or slightly longer with hand mixing and folding. At first, gluten develops in a sort of haphazard way, especially during the autolyse step. The mixing process aligns the gluten chains into straighter strands, strengthening the structure. It's hard to overmix dough by hand, but in a machine, the speed and total mixing time can make a difference. When dough is overmixed or overheated, the gluten becomes so stressed that the bonds begin to break down, and the dough goes slack and sticky. You're looking for that mixing sweet spot when the dough has a balance of both elasticity and extensibility: it should

hold together, pull back to hold its shape when stretched slightly, *and* stretch easily without shredding or tearing.

To test the dough, tug on a piece. When the gluten is fully developed:

1. The dough clings to itself instead of to your hands or the bowl.
2. It's less sticky than when you started mixing.
3. It's elastic and pulls back when stretched.
4. It looks smooth and shiny instead of ragged and dull.

You can also do the windowpane test: tear off a piece of dough and coax it out into the thinnest sheet you can. If it stretches so thin—without tearing—that some light shines through like a windowpane, the gluten has developed and the dough is properly mixed. However, the windowpane test is less reliable with whole-grain doughs. Use the four markers outlined above, and go by texture, not time. If a recipe says to machine-mix for four minutes and the dough hasn't come together in a ball and clung to the dough hook, you may want to keep mixing. If the recipe says to give two gentle folds during the rest period but the dough hasn't come together after the two folds, maybe give it a few more folds. Keep in mind that gluten develops from a combination of (1) putting some kind of force or pressure such as mixing, folding, dividing, and/or shaping on the dough and (2) just giving the dough more time.

Undermixed dough   Properly mixed dough

MARK AND FRAN FISCHER

Castle Valley Mill | Doylestown, Pennsylvania

Mark and Fran Fischer own and operate Castle Valley Mill in Doylestown, Pennsylvania. The mill was built on land originally owned by William Penn, and the first regional grains were ground there in 1730. After the Industrial Revolution in the 1800s and the agricultural revolution in the 1900s, the mill was largely abandoned and had fallen into disrepair. Mark's grandfather Henry Fischer preserved the mill in 1947, and Mark later restored the mill. Mark and Fran continue that work to this day, reviving antique stone mills and grain-processing machines and putting them back into operation. Today, Castle Valley Mill grinds only local and regional non-GMO grains, triple-cleaning the grains before a single pass in the stone mill.

> Most people don't know the difference between commercial grains and the heritage grains and flours that we make. But once they taste our grains, and bread made with our flours, they are blown away. And hundreds of people have told us that they can eat our products even though they had stopped eating wheat. They're thrilled to be able to eat pancakes again!
>
> I call our community the grain train: you've got to get the farm train moving along or we don't have good grains to mill. And the consumer train has to be moving, or there won't be any demand. That's what creates the push-pull to keep the train moving.
>
> We offer farmers more money for the grains that we're looking to mill. Farmers are realizing that you can actually make money farming better grains because there is demand, and they are not competing in the commodity wheat market.

If you're already an experienced bread baker, it also helps to keep in mind that the doughs in this book are going to feel stickier and weaker to you. They won't necessarily have the slick, rubbery, chewing-gum characteristics of dough made with refined white flour. That's the general effect of fresh milled and whole-grain flours. It's okay. Try not to overmix in an attempt to eliminate stickiness.

BE AWARE OF TEMPERATURE AND HUMIDITY

Similar to yeast, bread dough likes to be about the same temperature we like to be. Above 75°F feels a bit warm. Below 65°F starts to feel cool. Humidity is also a factor: below 40% relative humidity makes a room feel dry and could slow down fermentation, although high humidity of 75 to 85% tends be a nonissue with dough. For most breads, try to keep the dough within those general temperature and humidity ranges during the "room temperature" stages of bread making: 65° to 75°F temperature and 40 to 75% humidity. For recipes that specify "cool room temperature," shoot for 50° to 65°F, and for "warm room temperature," shoot for 75° to 85°F.

In a professional bakery, a lot of attention is paid to water temperature, but that has to do with the way large amounts of dough hold heat and with hitting consistency targets in the context of daily production. At the end of mixing, the ideal temperature for most doughs is between 76° and 80°F. At home, just use room-temperature water. The home-baker batches in our recipes are so small that the room you're mixing in will have a bigger effect on your final dough temperature than the starting temp of your water. For instance, if you have the heat on in the winter or the AC on in the summer or the windows are open and the fans are going, those conditions will cause wide fluctuations in temperature and humidity. Plus, in the end, the dough's temperature has less to do with mixing and gluten development and more to do with fermentation (more on that in the next chapter). Just be aware.

BAKER'S MATH PROVIDES A SNAPSHOT OF THE BREAD

Bread recipes, including the ones in this book, are usually written in a standard format that shows you at a glance how one bread compares to another. These baker's formulas allow you to easily change a recipe or scale it up or down without altering the basic proportions. Learning basic baker's math can help you progress from beginning to intermediate baking. It's all just simple arithmetic. And it's all used to calculate the *weight* of each ingredient. Weight is a much more precise measurement than volume (see page 4 for details). That's why serious bakers weigh their ingredients. The recipes in this book list the metric weight of each ingredient in grams first, followed by cups or tablespoons for reference. We strongly encourage you to weigh your ingredients. That move alone will automatically improve your chances of success with bread recipes.

Since everything is based on ingredient weights, the basic idea of baker's math is that you can make any quantity of bread you want. The formula itself is written out as percentages. The flour weight equals 100%, whether it's a single type of flour or a mix. The weight of every other ingredient is written as a percentage of the flour. All the ingredient percentages are then summed up, which gives you the total formula percentage. This total percentage is always more than 100%, something that throws beginners off. Get used to it!

For example, here is the baker's formula for Simple Sourdough Table Bread (page 149), a very standard formula:

INGREDIENT	%
flour	100
water	75
starter	20
salt	2.3
Total	197.3

To start calculating the weights of each ingredient, we scaled this bread for two medium-size loaves, the total amount that fits on a typical home oven baking stone. We chose 700 grams as the weight for each loaf (before baking), but you could choose another loaf weight. This makes the total dough weight 1,400 grams. Your total dough weight equals the total formula percentage. We already know that total percentage is 197.3%. To find the weight of the flour, you take the total dough weight, 1,400 grams, and divide it by the total formula percentage, 1.973 (remember, another way of writing 100% is simply 1). So, 1,400 g ÷ 1.973 = 710 g. That's your flour weight, or the weight corresponding to 100%.

To get the weights of the remaining ingredients, you multiply the flour weight by the percentage for each ingredient. For the water, 710 g × 0.75 = 532 g. For the starter, 710 g × 0.2 = 142 g. For the salt, 710 g × 0.023 = 16 g. To cross-check your math, add all the ingredient weights and make sure they equal the total dough weight that you wanted. Here's what the bread formula looks like with all the weights shown:

INGREDIENT	%	GRAMS
flour	100	710
water	75	532
starter	20	142
salt	2.3	16
Total	197.3	1,400

Not so bad, is it? The beauty of baker's math is that if you want to make a bigger batch or smaller or larger loaves, you just choose a different dough weight. The percentages remain the same. Even if you're not ready to start calculating baker's math yourself, do look at the percentages in our recipes to notice things like the bread's hydration, the professional term for the proportion of the water relative to the flour. The sourdough bread in this example has 75% hydration, making it a moderate-hydration dough. The dough for Bagels (page 97) has 55% hydration, a dry dough. Pane di Genzano (page 155), at 80% hydration, is a fairly high-hydration dough. You can glean a lot of information about a bread, such as how enriched it is and how the dough texture may feel, just by looking at the formula. You'll also notice that many breads hover around 2% salt.

USEFUL DOUGH TOOLS

People having been baking bread with primitive equipment for millennia. There's a huge variety of bakery tools you could buy. But unless you're deep in the dough matrix, just get the big things you need and maybe one or two tools you think would be fun to have. Here's a list of essentials, plus a few fun things. Most of these items can be found at restaurant supply stores, cooking supply stores, and baking supply websites.

Bannetons/proofing baskets. If you're just starting out, a round bowl lined with a tea towel makes a sufficient proofing basket for a round loaf. If you get into the bread habit, bannetons are easily obtainable and do a better job. They're traditionally made of wicker or bamboo and available in both round and oval shapes. They help to support the shape of the dough and maintain the correct level of moisture on the outside. Medium ones (8- to 9-inch diameter) are the most useful, but it's nice to have large ones (10- to 11-inch) on hand for some breads. Bannetons are sometimes sold with a fitted cloth liner. Use the liner if your dough is wet and you're worried about sticking, or if you want a less floury crust on the finished bread. Just flour the loaf before setting it in the cloth-lined banneton. If you're not worried about sticking, or if you really want the lovely basket print from the dough rising directly in the banneton, then skip the liner. In that case, the trick is to dust both the dough and banneton but avoid using so much flour that your finished loaf is caked with raw flour.

Beeswax wrap. Anywhere that we call for plastic wrap, you can easily use beeswax cloth. These wraps are trendy now, but it's an old technology: a piece of fabric dipped in a mixture of beeswax and oil that makes it flexible, moldable, waterproof, washable, and reusable. Claire is a huge fan and uses them for everything . . . to cover dough, to tent a banneton for proofing overnight, and to wrap cut pieces of bread. Not essential, but super nice to have.

Bench knife. Pro-bakers can't live without these, but a spackle knife from the hardware store also does the job. They're usually square with a flat metal spade-type blade and a wood or plastic handle. Buy one with a crisp metal edge, and do not use it to pry open cans. The straight edge is the whole point. Do not bend it.

Couche. A tea towel is a good stand in to start, but a couche (pronounced *koosh*) is nice to have if you're baking regularly. This natural flax linen fabric is arguably more versatile than a banneton because you can arrange it to support almost any dough shape. And it's essential for baguettes. Just dust it with flour and set the baguettes seam-side up on the couche about an inch apart, then you can make a fold in the couche and slide one baguette right next to its neighbor with the couche folded between them. This nesting system supports the final shape of the baguettes while regulating the temperature and moisture of the dough. When new, a couche is somewhat stiff, but it loosens up over time.

Digital scale. These are affordable and absolutely essential. Measuring by weight will improve your success rate dramatically. That's because volume measures like cups and tablespoons simply cannot match the precision of exact weights. Look for a digital scale with a minimum 5-kilogram (11-pound) capacity that measures in 1-gram increments. For these small home baker batches, it's also helpful to have a little pocket scale that can measure tiny amounts of dry yeast, such as 0.03 grams.

Dough proofing bucket. For bulk fermentation, find a dough bucket that's at least 4 quarts with a lid. It should fit in your fridge, and clear plastic is nice, so you can check on how much the dough has risen. They are inexpensive.

Dough scraper/pastry card. These flexible plastic or silicone scrapers come in various shapes and sizes, cost less than $1, and are super handy for folding dough and scraping dough from your bowls, hands, and countertop. If you find one large enough and with a tapered straight edge, you could even use a dough scraper in place of a stiff metal bench knife.

Mixer. This is the biggest investment, so get a mixer if you'll use it for other tasks as well as baking. Lower-end mixers aren't great for stiff bread doughs. Buy one that's at least 500 to 600 watts to avoid burning out the motor. And you want at least a five-quart bowl with a spiral dough hook attachment. Those funny C-shaped Captain Hook dough hooks won't do you much good, so avoid them. KitchenAid is a solid choice, and the array of available attachments makes it extremely versatile for rolling pasta, grinding meat, and even milling flour with a stone-mill attachment (see page 17).

Sourdough crock. Find a container or two for your pre-ferments and/or Sourdough Starter (page 147). Glass jars allow you to see fermentation activity through the side, but even plastic storage containers work.

Tea towels. Bread dough and fuzzy terrycloth towels do not play well together. You want a tight or closed weave. Linen works well, and oversized ones are particularly useful. Covering dough with a towel allows the dough to respond to environmental conditions like humidity and airflow. But if your room is dry or drafty and you're concerned about a skin forming on the dough, you can cover it with a lid, beeswax wrap, or plastic wrap instead of a tea towel. A couche also works anywhere a tea towel is called for.

Thermometer. An instant-read digital thermometer can help you get a sense of what 80°F dough feels like. Also, most breads are done when the loaf reaches an internal temp of 205°F, something you may want to check until you get more familiar with other signs of doneness. When it's crucial, we state the internal doneness temp in the recipe.

3

FERMENTATION

AFTER WE STARTED MILLING GRAINS AT VETRI, WE DECIDED TO MESS
AROUND WITH MAKING OUR OWN MALTED GRAINS AND MALT SYRUP.
Malting is a process of soaking grains in water to start germinating them
and then stopping the germination by drying the grain. Essentially, malting
makes it easier for grains to ferment and helps creates all kinds of flavors.
For instance, malt syrup tastes sort of like caramel but savory and only a
little sweet. It's so good, we started using it in everything. We glazed an
amazing foie gras dish with it, and we worked it into all kinds of breads,
like Malted Grain Sourdough (page 204). That bread has soaked malted
grain in it, too, which gives it these awesome little pops of malt flavor.

Around that time, we were getting ready for The Great Chefs Event, a fundraiser we've held every year for Alex's Lemonade Stand to benefit pediatric cancer patients. Great Chefs is going on fifteen years now! Sam Calagione, the founder of Dogfish Head Brewery, was coming that year and we started talking about malt syrup, something he knows a lot about. It's a key ingredient in beer making. He said if I could get him a gallon of our malt syrup, he could brew a keg of beer as a special collaboration to serve at the event—which sounded perfect.

We kept talking, and Sam told me about a trip he had taken to Cairo a few years earlier. On the wall of an ancient tomb there, he got to see the original hieroglyph that represented beer. He told me the symbol for beer is nearly the same as the symbol for bread. It makes sense. Both beer and bread were born in Egypt, and they both start with grains and yeast fermentation. When you think about it, the biggest difference is texture. Beer is liquid bread, and bread is solid beer.

Yeast—which makes the bubbles in bread dough and in beer—is at the heart of both products. But the truth is, those fermentation bubbles wouldn't even happen without something else: enzymes. These little guys kick off the entire fermentation process. Enzymes do the heavy lifting of turning a big grain into smaller components that the yeast can actually eat. That's why grains are malted to make beer: you soak the grains to release the enzymes. They break down the grain's larger nutrients into smaller ones. It's the same with bread dough: when you mix flour with water, enzymes start making food for yeast. Without enzymes, yeast fermentation would never happen, and bread would never rise.

Pretty cool stuff! Do you need to know all this science to make great bread? Or great beer? Of course not. People have been baking great breads and brewing delicious beers for way longer than scientists have been slinging around terms like "enzymatic activity." Bakers know from experience that those fermentation bubbles are what make a loaf of bread different from a wad of flour and water. But knowing a little more about the whole fermentation process may help you make even better bread. And a little is all we have room for here. Believe me, fermentation is a deep rabbit hole, and we're not gonna go all the way down it!! —MV

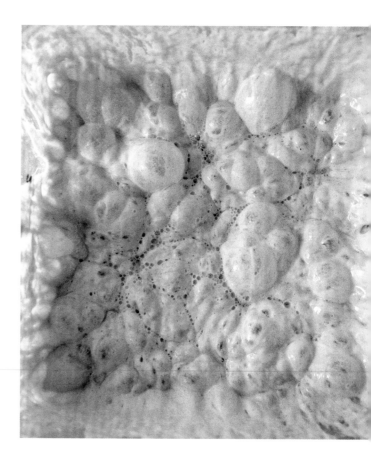

TWO TYPES OF FERMENTATION HAPPEN IN BREAD DOUGH

Fermentation is not like mixing, shaping, and baking. It's not really a "step" in the bread-making process. It happens the entire time you make bread, beginning as you mix. While it's not really an active stage for the baker, it's an active stage for the yeast—and it's critical. Yeast is a fungus, and as soon as it gets mixed with flour and water, it starts eating to survive. Yeast fermentation is basically the metabolic process of this little microbe feeding on sugars in the dough. As the yeast feeds, it gives off carbon dioxide and ethyl alcohol. The same thing occurs in beer making: yeast feeds on sugars and gives off carbon dioxide and alcohol. In bread, the carbon dioxide bubbles make the dough rise. If you don't ferment dough, you get crackers or dumplings. Your goal as a bread baker is to let this completely natural, beautiful process happen and guide it so it inflates the gluten structure you started creating during mixing. Then, when the dough reaches its full strength and full height, you bake the loaves. Simple, right?

Yeast fermentation is also known as alcoholic fermentation because of the alcohol it produces. Most of the alcohol disappears during baking. But there's a second type of fermentation at work, especially in sourdough breads: bacterial fermentation. This is the essential difference between yeast doughs and sourdoughs. In sourdough, there's a happy little community of yeast *and* beneficial bacteria (mostly lactic acid bacteria) feeding on the dough as well. These little microbes are the same kind that ferment other foods to make coffee, chocolate, vinegar, sauerkraut, pickles, kimchi, kombucha, yogurt, and fish sauces like Italian colatura. The bacteria in sourdough just prefer to feed on flour. They eat the sugars in bread dough and give off acids like lactic acid and acetic acid. Those acids are what make sourdough bread taste more sour. They also inhibit mold and make sourdough breads last longer when you leave them out. The acids help preserve the ingredients in sourdough bread just as they help preserve the ingredients in a jar of pickles.

FERMENTATION CREATES FLAVOR, DEVELOPS TEXTURE, AND IMPROVES DIGESTIBILITY

Flour, water, and salt bring their own flavors to bread dough, but yeast actually creates new ones. Yeast activity generates those incredible smells of fresh bread, those irresistible aromas that draw you in! This little microorganism transforms the mild-tasting starches in flour into all kinds of better-tasting flavors and aromas. The carbon dioxide that yeast gives off has a slightly sour taste, and the alcohol it makes can taste both sweet and bitter. Both carbon dioxide and alcohol dissipate when the bread is baked, but yeast creates other flavor compounds that remain and even intensify during baking. Those fermentation flavors can be buttery, fruity, sulfurous, spicy, and/or herbal. When feeding on high-extraction and whole-wheat flours, yeast can generate even more heady aromas like vanilla, rich and fatty nuttiness, and honeylike sweetness. Your flour and the yeast feeding on it are what make bread taste so good!

Naturally leavened bread dough, the pro-baker term for sourdough, brings even more flavor because there's a wider variety of these microorganisms in sourdough. The species that's in dry yeast is *Saccharomyces cerevisiae*, but a sourdough culture includes other species, and each one has a slightly different rate of feeding and likes slightly different temperatures. Some are better fermenters, and some produce really interesting flavor components like diacetyl, one of the flavors in butterscotch. That's reason alone to bake something like our Simple Sourdough Table Bread (page 149).

Then there are the flavors of bacterial fermentation. As the bacteria eat to survive, they transform sugars into acids. Some of them produce only lactic acid, and others produce lactic acid as well as acetic acid, carbon dioxide, and alcohol. That matters because lactic acid brings a slightly sweet, slightly tart taste to your bread. Think of the mild tang in yogurt. But acetic acid tastes more like vinegar. It's straight-up sour. The bacteria also break down proteins in the dough, allowing other flavors to emerge, like the scent of cooked potatoes or ground cloves. Really complex flavors! Depending on what flavors you're going for in your bread, you can kind of guide the bacterial fermentation process. Temperature is the key. Warmer temperatures throughout the bread-making process, but especially during bulk fermentation, tend to bring the more mellow flavors of lactic acid, while colder temperatures bring the brighter, sharper flavors of acetic acid. You know how using a touch of vinegar in cooking brightens everything up and makes it taste good? But if you use too much acid, it can overpower a dish? It's the same in bread! You can bring out some of those bright flavors in bread with cold fermentation. And you can get the best of both worlds—buttery and bright flavors—in breads like Panettone alla Vetri (page 275). That dough has a super-long fermentation time, but it's done at warm temperatures with a smaller amount of starter. All these little variations make subtle differences in the taste of your bread.

Time is another factor. The longer you let fermentation go at any point in the bread-making process, the more pronounced all the fermentation flavors get. With more time, you're basically allowing yeast, bacteria, and enzymes to transform more of the flour into more flavorful and aromatic compounds. But the party can go too far. If you forget about a batch of fermenting dough, some of the sweet-tart flavors and pleasant aromas we love in bread can develop into unpleasant odors, like the smell of paint fumes or nail polish. Just follow your nose: if it smells bad, it probably is! Let's say you're making sourdough and you notice those aromas; maybe your starter was left to ferment too long and needs more care and frequent feeding. A well-maintained starter will taste almost sweet and yogurtlike, with no off-putting aftertaste.

Yeast fermentation also affects the texture of bread dough. The carbon dioxide gas released by yeast aerates the dough; this makes the bread lighter and more pleasant to eat. Then, when the bubbles grow, they gently stretch the dough; this also strengthens the gluten, giving the bread better structure. The acids produced by bacteria also strengthen the gluten network even further. That's all good. But long fermentation times allow enzymes to continue breaking down protein in the dough. Overfermented dough can weaken so much that it loses its bubbles, and the bread fails to rise in the oven. You just have to watch to make sure things don't go too far.

For some bakers, fermentation is all about flavor. But it also makes bread more digestible and nutritious. Thanks to fermentation, some nutrients in flour, especially whole-grain and high-extraction flours, become more available to us to absorb. For instance, wheat bran—all bran, for that matter—contains phytic acid, which can inhibit your ability to digest protein and starch. Phytic acid also binds up iron, zinc, and various beneficial minerals. But the more thoroughly you ferment bread dough, the more phytic acid becomes neutralized, making your bread easier to digest and making it healthier, too. We're talking better flavor, better texture, better digestibility, and better nutrition. Fermentation for the win!

PREFERMENTS KICK-START FERMENTATION

Thoroughly fermenting dough makes better bread. That's why some bakers like to get a head start on the whole fermentation process—before they even start mixing. A preferment—quite literally—pre-ferments a portion of the flour that will go in your dough. If you're working with flour—like a freshly milled, high-extraction flour—that seems as if it might give you a looser dough, a preferment can help start strengthening the gluten early on. Preferments also begin developing flavor, texture, and digestibility without subjecting the entire batch of dough to the gluten-weakening effects of enzymatic activity.

If you use a preferment, you need to fit it into your baking schedule. Some preferments need less time, while some need more. There's a lot of confusing terminology among preferments because bread comes from so many baking traditions around the world. Here are the three main terms for yeasted preferments, the ones made with store-bought yeast. *Sponge* comes from the British baking tradition. This preferment usually has a lot of water that makes it pretty loose, and it's fermented for a relatively short time, thirty minutes to one hour at room temperature. *Poolish* is a type

Examples of sourdough starter on day 1 and day 14 demonstrate how it can be built up over a period of hours, days, or weeks to increase its activity and volume for use in a specific dough.

of sponge from the French baking tradition. It usually has 100% hydration (equal parts water and flour) and just a pinch of yeast, and it has a longer fermentation time, around eight hours at room temperature. *Biga* is Italy's yeasted preferment. It's a bit stiffer with lower hydration, a small amount of yeast, and an even longer fermentation time—more than eight hours at room temp. There's also *pâte fermentée*, which is just a portion of fermented dough reserved from a previous batch of bread for use in a future batch. Modern bakers borrow from all of these traditions because they make us better equipped to produce the breads we want. But the downside is that there is some inconsistency in the language we use to describe what are, essentially, variations of the same thing. Depending on the bread, we use both *biga* and *poolish* in the recipes in this book.

The preferments mentioned previously are made with commercial yeast, but there is a whole other category of naturally leavened or sourdough preferments. The term "naturally leavened" is synonymous with "sourdough," but we often prefer naturally leavened because it's more general. Among these naturally leavened preferments, you see all kinds of terms such as *sourdough starter*, *mother*, and *levain*. They're all essentially the same thing. Starter and levain are the most common terms. Some bakers use the term starter when talking about the continuously maintained culture, and levain only for the portion that's broken out and built up for a specific mix. Otherwise, these terms are interchangeable. And the most common hydration here is 100%. Why? Because it's the easiest math! To build up your own sourdough starter, see the recipe for Sourdough Starter on page 147. Or get one from a friend! Which is the better preferment, yeasted or naturally leavened? It depends on your preference: generally, yeasted preferments are more convenient to use, while naturally leavened preferments are more flavorful.

THERE ARE TWO MAIN PHASES OF FERMENTATION

Whether you use a preferment or not, once you mix your bread dough, the dough is often fermented in one "bulk" mass before you portion and shape it into loaves. This is called bulk fermentation and is the first main phase of fermentation. If you let dough ferment in bulk for a long time, the whole mass gets puffy and huge. With shorter bulk fermentation, you may just begin to see some bubbles form, and the dough volume may not change dramatically. Bulk fermentation ends when you divide and shape your bread. That is when the second phase, called final fermentation or proofing, begins.

You can lean more heavily on bulk fermentation or final fermentation in your bread-making process. Some of our doughs, like the one for Pita (page 77), have a longer bulk fermentation time and then don't rise much before baking. Others, like the dough for Bagels (page 97), are bulk fermented pretty quickly, then shaped and retarded, leaning more on final fermentation. You can only ferment dough so much. If you lean more on bulk fermentation, you tend to get a finer crumb structure in the bread, but that also means you don't have as much time for preshaping and shaping the loaves before they'll be ready to bake. If you lean more on final proofing, you tend to get a more irregular crumb structure in the bread.

RETARDING DOUGH CREATES MORE COMPLEX FLAVORS AND TEXTURES

Retarding, or chilling your dough in the refrigerator at either phase of fermentation, deliberately slows down and extends the whole fermentation process. A longer fermentation time brings out more complex flavors and textures in your bread. More acids are created, making the bread tangier and making the crust thicker and chewier. Because fermentation slows down, enzymes have more time to break more starch into sugar; this rounds out the bread's flavor and gives it a deep, dark, caramelized crust. Some fruity aromas also emerge from bacterial fermentation that happens at a cooler temperature.

If you decide to retard, you can do it during bulk fermentation or final fermentation. Each has a slightly different effect. Dough that's bulk fermented, shaped, and then retarded tends to develop a more irregular crumb and a more distinct, caramelized crust. Dough that's retarded in bulk, then shaped and baked, often has a more even, lacy, tender crumb with a less assertive crust.

When you start playing with all the variables, from pre-ferments to fermentation times and temperatures, you can really start to dial in the flavors and textures of the bread you want to make. That's what makes bread so infinitely interesting! If you're making a crusty sourdough like Omni Bread (page 169), you probably want more sour flavor and more acetic acid; this means you probably want to retard the loaves. For that bread, we use a pretty ripe starter (and not too much of it), then shape into batards (ovals), retard them overnight, and bake the loaves the next morning. But if you're making a softer, sweet bread that's naturally leavened, like Sourdough Brioche (page 207), the buttery, creamy flavors of lactic acid will probably be a more pleasant experience. In that bread, we use a fair amount of starter, bulk ferment the dough at warm room temperature (about 77°F), then proof the loaves overnight in a spot that's somewhat cool but not cold, to discourage acid production.

Now we're getting deep into the baking matrix! You might know you're a serious baker if you're never done juggling all the fermentation options. Just be observant as you make the dough. If you're a sourdough baker, get to know when your starter is at peak ripeness and ready to do its leavening work. Find a few spots in your home that tend to be warmer or cooler, so you can alter your starter or dough temperature simply by moving the starter or dough to a different spot. Get used to touching the dough and your countertop and noticing the temperature of a sunny windowsill or a shady corner of the room. Managing dough temperature is another aspect of how you manage fermentation. If you really want to get precise, you could invest in a small bread proofer, which allows you to specify the proofing temperature anywhere from 70° to 120°F. There are decent models available online for about $150.

ENZYMES FACILITATE FERMENTATION BUT EVENTUALLY WEAKEN BREAD DOUGH

Remember those little guys that kick off the whole fermentation process? The ones that make food for the yeast when you mix bread dough and when you malt grains for beer? Keep enzymes in mind as your dough ferments. They are constantly at work. Amylase in the flour is always breaking down complex starches into simple sugars. Have you ever noticed that when you eat rice or potatoes, the rice or potatoes start to taste a little sweet as you chew them? That's because your saliva also produces amylase enzymes, and they start converting the starches in the rice or potato into simpler sugars to help you digest the food. The same thing is happening in fermentation. In addition to the amylase, protease enzymes are also breaking down large protein molecules into smaller amino acids, which are easier to digest. Yeasts and bacteria feed on those simpler components, and fermentation gets rolling. For the most part, fermentation activity brings positive attributes to the dough. For instance, proteases help make bread dough more extensible, easier to shape, and more flavorful.

But, as we discussed earlier, sometimes things can get out of whack. If you leave your dough to ferment for too long, proteases have time to break down so much protein that they weaken the gluten structure. Then your dough may start to fall apart before you get it in the oven. Sad loaf! Or if your flour has a lot of enzyme activity (sometimes the case with freshly milled whole-grain flour and flour milled from grain that has germinated), you might get a more dense and pasty texture in the bread because the extra enzyme activity has weakened the gluten structure. Or if you use a lot of malted ingredients in the dough, the extra enzyme activity in the malted grain means you have to work fast to keep the dough from weakening too much. That's why we mix and shape the dough so quickly for Malted Grain Sourdough (page 204).

Another advantage of sourdough breads is that the acids in the sourdough slow down enzymatic activity. That helps prevent the bread from developing a pasty crumb and a weak gluten structure, so it rises better in the oven and tastes better in the mouth. Sourdough starter is especially useful when making rye breads because rye flour contains enzymes that keep working at pretty high temperatures, unlike the enzymes in wheat. The acids keep these enzymes from ruining your rye bread.

But, really, you don't absolutely have to know all this science. It's only useful insofar as it helps you make better bread! Enzymes are just another factor to be aware of, especially when using freshly milled flours.

IS THE DOUGH READY TO BAKE?

The bottom line in all this is that fermentation creates flavor, and thoroughly fermented breads taste better. Fast-fermented breads lack all those complex flavors and aromas we talked about on the previous page. That's why mass-produced breads usually don't taste as good, and it might be why some people have trouble digesting them. Just give your dough time for fermentation to work its magic. How much time? How do you know when the dough is ready to bake? It's a judgment call. Look at the dough and feel it.

Observe the dough's size as it goes through bulk fermentation and especially when you shape it. With most of our doughs, you're looking for a 30 to 50% increase in the volume of the shaped loaf before it's ready to bake. That said, some doughs may not rise much, and some are more forgiving than others. Depending on things like the health of your yeast or your starter and the temperature of your room or refrigerator, your loaf could be tall and puffy or pretty close to its original size when it's ready to bake. And either size may work. If your loaf is looking pretty small and you're trying to get a really good rise out of it in the oven, maybe score the top of it extra deeply before baking, because scoring helps bread dough expand. Or let's say you have a very puffy loaf that looks as if it's on the brink of collapse. Maybe you want to score that loaf short and shallow and load it gently into the oven.

Some bakers use the poke test to judge dough readiness. Poke the dough with your finger: if the dough doesn't bounce back or does just a little bit but you can still see the indentation, the dough is probably ready to bake. If the indentation bounces back immediately, the dough probably still has some strength to give up and may rise higher. Let it ferment a little longer. If the indentation from your finger not only stays but also seems to deflate the dough a bit, its strength is probably gone and the dough may be overproofed. Bake it immediately.

But we usually don't use that test. It works well with warm-fermented yeast breads but not as well with cold-fermented sourdoughs. It's not that we don't touch the dough. We do, but we're looking to get more information than a simple measurement of our fingerprint's spring-back or lack thereof. We also touch the dough to feel its temperature and to get a sense of how firm it is. Is the dough cool or warm? Is it full of air? You learn something about your dough with every touch. What you learn tells you if the dough is ready to bake.

The truth is, you have to learn to read your dough to know how well the fermentation has gone. By the end of the process, underproofed dough just won't have enough gas in it to expand in the oven and raise the loaf to its fullest height. In overproofed dough, the bubbles will have exerted so much pressure on the gluten network that the cell membranes tear, releasing gas and deflating the dough.

Once the dough is mixed, you control fermentation by adjusting times and temperatures. These decisions are really what define a baker's skill. You have lots of options. Mastery means dedicating the time to honing your powers of observation, so when you're faced with a choice, you can make a good call. Over time, you get a sense of what it is you're seeing and feeling in the dough as well as understanding the science behind it. This is one of the most frustrating and infinitely interesting things about bread: you can't comprehend it thoroughly if you don't actually make bread! If you are new to baking, there will be a huge period of time where you are just following instructions that you may not fully understand. That's okay. Actually, it's important. Do the motions described, handle the dough, observe it as it ferments, and you'll come to know. At some point, the things you notice will snap into place with the things that you've read. You'll start seeing how your flour, the mixing, your baking environment, and even your own hands play their roles in creating the flavor and texture of your bread. But accept the fact that after you do come to understand something that you've read and how it plays out in the dough, something new will pop up that makes you feel as if you don't know a damn thing. That's okay! There are lots of tiny epiphanies to be had in bread making. Both the understanding and the doing are what help you advance as a baker.

BRETT STEVENSON

Hillside Grain | Bellevue, Idaho

Brett Stevenson is the founder and head miller at Hillside Grain at the headwaters of Silver Creek in Bellevue, Idaho. Hillside is both a family farm working on regenerative agriculture and a mill that grinds flour from grain grown right at the farm. Brett's father, John, began farming the land in the early 1970s, and his award-winning barley became widely used in the brewing industry. Brett has a master's degree in environmental studies, and now she and her brother, Justin, are expanding the farm, improving water and soil management, and growing various types of wheat and other grains. They continually experiment with grain varieties to find out what grows best on the farm and what can be milled into the most flavorful, wholesome, fresh flours for regional bakers and cooks.

"I grew up on the farm. Our valley, our community, the farm, and my family all mean a great deal to me. My connection to my place and the land is deep. As a grain grower and miller, I feel a sense of responsibility to help change the status quo—to be better stewards of the land and improve food options.

I built the mill to build on our family farm. I wanted to provide fresh high-extraction flour from clean grain. I want bakers and consumers to not be scared of flour and bread. Bread should taste great and be good for you.

My dad has been growing high-quality malt barley for the brewing industry for a long time. More recently, we reintroduced wheat into our planting plan. I have been experimenting with heritage grains, including rare varieties from Rocky Mountain Seed Alliance, varieties from the Washington State University Bread Lab (see page 13), and Kernza, a perennial wheat from the Land Institute.

I recently started baking bread and am loving it. I find it intriguing, humbling, and, most important, rewarding. My starter reacts much faster when I use my own fresh flour. I also notice a lot more flavor. Our early adopters are loving the flour, too. The feedback from our community has been excellent, which is really encouraging."

4

SHAPE

BAKERS DON'T HANG OUT LIKE NORMAL PEOPLE. We socialize at five o'clock in the morning around a table piled with dough. Bench work is usually group work, and everybody gets to know each other. You shape loaves, shoot the shit, and talk about your lives and the world. It's one of the better aspects of baker life.

The bench is usually the first station you get put on in a bakery. Someone models how to shape the loaves so you can do it right. Then you do it. It's a safe spot for new people because you're only handling one loaf at a time. If you make five wonky ones and then one hundred good ones, that's fine. On the other hand, if someone inexperienced gets put on the mixing station, they can ruin an entire day's work before anyone catches the problem. So yeah, new bakers stay on the bench.

Bench work requires zero brain power. It is rote muscle memory. In a bakery, you might shape a couple hundred boules, a couple hundred batards, and a couple hundred baguettes. Divide, shape, divide, shape. If you have a romantic notion of working in a bakery, let me dispel some of that. It's super repetitive. A new baker will typically be tasked with something like shaping hundreds of hamburger buns, day in, day out. Then, if they keep showing up after a few months, it might be worth developing their skill on the bake, which is a medium-level skill, and then on the mix, which is the most highly skilled station in a bakery.

I feel a little bad for home bakers. Most aren't making enough bread to develop the muscle memory that makes shaping easy. That said, you're handling the dough at a transitional moment, so it is a good time to correct any potential problems. And even if your handwork isn't perfect, you're not likely to ruin everything. So that's nice. **—CKM**

DIVIDING IS THE FIRST STEP OF SHAPING

After bulk fermentation, you divide and shape your dough. At home, you just scrape the bulk dough onto a countertop, then eyeball it or weigh the pieces. The only tools needed are a bench knife (see page 32), some water, some flour, and maybe a scale.

If your batch size is two loaves, you can eyeball it and cut the dough in half. Who cares if the loaves are 50 grams off from each other? Eyeballing can also help reduce how much you handle the dough, which is a good thing.

Then again, it's totally valid to scale the pieces. Weigh the first one before cutting the rest, so you have a visual on the correct volume. But remember that every time you make another cut, you're working the dough, making it tighter and harder to shape.

Dos and Don'ts with Your Hands

When shaping dough, an underhandled loaf is generally better than an overhandled one.

Use a light, quick hand. The longer your hand lingers on the dough, the more likely it is to stick. Shaping bread dough is not like sculpting clay. You don't want to grab the dough and squeeze it. Guide it with brief touches. Think of it like playing hot potato with the dough.

Make your hand a paddle. Most things in life we do with our fingers. But for shaping, you generally want to turn your hand into a paddle. Bring your fingers together. Look at the tools used for handling dough. A scraper. A bench knife. They are more like spades than rakes. You want a broad surface for scooping and stretching the dough. Think of your hand as a paddle or a mitten and you'll get more control.

Minimize handling. If you attempt a shape and it goes sideways or is imperfect, hesitate before handling it again. The more you manipulate bread dough, the less likely it is to hold a shape. And if you handle it too roughly, you can tear the dough, knock out some gas, and reduce the volume. An imperfect first pass is better than a mangled second attempt. To minimize handling when removing your hand from a sticky loaf, swiftly peel it off instead of lifting straight up.

Try using water. We often work with a wet hand instead of a floured hand. Water is slippery and makes you less sticky. When you do use floured hands, periodically rub them together to get rid of extra dough. See page 48 for details on when to use water and when to use flour when shaping.

Learn to be like Teflon. The dough will want to stick to you, especially high-hydration doughs and ones made with freshly milled or whole-grain flour. You have to develop these manual skills, and in time you'll come to be nonstick.

PRESHAPING HELPS STRUCTURE
THE FINAL LOAF

Some loaves call for preshaping, where you give the dough pieces a uniform starting point before final shaping. Preshaping also starts creating some structure. Basically, you do a light round of shaping to establish what will be the top and bottom of the loaf and then allow it to relax briefly before going into the final shape. We mostly preshape on a wet countertop, although some recipes call for the more traditional light dusting of flour.

A typical preshape is to picture the piece of dough with four sides, then fold each side in toward the center and roll the loaf over so it rests on its seam (see four-fold photos on page 28). For longer loaves like Ursa Baguette (page 81) and Olive Filone (page 100), just take your shapeless wad of dough and roll it over into a loose coil, then put it seam-side down so the weight of the dough helps to seal it.

SHAPING CREATES TENSION
THROUGHOUT THE LOAF

Shaping isn't strictly necessary. You could just load a mass of dough in the oven. If it's been mixed and fermented properly, the bread would be okay. You'll probably get a flatter loaf, but that might be fine. We have a few slab-style breads that are minimally shaped and meant to have a somewhat flat profile, including 100% Sonora Slab (page 161), Ciabatta Grano Arso with Einkorn (page 173), and Red Onion Focaccia (page 84).

For a loaf with a higher profile, shaping coaxes the structural foundation you laid during mixing into whatever final form you want. It creates tension that helps the loaf hold its shape. Without that tension, the loaf may not hold its shape. To increase the tension, you typically fold and roll the dough in a way that doesn't break the skin. Notice any slack on the dough and try to get rid of any excess slack as you shape. If you're a new baker, notice which manipulations

For a typical preshape, picture the piece of dough with four sides, then fold each side in toward the center.

In final shaping, tighten up any slack to increase tension.

As you shape, aim for developing tension throughout the loaf.

are effectively tightening the dough and which are making it looser. Sometimes just picking up or moving a loaf will stretch it in a way that loosens the structure.

We bakers talk about surface tension a lot, but in an ideal world, shaping will create tension throughout the entire loaf rather than just on the surface. It is this tension that allows a loaf to expand up and out dramatically in the oven. To avoid a flat loaf, aim for developing the tension throughout the loaf as you shape.

WHEN TO SHAPE ON A WET OR FLOURED BENCH

We tend to shape boules and batards on a wet bench. We feel it's generally better to introduce a little water rather than flour into dough. Water also makes things less sticky, so the dough doesn't glue itself to your hands or the countertop as much. It's cleaner, allowing you to work faster. And it keeps the dough from forming a skin too quickly. Just drizzle a little water on your countertop and spread it around so the surface is wet and shiny. You don't want a big puddle. Whenever the dough sticks to your hands, re-wet your hands.

We sometimes use flour for boules and batards, but more often we use flour for doughs that are rolled out, like Pita (page 77), Beignets (page 133), and Cornetti (page 137). We also flour the bench for more extensive shaping, or taking a little piece of dough and shaping it into a long, skinny Ursa Baguette (page 81). With stiffer, drier doughs such as the one for Bagels (page 97), we only use flour as needed, if needed at all.

You often need a steady supply of bench flour, so it's a good idea to keep it on hand. It doesn't really matter what bench flour you use. For consistency, you can use whatever's in the dough. Or if you want to save a flour you enjoy working with, use something that you didn't like or whatever cheap flour you want to burn through.

HOW TO SHAPE A BOULE

A boule is a ball or round loaf of bread.

1. If your dough is especially slack, you may first want to repeat the preshape, flipping the seam back up and tucking the sides in.

2. Then you can roll it back onto its seam and tighten.

3. Now, to finish the shape, cup your hands around the dough and start dragging it in a circle with gentle pressure. Increase the tension all around the loaf by catching up any slackness underneath.

4. As you move, the seam should stay in contact with the countertop; this smooths it out and seals it. For large boules, it's easiest to use two hands. For small pieces made into rolls, use one hand. To transfer a large boule to a banneton, coat the top and sides liberally with flour, then transfer it into a floured banneton so the floured side of the loaf is down.

HOW TO SHAPE A BATARD

A batard is an oblong loaf of bread.

1. After preshaping, position the loaf seam-side up like a rectangle, with short sides left and right. Gently stretch the right side outward and then fold it in toward the center.

2. Repeat with the left side, gently stretching the left side outward and then folding it in toward the center.

3. Pick up the edge closest to you.

4. Then tuck and roll that edge in about a third of the way up the loaf.

5. Continue rolling away from you, tucking the dough into itself as you go.

6. Shape the dough into a taut blunt log. Avoid tearing the outside of the loaf, since that can lead to sticking issues or an irregular final shape. Seal the seam by pressing along it with the heel of your hand if necessary. To transfer a batard to a banneton, coat the top and sides liberally with flour, then transfer it into a floured banneton so the floured side of the loaf is down.

HOW TO SHAPE
A BAGUETTE

A baguette is a long, narrow loaf
of bread.

1. After preshaping, begin stretching the dough by lightly patting it out to a rectangle about 5 inches long.

2. Then gently lift the long edge closest to you, and tuck it in about a third of the way up the loaf.

3. Continue rolling away from you, curling the dough into itself as you go. You will have a blunt log.

4. Use your palms to gently roll the log back and forth from the center to the ends, extending the baguette.

5. Continue rolling back and forth from the center outward with even pressure until the baguette reaches its full length of 16 to 18 inches. As you get to full length, press down on the last inch or so to taper the ends slightly. If the seam hasn't sealed well, use your fingers to gently pinch and seal the seam along the length of the dough.

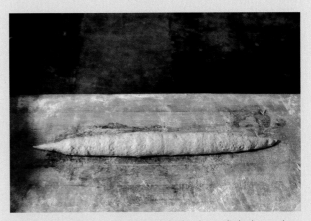

6. Keep in mind that the baguettes in this book are a little shorter than traditional baguettes, so that they will fit on home baking equipment. Note the length of your baking stone before shaping baguettes.

HOW TO SHAPE A ROUND BRAID

This round braid begins with four ropes.

1. Divide the dough into four equal pieces, then roll the pieces into ropes, each about 16 inches long and 1 inch thick. Lay one rope down horizontally on the countertop (ends to your left and right). Lay the second rope down vertically, perpendicular to the first, slightly right of the center of the first rope.

2. Lay the third rope over the second, parallel to the first, with a ½-inch space between them. That space helps prevent the center of the braid from binding up too tightly.

3. Now lay the fourth rope over the third, parallel to the second, and then cross it under the first rope. The ropes should now all be symmetrical and in pairs pointing up, down, left, and right.

4. Think of the ropes like a clock. Start with the rope that's just shy of six o'clock. Moving clockwise, lay that rope over the one next to it.

5. Next, lay the rope at nine o'clock over the one next to it, and tug that rope down slightly.

6. Then lay the rope at twelve o'clock over its pair, tugging that rope to the left slightly.

7. Finally, lay the three o'clock rope over the one next to it, tugging that rope up slightly. You just crossed the ropes of each pair moving in the same direction around.

8. Now, switch directions and move counterclockwise. You will be breaking up the original pairs. Start at the six o'clock rope that is under its pair and lay that rope over the very next rope to the right of it.

9. Continue moving counterclockwise and lay the next rope over the rope to the left of it near twelve o'clock.

10. Move counterclockwise and lay the next rope over the rope to the left of it near nine o'clock.

11. Move counterclockwise and lay the next rope over the rope below it near six o'clock.

12. Now, switch directions back to clockwise. Lay the six o'clock rope over the rope to the left of it.

13. Continue moving clockwise and lay the next rope over the rope above it near nine o'clock.

14. Move clockwise and lay the next rope over the rope to the right of it near twelve o'clock. Note how ropes that were under now go over.

15. Take each of the loose ends and connect it to its nearest partner in the circle, pinching the ends together.

16. After pinching the ends all the way around the loaf, the perimeter will look sort of ragged, and the loaf will be flat. To clean it up, tuck the pinched ends under, cupping the dough in your hands to create a pert, symmetrical round loaf.

HOW TO SHAPE AN OBLONG BRAID

This oblong braid begins with four ropes.

1. Divide the dough into four equal pieces, then roll the pieces into ropes, each about 10 inches long and 1 inch thick, tapering the ends to a point. Line up your four ropes vertically on the countertop with an inch or two between each. Pinch the top ends together to seal.

2. Number each rope position 1 through 4 from left to right. Begin braiding by laying rope 1 over ropes 2 and 3 moving from left to right.

3. Then place rope 4 over rope 1, moving right to left.

4. Now return to the left-most rope, which is now in position 1. Repeat the pattern, laying 1 over 2 and 3, moving left to right.

5. Then lay 4 over 1, moving right to left.

6. Repeat the pattern as many times as needed to finish the braid.

7. Pinch the ends together.

8. Then tuck the ends under to create a symmetrical oblong loaf.

KELLY WHITAKER
Noble Grain Alliance | Boulder, Colorado

Kelly Whitaker is the chef and owner of Basta and Dry Storage restaurants in Boulder, Colorado, as well as The Wolf's Tailor and Brutø restaurants in Denver. He co-founded the Noble Grain Alliance to connect farmers and chefs, restore local heritage grains to Colorado regional farms, and help distribute high-quality grains and freshly milled flours to chefs and bakers in the area. Heirloom wheat varieties and fresh flours form the backbone of the menus at his restaurants. Dry Storage is both a café and milling operation that grinds heritage grains into flours for the restaurant and for local chefs and bakers.

"

There are so many misconceptions surrounding bread. One of the biggest is that the bread-making process is more important than the flour you use.

Our nonprofit's mission is simple: support regional heirloom grain practices so that everyone has access to good whole grains. This has connected us with lots of folks who are interested in changing the grain landscape of Colorado and beyond.

Chefs care about sustainable seafood and the problems of the oceans. Wheat fields are the oceans of the land, and the problems facing these natural landscapes are the same.

In Boulder, people expect local ingredients, but nobody expected us to be milling flour in the back of the kitchen. When we show them the mill and the seed trials in our garden, they connect intensely to the food they just had.

"

5

BAKE

AT MY FIRST BAKING JOB IN NORTHEAST PHILLY, I LEARNED ALMOST AS MUCH ABOUT FIRST AID FOR BURNS AS I DID ABOUT BAKING BREAD. One day, I was pulling loaves from a tall convection oven that spins an entire rolling rack of bread inside. Sometimes this oven would stop rotating, leaving dozens of loaves stranded mid-bake and an aggressive fan blowing on one side. I would have to manually pull each tray of bread off the rack. That day, I was baking large, long pan loaves, and each tray had three heavy pans baking at 400°F. When you pull a heavy sheet pan like that, it's tippy, so you have to support it near your body. When I jerked one of the trays near the top of the rack, I pulled it right into my throat.

I don't want to come off as accident prone, but I did get another memorable burn in New Orleans, while getting ready to teach a bread class at Bellegarde Bakery. This one was pretty recent. I was loading the deck oven, chatting with another baker, and I accidentally steamed the deck I was about to load instead of the one I had just loaded. When I opened the oven, there was a ton of steam in the deck, and I was standing super close to the door. The steam completely blasted my face and chest. I taught the whole class trying to pretend I wasn't in pain. Three days later, I had a 3-inch blister on my chest. Four months later, a blotchy scar.

Anytime I'm working on a new setup, I just know I'm going to burn myself. I've accepted it. There's so much muscle memory from working my usual setup that I'll inevitably bump an unfamiliar oven door or touch a slightly higher rack or lower tray when I'm getting used to a new space. If you haven't done much baking in your home oven, you may not be used to moving hot stuff around in it. Of course, I don't want you to burn yourself. But I want you to know that you probably will. If it happens, know that the burns aren't so bad. Scars fade. If they didn't, both of my arms would look insane. And there's always a good story to tell, even if folks are too shy to ask.

Oh right, then there's the one where I burned my forehead on my last day working at Fork restaurant in Philly. Very dignified. —CKM

WHAT HAPPENS IN THE OVEN

During the bake, some dramatic changes take place. Your loaf should already have a lot of air bubbles in it. The fermentation begun hours or days earlier reaches its peak in the oven. When the dough heats up, yeast activity briefly speeds up until the yeast becomes so hot that it dies (around 140°F). Before that happens, the yeast gives off a big burst of carbon dioxide and alcohol. The vapors further inflate the bubbles in the dough, the gases expand from the heat, and the loaf enlarges. This "oven spring" tends to happen within the first ten minutes. That stage of baking is particularly important for hearth-style breads, which are baked freeform (without a pan) directly on the deck or floor of an oven. To replicate the effects of a hearth oven, you want to maximize the initial expansion for good loaf volume.

What happens next is not quite as visible to the naked eye. As the dough temperature climbs, the gluten proteins in the dough start coagulating, solidifying the crumb. Simultaneously, the starches gelatinize, giving the crumb a somewhat creamy texture and, in some cases, a translucent appearance. When the internal temp of the loaf reaches about 200°F, the bread's crumb structure is formed. The inside of a loaf will dry out with continued baking, which may or may not be desirable, depending on the character of the bread. Outside, the surface gets hotter and continues to dry and brown, developing the crust. Depending on the dough and the baking environment, the crust can be thin or thick, crisp or soft or chewy, light tan in color or nearly burnt, and relatively mild tasting or full of intense, bittersweet, roasted flavors.

STEAM IMPROVES OVEN SPRING AND CRUST FORMATION

It helps to think of baking as two stages: the oven-spring stage and the crust-setting and darkening stage. The first is more humid; the second is dry.

To optimize the first stage, modern ovens use steam injection, creating a moist environment at the beginning of the bake. Steam improves oven spring by delaying crust formation. And since water transfers heat faster than air, the steam very quickly gelatinizes the starches on the outside of the loaf, making them extra stretchy and shiny, which leads to a crust with an attractive color and crisp texture. So, steam helps you get both the dramatic oven spring and satisfying crust that characterize beautiful hearth-style breads like Spelt Sourdough Boule (page 157). Our basic home-oven method, using a baking stone and a metal pan over the dough, approximates the baking environment of a steam-injected oven.

There are many other bread styles, of course. Some gorgeous breads, like Schiacciata con l'Uva (page 209) and Ursa Challah (page 119), have minimal oven spring and don't benefit much from steam. Instead of puffing up dramatically in the oven, these doughs rely more on being at the maximal state of proofing when you load them.

SCORING TECHNIQUES

Batard single score

One quick, moderately deep (½ inch) slash from end to end on the loaf, as on Simple Sourdough Table Bread (page 149)

Batard double score

Two quick, moderately deep slashes with about 2 inches of overlap between the end of one and the beginning of the other, both scores centered down the top of the loaf with about a ⅜-inch space between each score, as on Sesame Durum Bread (page 152)

Batard four score or diamond

Two moderately shallow (about ⅜ inch) parallel slashes about 2 inches apart, diagonally across the loaf from top left to bottom right and two more diagonally from top right to bottom left, like a diamond, as on Omni Bread (page 169)

Baguette scoring

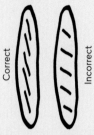

Up to five moderately shallow score marks down the center of the baguette with about an inch of overlap between the end of one and the beginning of the other and with about a ¼-inch space between the slashes, as on Ursa Baguette (page 81). The most common scoring mistake I see on baguettes is cutting too diagonally with the cuts too far apart. While the loaves are scored on a bit of a diagonal, it's not much. Imagine a ½-inch-wide column down the center of the baguettes and keep the cuts within that ½-inch column, running the cuts parallel to each other. The cuts should be side-by-side for about an inch on the ends of each cut.

Boule or miche four score or square

Four moderately deep slashes that meet or slightly overlap on their ends, forming a square on the top of the loaf, as on Buckwheat Buttermilk Bread (page 167)

Boule or miche cross or X scoring

Two ½-inch-deep, long crosscuts all the way across the loaf, as on Chocolate Rye Sourdough (page 189)

Epi scissor cutting

Deep angled cuts with a pair of scissors three-fourths of the way through a baguette down the length of the loaf with the cut pieces of dough set at alternating sides along the length of the loaf to mimic a head of wheat. This scissor cut is an alternative to scoring a baguette.

Wheat-stalk scoring

To mimic individual grains along a stalk of wheat, nick one vertical and four angled, staggered cuts (about ¼ inch deep) on almost any shape, such as Olive Oil Durum Rolls (page 121). This pattern is both decorative and functional.

Sausage/stripe scoring

A series of shallow (¼ inch) slashes running at a slight angle across the loaf with about an inch between cuts, as on Deli Rye (page 199)

SCORING IMPROVES OVEN SPRING

You know those diagonal cuts you see on the top of a baguette? They're not just decorative. Slashing, or scoring, the dough allows it to expand as much as possible in the oven. When you score a loaf, you're creating a guided weak point for the expanding dough to fill. If you don't score, you're likely to get a compact, tight loaf. Or the expanding gases in some loaves will build up so much pressure that the oven spring overcomes the dimensions of the crust and it will blow out, probably in an uneven and unattractive way. Scoring dough helps prevent that.

There are some bakers who favor incredibly elaborate scoring patterns with dozens, if not hundreds, of tiny scores over a loaf. That's not our style. Generally, we like just two to four cuts. You get better oven spring that way. On a batard, a single score along the top maximizes an open crumb by creating a dramatic rise along the entire length of the loaf. But let's say you want a more evenly risen loaf. Or maybe you want a crust that looks smoother when the bread is sliced. In those cases, make multiple score marks instead of just one. The little strips of dough between the scores act like belts, holding the dough up so it rises up evenly instead of just out. And the scored dough rises up along the score marks, curling slightly into crispy little flaps or "ears." If you're worried about a boule flattening out, you can make several smaller slashes, so the areas between the slashes will puff up. On the other hand, a dough you expect to spring a lot will benefit from longer, connected cuts. See the Buckwheat Buttermilk Bread (page 167) for an example. The square slashed into the top of that dough releases tension all around the boule, allowing lots of expansion. It also creates a nice square cap on top.

When you score a loaf, do it quickly and with purpose. Slice it like you mean it! If you move too slowly, the dough will bunch up instead of cutting cleanly. To help the dough expand fully and help prevent the score mark from sealing up, hold the blade at an angle instead of cutting straight down. The flap of the cut prevents the expanding area from setting too soon. We think the best tool for the job is a double-sided razor blade. But you can also use a baker's lame (see page 64). A thin serrated knife is the next best thing. Either way, score your loaves immediately before they go in the oven, so the score mark doesn't seal up before baking.

HOW TO USE THE BAKING STONE–HOTEL PAN METHOD

For hearth-style baking, you want to maximize humidity at the beginning of the bake. A lot of artisan bakeries now rely on steam-injected deck ovens with sealed chambers for minimal air movement. These ovens also have dampers that can be opened to vent humidity toward the end of the bake and finish forming the crust.

Home ovens are coming along. Some have proof settings or convection fans that can be set at different speeds. Some high-end ones even have steam injection. But you really don't need all that. You can make world-class breads in a regular old home oven. That's how we make most of our breads at Vetri. That's how the breads in the pictures in this book were baked. We wrote all of the recipes for a standard home oven that could be gas or electric. You don't need convection or steam injection.

To replicate the baking environment of a hearth oven, we like to place the dough on a large hot baking stone in the oven and set a large metal pan, called a hotel pan, over it to seal the baking chamber. That setup traps steam and allows you to bake multiple loaves at once. It's similar to the Dutch oven method that many home bakers use. But it's more versatile. It's a piece of cake to lay a couple loaves of virtually any shape on a baking stone and cover them with a pan. But if you're baking a single small or medium boule or batard, the Dutch oven method is also great (see page 65).

For this stone-and-pan method, preheat your oven with the baking stone inside for at least 45 minutes. An hour is better. It can take that long for the stone to fully preheat. The stone increases the overall thermal mass of your oven, approximating the conditions of hearth baking. The stone's high heat capacity and its direct contact with the dough transfer tons of energy into the dough, improving its oven spring. If you try to bake a hearth-style sourdough loaf in a home oven without fully preheating the stone, or with no stone at all and just a sheet pan, you'll probably get unsatisfying results.

It's best practice to preheat the hotel pan, too. You want everything in the baking environment fully charged with energy. A full-size hotel pan and a large rectangular baking stone (see "Useful Baking Tools," right) allow you to bake two or three loaves at a time. Large-format loaves such as Farro Miche with Whey (page 164) also do well with this setup.

Once everything's preheated, the basic load-in goes like this: move the hot hotel pan to your stovetop (use dry kitchen towels or hot pads!) and load the loaf or loaves onto the stone. Then set the inverted hotel pan over the loaves, resting the back side of the pan on the stone, while spraying water into the top of the pan to trap steam, and finally cover the loaves with the inverted pan. A spritz of water upward into the pan gives the loaves a nice infusion of moisture at the beginning of the bake. Later in the bake, steam comes mostly from the loaves themselves. For some breads like Horse Bread (page 194), instead of spritzing water into the baking environment, we boost humidity by placing a metal bowl or pan of hot water on a lower oven rack. Adding rocks to the water bowl is even more effective: they increase surface area, absorb and retain heat, and produce more steam throughout longer bake times.

Another pro tip: keep your kitchen towels or hot pads, razor, and spray bottle in the same spot every time you bake. That way, your load-in movements will be smooth and quick. It's easy to get flustered when you're loading. Develop a consistent flow and you'll simplify load in and minimize the time your oven door is open, maximizing oven heat. And you're less likely to get burned.

When stage one of baking is complete (the bread puffs up from oven spring), typically around 20 minutes, remove the hotel pan for stage two: crust setting and darkening. In this stage, you want to dry out the exterior of the loaf so it caramelizes, darkens, and thickens as the crumb is setting inside the loaf.

USEFUL BAKING TOOLS

You don't need much. A baking stone and a big pan to cover it are the most important tools for hearth-style breads. The rest of what's covered here is somewhat optional.

Baking stone. The ideal baking stone will come as close to covering an entire rack of your oven as possible. At the very least, the stone has to be larger than the hotel pan you'll cover it with to trap steam. Otherwise, there's no point in doing the baking stone–hotel pan method. To accommodate a full-size hotel pan, look for at least a 12 by 20-inch baking stone. Up to a 14 by 20-inch will fit in most home ovens. At least ½ inch thick is good, but thicker is better because that means more heat capacity. We like to leave our baking stone in the oven on a lower middle rack. Bread cooked on a sheet pan will burn on the bottom if you put the pan right on the hot stone. So, we usually bake sheet-pan items on a separate higher rack.

Bread knife. The whole point of a bread knife is the sawing action. Get a long one, especially if you bake a lot of large boules. It doesn't need to be expensive.

Cooling rack. We cool most breads on a wire rack. It's helpful if the rack fits into a half-sheet pan, so you can use them together for things like draining fried Beignets (page 133).

Dutch oven. If you want to use the Dutch oven method (see page 65), you'll need a 6-quart or larger Dutch oven. A nice alternative to a true Dutch oven is a cast-iron combo cooker. It's a deep pan and a shallow pan that fit together. You can use the shallow pan as the base and then cover it with the deep pan as the lid. No more dropping loaves all willy-nilly into a deep Dutch oven. No more reaching your hand into a super-hot Dutch oven to score your loaf.

Hotel pan. These are the rectangular pans you see at buffet steam tables. We use them as lids in our home oven hearth-style baking method. You need only one of these pans, and they're pretty inexpensive. If you can spring for it, get a thicker one, about 20 gauge. Go for a full-size hotel pan (20 by 12 by 6 inches). You can also get away with a

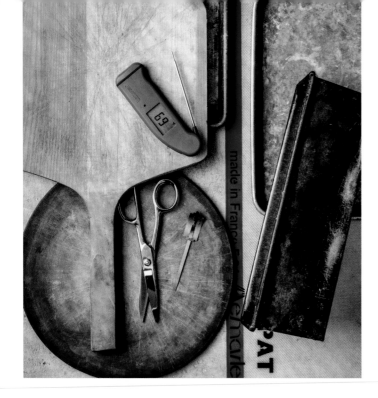

Loaf pans. We did all our recipe testing in metal loaf pans. They're the most versatile and durable. If you want to bake in ceramic or glass, adjust the baking time up and temp down (for glass) or get to know your ceramic pans (results will vary). The standard loaf pan we use is 9 by 5-inch, slightly larger than 8½ by 4½-inch, another common size. If you have the 8-inch, you can still bake our pan loaves in it; just keep in mind that its total capacity is about 2 cups less than the 9-inch. One or two recipes also call for special baking pans like a lidded Pullman pan for Brioche (page 115). But you can change the pan size and your loaf shape if you like. Instead of baking brioche in a Pullman pan for perfectly square slices, you can bake it in a 9 by 5-inch pan. Just try to match the capacity from pan to pan (measure the capacity of a pan by pouring water into it, then pouring the water into a measuring cup). Or if you bake a large volume of dough in two smaller pans, remember that bread bakes faster in a smaller pan.

4-inch-deep one for many of our breads. Either way, the pan needs to be slightly smaller than your baking stone so that the pan sits on top of the stone, covering the stone's surface. For round and oblong breads, you could even use a metal mixing bowl as a lid instead of a hotel pan. But hotel pans are inexpensive and easy to find. Pick one up at a restaurant supply store.

Kitchen towels. We generally prefer kitchen towels or hot pads to oven mitts. The mitts are cumbersome to take on and off when lifting hot lids, scoring loaves, and loading the loaves into the oven. Mitts also tend to burn through in the spots where you need the most heat protection, rendering them useless. Towels and hot pads are more versatile. But essentially, these items are interchangeable.

Lame. Pronounced *LAHM*, this baking term refers to a razor with a handle, used to slash the tops of bread before baking. There are all kinds of fancy, expensive lames out there; you don't need them. Just buy the simple, straight-handled kind that looks like a coffee stirrer. But a handle isn't strictly necessary, either. You can also just buy a few ten-packs of the double-sided razors that barbers use, available at most pharmacies and hardware stores. (One-sided razors are too thick.) A final option is a thin serrated knife, but it's only a meh-okay substitute that doesn't work as well as the other two.

Parchment paper. We often line sheet pans with parchment paper. It comes in handy for loading, too, because you can slide the parchment and loaves onto your baking stone in one easy movement. Instead of using parchment paper, you could line a sheet pan with a Silpat, a reusable nonstick, flexible baking mat made of silicone and fiberglass mesh. A Silpat is too grippy to use as a peel for loading and unloading, but it's perfect for baking pastries like Sonora Graham Crackers (page 216).

Sheet pans. We use sheet pans quite a bit, mostly half sheet pans (18 by 13 by 1 inch). Lined with parchment, an inverted sheet pan comes in handy as a makeshift peel for loading loaves into the oven. Sometimes we bake directly in sheet pans, as in Red Onion Focaccia (page 84) and Lemon Durum Cake (page 215).

Spray bottle/mister. An essential item for steaming your loaves with the stone-and-pan method. Any cheap mister will do. If you're being picky, look for one that produces a large volume of fine mist with every squeeze.

Thermometers. Hopefully, you already have a few thermometers like a digital oven thermometer, an instant-read thermometer, and a frying thermometer, which is useful for making Beignets (page 133).

HOW TO USE OTHER BAKING METHODS

If you're already used to the Dutch oven method, our preferred stone-and-pan method might sound familiar. The two methods are pretty much interchangeable. As with the stone-and-pan method, you preheat your oven with the Dutch oven (and its lid) inside for forty-five minutes to one hour. Then load the loaf into the hot Dutch oven, score the loaf, put on the hot lid (using a towel or hot pad), and bake. We use the Dutch oven for our Simple Sourdough Table Bread (page 149). But overall, the Dutch oven method is less versatile than the stone-and-pan setup because the dimensions of your Dutch oven limit the size and shape of the

bread you can bake. And, unless you have more than one Dutch oven, you have to repeat the process for each loaf, whereas the stone-and-pan method allows you to bake several loaves at once.

We'd like to say that a baker's cloche (a ceramic base and lid) is a great option, but it's just not versatile enough. At least you can cook other stuff in a Dutch oven. With a cloche, you can bake only one shape of bread. Or you have to buy several, and that gets pricey. Would someone please make a big rectangular cloche that can accommodate a variety of loaf sizes and arrangements?

Don't have a baking stone or a Dutch oven? And don't want to buy either? No problem! Not all breads

GRAISON GILL
Bellegarde Bakery | New Orleans, Louisiana

Graison Gill is the baker-owner of Bellegarde Bakery in New Orleans, Louisiana. He trained at the San Francisco Baking Institute and has been baking professionally for more than ten years. Bellegarde mills thousands of pounds of flour each week and bakes bread for local restaurants and retailers. All breads at the bakery are made by hand, with sourdough and fresh stone-ground flours milled in-house from identity-preserved, single-origin grains. Bellegarde's mission is to connect community and ecology through gastronomy. The bakery sells bread, pasta, and flour direct to customers, and hosts monthly baking and tasting workshops for both the general public and professional chefs and bakers.

"In New Orleans, we don't live in a grain belt. In the Northeast or California, you can use all local wheat, but we don't have the climate to grow grain. That's why we've been building our growers' network for more than ten years.

Flour is the same as coffee, tomatoes, oysters, grapes, or any other ingredient. It has a relationship to the land. That relationship is terroir.

At the end of the day, it's about taste. We spend a lot of time finding the best grains we can, and in doing so we hope that we are making others more accountable, traceable, and transparent in their choices. But no matter what, it's all about the bread. If it tastes great, the flavor will evangelize the message, no matter what that is.

The intimacy and ritual of making bread is why most bakers are drawn to doing this work. At Bellegarde, we sell mostly wholesale. That keeps us focused on raising the bar for our bread, not on salads, cupcakes, or Wi-Fi passwords."

need that kind of oven spring. An oven and a sheet pan are all you need for breads like Potato Bread (page 110), Grissini (page 113), Olive Oil Durum Rolls (page 121), Ursa Challah (page 119), Pane alla Zucca (page 130), and Cornetti (page 137), and for pastries like Prune Scones (page 219), Fennel Orange Biscotti (page 223), Hazelbutter Cookies (page 224), Lemon Durum Cake (page 215), and Taleggio and Strawberry Stuzzichini (option, page 230). A plain old loaf pan is all you need for Cinnamon Raisin Pan Loaf (page 129), Einkorn Pan Loaf (page 160), Seeded Schwarzbrot (page 183), and Sourdough Brioche (page 207). Easy peasy.

DIFFERENT BREADS BAKE AT DIFFERENT TEMPERATURES

Generally, higher baking temperatures (around 500°F) are best for wetter, leaner doughs like Ursa Baguette (page 81), Spelt Sourdough Boule (page 157), and Omni Bread (page 169). A hot oven gives you great oven spring and a legit crust. Drier doughs, such as the one for Bagels (page 97), do better with moderate temperatures that allow more time for the heat to travel through the denser bread without burning the outside. With enriched doughs, such as Ursa Challah (page 119), the sugar, fat, and/or eggs make the crust darken sooner, so to avoid burning, they're usually baked at even lower temperatures, around 350°F.

Overall, the crust on bread is a bigger consideration with lean doughs, particularly lean sourdoughs. If you like, you can achieve a thicker, chewier crust with some crunch in it on these breads. To get that kind of crust, turn the oven temp down a notch so the exterior of the loaf has more time to dry out. Or, if you want your sourdough bread to have a thinner, softer crust, bake it in a hotter oven for less time. But we're talking factors of 15 degrees and a difference of maybe five to ten minutes. You still need to make sure the dough is baked through. And with relatively long baking times, you don't want to completely carbonize significant parts of your crust. A little burn is good. It gives the crust character—just as it gives a person character!

HOW TO JUDGE DONENESS

Doneness is one of those spidey senses you develop over time. The good news is that there's a decent threshold of acceptability. You can poke your loaf with a thermometer and see if you're at 200°F, but we've never enjoyed stabbing our loaves right as they come out of the oven all beautiful and promising. Weight is a pretty good test. With lean doughs, you should be able to feel that a lot of the moisture has baked off. A fully baked loaf feels somewhat light for its size. Visually, the crust should look completely set, especially along the bottom. And the bread should have good color.

When in doubt, let the loaf bake. If your crust isn't burning, there generally isn't much harm in letting it go a little longer. The darker the crust gets, the more flavorful the bread will be. If you scored the loaf, you can judge doneness by taking a look at the lip around the score mark. It will pull up and get darker than the rest of the loaf. To the untrained eye, it may even look burnt. But there's a black that is very dark yet still brown and delicious. That's the level of browning you're going for in some sourdough breads, like Pane di Genzano (page 155).

Some people use the thump test, where you rap the bottom of the loaf and listen for a hollow sound. We don't think that's a great test, as satisfying as it may be. Weight and color are better indicators. We still do the thump but just for pleasure.

If your crust darkens too quickly, you can tent the loaf or lower your oven temperature. That will allow more time for heat to travel through the loaf and finish baking the crumb. With some larger-format hearth-style loaves, you can even turn the oven off to finish setting the crust without drying out or burning the bread.

COOLING HELPS SET THE CRUMB

Cooling is the last stage of baking. When you pull a loaf from the oven, the crumb is still setting up and releasing moisture. Cooling the bread allows moisture to dissipate throughout the loaf; this does soften up the crust a bit.

Cooling also lets some air pressure out of the bubbles in the crumb, compacting it a little. You can hear a crusty loaf crackle as it cools and shrinks.

Cooling is especially important for larger loaves because they take longer to cool off. If you cut a large boule too soon, it will go stale more quickly because it loses so much moisture. But for smaller and thinner breads, like dinner rolls and focaccia, it's okay to enjoy them warm. Then there are breads like All Rye (page 186), where it's not just about cooling them off. For rye bread, this last step is better called curing. Long cooling vastly improves the flavor as well as the texture because enzymes are still active in these breads even after they have been removed from the oven. Let your rye bread cool completely, even overnight, and you'll get a stronger, tangier, sweeter loaf. Cool your loaves on a wire rack to keep steam from making the crust soggy. After cooling, ryes can be moved to a bread box to cure.

Cutting into the finished loaf is the big reveal of the success of every step that was taken hours or days earlier. It can be elating or crushing. It's only after you slice the loaf that you can start troubleshooting for next time (see page 70).

Ways to Store Bread

After it's baked, your bread may be good for twenty-four hours or up to a week. Larger-format loaves that are naturally leavened and higher in whole grain tend to last longest. Enriched doughs also have a long shelf life. Lean breads and smaller-format loaves have a shorter shelf life of maybe one to two days.

At home, we like to store bread in a bread box, an old-fashioned tin on the counter. A cabinet works well, too. Try to keep your bread in a not-too-humongous container that's also not too airtight. You want a little airflow but not a full draft. That's why paper bags work well. If you're in a really dry environment, plastic is helpful. Or try beeswax wrap (Claire's favorite). It easily forms itself around a loaf and lets air both in and out. If your bread seems to be going stale, get more life out of it by making Bread Crumbs (page 240), Croutons (page 241), Panzanella (page 246), or Ribollita (page 248).

Bread freezes well, so you can always store it that way. Maybe cut a large loaf in half, eat half over a few days, and freeze the rest in a zipper-lock bag until you're ready. Or slice the whole thing and freeze it, then pull slices from the freezer as you need them. You can thaw bread at room temperature or even toast slices directly from frozen. After freezing, you have a three-week window when frozen bread will come back to essentially good as new. After that, the bread may be good, but it'll be a bit dried out.

Troubleshooting Bread

All kinds of things can go sideways in bread baking. Undermixing, overmixing, underfermenting, and overproofing can cause everything from flat loaves and a lack of flavor to a crumbly or dense crumb. Each time you bake, assess your loaves and make notes for next time. The flour makes a huge difference. We strongly encourage using fresh milled and whole-grain flours for both flavor and texture. These flours do tend to create stickier, weaker doughs. Keep that in mind. But be careful about overcorrecting. Subtle changes can create big differences in the final bread. If you spot a problem, don't make all the potential changes. Make only one tweak at a time. Then jot down the results on the recipe itself or in a baking notebook. That way you can refer back to the tweaks to keep improving your bread with every batch.

When applicable, the most likely culprit for the problem is placed at the top of each list that follows.

Flavor Problems

Dough Lacks Flavor

- Try longer bulk fermentation
- Try using freshly milled flour
- Try warmer fermentation
- Try increasing the leavening

Dough Lacks Tanginess

- Try cooler, longer fermentation

Dough Flavor Is Too Acidic or Funky

- Try decreasing fermentation
- Try not retarding the loaves
- Try feeding sourdough starter more frequently

Sweet Dough Lacks Sweetness

- Try decreasing fermentation time
- Try using osmotolerant yeast (see page 25)
- Try adding more sweetener

Crumb Problems

Crumb Has No Bubbles, Tiny Bubbles, or Stray Large Bubbles

- Try longer bulk fermentation
- Try warmer fermentation
- Try increasing the leavening

Bread Has Great Oven Spring, but Crumb Is Dense

- Try warmer final fermentation
- Try longer final fermentation

Crumb Has a Large Hole under the Crust, Crumb Is Dense, or Bubbles Stretch Left to Right

- Try decreasing fermentation time
- Try colder fermentation

Crumb Is Pasty

- Try reducing the hydration a few percent
- Try letting the loaf cool completely before cutting
- Try baking the loaf longer
- Try a different flour blend

Crumb Is Doughy Even Though Crust Is Dark

- Try baking at a lower temperature for more time
- Try reducing fermentation time

Crumb Is Too Crumbly

- Try mixing longer (or less if you went too far!)

Crumb Edges Are Good, but Core Is Too Dense and Tight

- Try extending final fermentation (baked too soon)

Crust Problems

Crust Is Pale, Dull, and Set Too Early

- Try using more steam
- Try creating a more sealed baking chamber

Crust Is Too Shiny and Chewy

- Try venting baking chamber sooner
- Try using less steam

Crust Is Too Thick and Chewy

- Try baking at a higher temperature for less time

Crust Is Too Thin and Dark

- Try baking at a lower temperature for more time

Crust Is Unevenly Browned

- Try rotating loaves halfway through the bake for more even browning

Bottom Is Burnt

- Try placing baking stone higher in oven (most ovens have strong bottom heat)
- During stage two of bake (drying/venting), try moving the loaf to a rack or slip a flat cookie sheet between the stone and the loaf

Loaf Volume Problems

Low-Profile Loaf: Bread Is Too Flat

- Try reducing the hydration
- Try using a different flour or mix of flours (problem could be gluten qualities or enzymatic activity)
- Try mixing longer (or less if you went too far!)
- Try fermenting less if you went too far
- Try increasing tension during shaping
- Try sealing seams better during shaping
- Try baking at a higher temperature

Overly High-Profile Loaf: Bread Is Blown Out or Too Round on Top and Bottom

- Try proofing longer
- Try increasing the hydration a few percent
- Try making more score marks on the loaf

6

YEAST BREADS

I WAS SITTING WITH MY FRIEND KELLY WHITAKER IN DRY STORAGE, HIS NEW CAFÉ/BREAD SHOP IN BOULDER, COLORADO, WHEN OUT CAME THIS AMAZING THING ON THE MENU CALLED TOAST. It was basically seven different breads that Dry Storage makes with all of their carefully sourced, freshly milled flours, using grains from all over the country. It's beautiful. There was a rye, a smørrebrød, a multigrain bread, a focaccia, a sourdough, a seeded sourdough, and a gorgeous pain de mie sandwich bread. The pain de mie was one of the best I've ever had. I asked Kelly about it, and he told me this yeast bread is the one he's been working on really hard to make with 100% whole-grain flour.

"But some people just want a white bread," he said. "So, we make a beautiful freshly milled loaf in the Wonder Bread style." Yet when I tasted the one he served me, I noticed the flavor of bran in there. "This isn't just white flour, is it?" I asked. "No," he said, "this one was made with bolted Sonora wheat flour along with another flour." Then he said, "we like to give people the option of white or wheat."

That's when we both started laughing. Get it? White bread *is* wheat bread. It's just that white bread is not whole-grain bread; it's not *whole* wheat.

Well, I'm here to tell you there is a third way, a middle way: breads made with bolted wheat flour. This kind of flour is not 100% whole wheat, and it's not completely refined white flour either. Bolted wheat flour is just what it sounds like: whole grains of wheat that have been milled fresh and lightly sifted to remove some of the larger bran flakes. That's what you find at a lot of local farmers' markets, mills, and artisan bakeries these days. And that's what was in the "white" pain de mie that Kelly had served me. Bolted wheat flour is what we call for in many of the recipes in this book. Trust me. You want this flour. It makes bread taste soooo much better.

You see, flour is like any other ingredient. It's best when fresh. The problem with most store-bought whole-wheat flour is that it's been sitting on the shelf for weeks or months, getting stale, and the fat in the bran and germ starts to taste bitter and rancid. That's why most people have a negative association with anything "whole wheat." But when you mill the whole grain fresh and sift out some of the bigger bran flakes, it tastes amazing. You smell things like fresh grass, wildflowers, popcorn, and butter! You can smell it in the fresh flour, and some of those flavors end up in the bread. Wheat is not supposed to be this bland, white, flavorless ingredient. Wheat has flavor, and that's what I'm looking for in everything I cook and bake.

As I was leaving Kelly's place, he mentioned that he was doing a grain dinner with four courses, each course highlighting an heirloom grain variety that he raises on his farms: Rouge de Bordeaux wheat, Yecora Rojo wheat, Sonoran wheat, and Ryeman rye. The idea is to show how different wheat varieties (and the rye) bring different flavors and textures, not only to the bread but also to every dish made with the freshly milled flour. Amen, Kelly.

This is exactly what we have been doing since we began the Vetri Grain Project in 2014. When I first got into fresh milling, I started making pastas to highlight particular flours. When Claire came on board, she grew the bread program exponentially. We wanted to highlight all the breads and these amazing flours in the same manner that we call out the high-quality ingredients in our other dishes. We came up with a system to serve three breads throughout the evening, one for each course: something richer and nuttier or fun, like Seeded Schwarzbrot (page 183) or Spelt Pretzels (page 91), to accompany the appetizers; always our durum focaccia to soak up the sauce in our pastas; and then some kind of complex sourdough loaf, like Farro Miche with Whey (page 164), for the entrees. As it turns out, the bread and the grain varieties fascinate people as much as the other dishes. For the first and the third courses, we are constantly changing things, trying out new combinations, and working with the chefs to create dishes that complement the breads. I love how it motivates everyone to come up with new and interesting ideas.

But still, like Kelly had said, some people just want white bread. It's maddening, I tell you! We search the globe for heritage grains packed with flavor and nutrients, buy them whole, mill them in-house, and mix, ferment, coddle, and create beautiful breads to accompany mind-blowing dishes. These breads are all over this book, breads like 100% Sonora Slab (page 161), Spelt Sourdough Boule (page 157), and Ciabatta Grano Arso with Einkorn (page 173). They are completely delicious! And I believe it is of the utmost importance to keep pushing a local grain economy forward with heritage grain farmers and millers, farmers' markets, artisan baking, whole grains, teaching, and awareness.

Yet, some people just want white bread. This chapter is our nod to those types of breads, the ones you see every day, everywhere, made with flavorless refined white flour. No, we don't call for white flour in our recipes. That's not what this book is about. We call for bolted wheat flour, the middle way between white and whole wheat. This kind of flour allows you to create those familiar breads, like bagels and pretzels, but with more flavor and nutrients from the bran and germ. Our Red Onion Focaccia (page 84) is light, airy, and made with freshly milled bolted Redeemer wheat, a heritage variety grown just outside of Philadelphia. Some other breads include a combination of bolted and whole-grain flours. But most of the breads here just call for bolted hard wheat flour. Use whatever local wheat varieties you can find. Mill the grains fresh and sift them quickly to remove the bigger bran flakes. Or just buy freshly milled flour at a local farmers' market or mill. It's that simple. (See the regional grain sources on page 284.)

The point is that you can make these ubiquitous, every-day breads markedly better just by using higher quality flour. You can even elevate something as humble as a hoagie roll. Our Hoagie Rolls (page 94) are probably the most no-brainer, simple, down-and-dirty bread recipe in the book. That's the beauty of breads made with dry yeast. Sure, we could have made yeast breads with a bunch of preferments and long fermentation times. But we wanted the breads in this chapter to be super approachable with a low time investment and simple instructions. The Pita (page 77) are ready start-to-finish in only three hours. And they're so fun to see all puffed up when they bake. Likewise, the Olive Filone (page 100) and many of the other breads here are ready in just a few hours. This chapter is kind of like the shallow end of the pool. If you're new to baking bread, especially with freshly milled flours, start here.

Since the doughs are uncomplicated, the fun of this chapter is really in all the different shapes, from Spelt Pretzels (page 91) and Bagels (page 97) to Artichoke Fougasse (page 87). The Ursa Baguette (page 81) is kind of its own thing. The instructions for making the baguettes are a little more detailed but, at heart, baguettes are simple breads. On the whole, these are not complex breads with tricky fermentation times and temperatures (see chapters 8 and 9 for those). And for simplicity's sake, these doughs are all mixed in a machine. You could hand-mix them for five to ten minutes instead, and you'll get fine results. But "easy" is the name of the game here.

If you're in a white-bread kind of mood, try the familiar breads here. Each one gets a flavor and nutrition lift by using freshly milled bolted wheat flour. These yeast breads will give you a great foundation to build on. —MV

TOM AND DAVID KENYON

Aurora Farms and Nitty Gritty Grain Company | Charlotte, Vermont

Tom and David Kenyon own and operate Aurora Farms and Nitty Gritty Grain Company in Charlotte, Vermont. Their family has been farming grains in the region since the 1770s. Thirty years ago, the Kenyons began growing organic grain for the commodity industry, and ten years ago, they opened Nitty Gritty Grain to provide certified organic wheat, corn, and other grains to bakers, restaurants, and home cooks throughout the Northeast. One of their well-known customers is Jim Williams, who moved to Charlotte in 2019 from Providence, Rhode Island, where he ran the popular Seven Stars Bakery.

Soil is everything. We look for a certain protein level in hard red wheat and strive for consistency. But soil changes. It's important to understand that even a single wheat variety from year to year can change in protein content.

There's this perception that bread is bread is bread. But a hamburger bun made from organic wheat and fresh milled flour is not the same thing as a fast-food hamburger bun.

Wheat varieties taste different in the same way that different varieties of tomatoes taste different. That's what makes bread interesting regionally. The Redeemer wheat variety grows well in Vermont but not so well in Arizona.

Regional grains and fresh milling aren't just trends. They're here to stay. People want to connect more with their food, where it comes from and who's growing and making it.

PITA

MAKES ABOUT 20 PITA,
ABOUT 7-INCH DIAMETER

1 hour active time
over 3 hours

These jawns (that's Philly-speak for "things") are easy, quick, and foolproof. Plus, they're fun. They puff up like balloons after just a few seconds in the oven. Pita are great to make with kids because you just roll out the dough with a pin, and they're portioned pretty small. Some pita recipes call for yogurt or ghee, but I didn't want to complicate things. I like just a little oil in the dough to make the bread tender. —CKM

bolted hard wheat flour	719 g (5¾ cups)	100%
water	475 g (2 cups)	66%
extra-virgin olive oil	48 g (3½ tablespoons)	6.7%
dry yeast	4 g (1¼ teaspoons)	0.6%
salt	21 g (3½ teaspoons)	2.9%
TOTAL	**1,267 g**	**176.2%**

MIX. Measure the flour and set aside. Combine the water, oil, yeast, flour, and salt in the bowl of a stand mixer. Mix with the dough hook on low speed for 1 minute, then switch to medium speed and mix until the bread clings to the hook and clears the sides of the bowl, about another 6 minutes. The mixer will really get rocking and rolling, so do not leave it unattended or it might just walk off your countertop. A damp towel placed under the mixer will minimize this scooting around. (This trick works well to keep cutting boards in place, too.)

BULK FERMENT. Transfer the dough to an oiled bowl and cover with a tea towel or slip a plastic grocery bag, plastic wrap, or beeswax wrap over the bowl if the room is very dry. Leave to rise at room temperature (65° to 75°F) for 1½ hours. The dough should nearly double in size.

SHAPE. After bulk fermentation, place a baking stone on a rack set about two-thirds of the way to the top of the oven. Preheat your oven to 500°F.

Turn the dough out onto a floured countertop and divide it into 60-gram pieces. Keep in mind that making too many unnecessary cuts will make the dough tougher to shape, so get a sense of the amount of dough you need with the first few pieces and then try to get close to the correct size for

the rest of the pieces in one or two tries. They certainly don't need to be exact.

Round each piece by patting out gently and tucking four sides in toward the center. Then tighten it into a ball by turning it over onto a dry part of the countertop, cupping your hand over it, applying gentle pressure, and rotating your hand in a circle, kind of dragging the seam against the counter to seal the seam and tighten the surface (see the first two photos on page 78). The seam should roll around but stay in contact with the countertop as you drag the dough in a circle, increasing the surface tension and rolling it into a ball. With practice you'll get a perfectly round ball, but if you're having a hard time, balls for pita bread don't need to be perfectly round. Cover all the balls with a tea towel.

Gather some flour for dusting, a rolling pin, a timer, tongs or hot pads, another tea towel, and a plate for stacking the baked pita on as they cool. I prefer to alternate between rolling and baking for a few reasons, but mostly because I'm impatient and I like to bounce around. But if you have a different temperament, you could do all the rolling, then all the baking. Either way, dust a small area on the counter liberally

CONTINUED

with flour. Take the first dough ball and flatten it with the pin. Flip it and roll it out more. Keep flipping, rotating, and rolling until you get a circle about 7 inches in diameter, dusting it with flour as needed to prevent sticking. The circle should be very thin, about ⅛ inch. Set it aside and repeat with a second dough ball. If your baking stone can comfortably hold three 7-inch circles, you could roll out a third dough. The pita will be baked in batches, and every few rounds, turn your broiler on and wait a few minutes to blast more heat to the top of the oven. Then turn the broiler off and turn the oven back to 500°F and continue to bake. You open the oven a lot in this recipe because of all the batches, and the broiler helps recover the heat that gets delivered to the top of the pita. If you don't have a broiler, expect your oven to cool more as you bake, so later rounds may take longer than the first ones. Try not to open the oven unnecessarily.

BAKE. I hope this goes without saying, but this part of the recipe—the oven work—is not kid-friendly. Set your timer to 45 seconds. Open your oven, pull out the rack, and quickly but carefully lay each rolled pita on the hot stone. I make this a bit more efficient by draping two or three pita rounds over my forearm; this leaves my hands free to open the oven and pull out the rack. Then the pita rounds are right there to lay one at a time on the hot stone. Quickly push the rack back, close the oven, and start your timer. The pita will be done in about a minute, give or take, depending on your oven, so start checking at 45 seconds. In a perfect world, the pita will fully inflate like a balloon with one large bubble, it will have singed in a spot or two, and it will still be soft and just barely done inside, so when you put it under a towel, it will steam itself. My ideal flavor comes when the pita bake really quickly and burn just a touch, but not all ovens get hot enough. Know that pita can go from soft and perfect to

crispy crackers quickly, so get them out of the oven before they dry out. When they come out of the oven, they are full of hot steam. Use tongs or hot pads to grab them and transfer them to a plate. Cover with a tea towel to allow the baked pita to steam and soften.

Roll out another set of pita and bake them off. To keep the pita warm and soft, I like to bury the freshly baked pita in the middle of the stack and cover the whole stack in a tea towel. That way the new hot pita steams itself and its neighbors. Once you have the hang of things, you can roll while you bake and minimize down time. Troubleshooting tip: if your pita aren't fully puffing, they probably aren't being rolled thin enough or don't have enough top heat.

Pita are best super fresh, but they do keep for several days in an airtight container at room temperature.

OPTION

If you don't have a baking stone, you can use a cast-iron pan in the oven. Even better—if you have a cast-iron griddle, you can bake two pita at once.

URSA BAGUETTE

MAKES 4 BAGUETTES,
16 TO 18 INCHES LONG

Day 1 → 5 minutes
active time with an
overnight rest

Day 2 → 50 minutes
active time over 4 hours

For years, baguettes were my favorite things to make, and I thought they were a distinct mark of a baker's skill. Then I swung the other way on them and saw them as a sad product of industrialized baking. After returning to the farmers' market scene recently as Ursa Bakery, I've warmed back up to them. They're my top sellers at the market, and it's gratifying to see a customer happily tuck her baguette under her arm, rip off the end, pop it in her mouth, and wander off to a produce stand. Oh, by the way, my favorite flour here is bolted (sifted) Redeemer, but any bolted hard wheat flour will work. —CKM

POOLISH

bolted hard wheat flour	194 g (1½ cups)	100%
water	194 g (¾ cup + 1⅛ tablespoons)	100%
dry yeast	0.27 g (⅛ teaspoon)	0.14%
TOTAL	**388.27 g**	**200.14%**

DOUGH

bolted hard wheat flour	579 g (4⅔ cups)	100%
water	377 g (1⅔ cups)	65%
dry yeast	1 g (⅓ teaspoon)	0.17%
poolish (from above)	388 g (2½ cups)	67%
salt	15 g (2½ teaspoons)	2.6%
TOTAL	**1,360 g**	**234.77%**

DAY 1: MIX POOLISH. Measure the flour and set aside. Choose a container with a tight-fitting lid and enough space for the poolish to triple in volume. Pour in the water and sprinkle in the yeast. Then mix in the flour, stirring just long enough to make sure all the flour is wet. Scrape the bottom of the container to get any stray clumps. Cover with the lid and leave at room temperature (65° to 75°F) to rest overnight, 8 to 16 hours. On the short end of that time, you may get a stiff dough. On the long end, you may get a very extensible dough due to the extra enzyme activity.

DAY 2: MIX DOUGH. Measure the flour and set aside. Combine the water, yeast, poolish, and flour in the bowl of a stand mixer, then mix with the dough hook on low speed for 4 minutes. Cover the bowl with a tea towel and rest at room temperature for 30 minutes.

Sprinkle in the salt and mix on low speed for another 4 minutes. Then switch to medium speed and mix for 3 minutes. At the end of mixing, the dough should look shinier than at the beginning. Tug on the dough with your fingertips. When pulled, it should feel cohesive, moderately elastic, and moderately extensible. If it feels super extensible, the dough may be a little overmixed. In that case, skip the first couple of folds in the next step. If it tears before stretching, give it another minute in the mixer. After mixing, test the dough temperature with an instant-read thermometer. It should be around 78°F. If it's lower than that, put the dough in a warm spot. If it's higher, pop it in the fridge for a few minutes. If it's both warm and feeling stiff, mix in about 17 grams cold water. During the winter or in a cold room, you may want to use warm water.

CONTINUED

BULK FERMENT. After mixing, transfer the dough to a lightly oiled bowl, cover with a tea towel, and rest in a draft-free place for 1½ hours total, with folds after 30 and 60 minutes (see page 28 for the dough-folding technique). With each fold, you should notice that the dough has become increasingly active, with bubbles of gas showing under the surface. If it doesn't, the dough may need a little more fermentation time.

PRESHAPE. After bulk fermentation, scrape the dough onto a lightly floured countertop. Divide the dough into four equal pieces, each around 340 grams. A very simple preshape is sufficient: take what looks like a short end, then tuck and roll the dough up into a thick tube like a fat jelly roll. Seal the seam with a couple pinches and repeat with the other pieces. Place them seam-side up on a floured surface. Normally we rest doughs seam-side down. But the next shape is intensive, and we don't want to have a bunch of flour on the inside (the seam side). If the room is dry, cover the pieces with a tea towel. Leave them for 20 minutes.

SHAPE. Place a large baking stone and hotel pan (see page 62) on the highest oven rack they will fit on. Preheat the oven to 500°F.

To get the final loaf shape, have a couche or a well-floured tea towel ready. Very lightly flour your countertop. A baguette is a fairly dry bread to begin with, so I use a minimal amount of flour on an as-needed basis. In particular, minimize flour along the seam side. To begin stretching, lightly pat out the dough to a rectangle about 8 inches long. Then, gently lift the long edge closest to you, tuck it into the dough, and gently roll forward to the opposite edge (see photos on page 51). Use your palms to roll the dough back and forth from the center to the ends, but don't squish it down too much. Continue gently rolling the dough back and forth from the center outward until the baguette reaches its full length of 16 to 18 inches, pressing down just on the last inch or so to taper the ends slightly. Since these are home-oven baguettes, they can only be stretched to the length of your stone, so keep that in mind: aim for 16 to 18 inches long. After resting, the loaves will ideally stretch out to their full length right away, but if you're feeling a lot of resistance from the dough (tearing skin or springing back), just stretch each piece partway out, let it relax for a few minutes, and then take it out the rest of the way. Once the baguette reaches its full length, if the seam hasn't sealed well, use your fingers to gently press and seal the seam along the length of the dough.

Set the baguette seam-side up on the couche or tea towel and repeat with the remaining pieces. Set each baguette down about an inch from the one before and then slide it right up next to its neighbor with the towel folded between them. This nesting system supports the final shape of the baguettes while regulating the temperature and moisture of the dough. It lets a little moisture out to form a thin skin. If the room is dry, cover the baguettes with another tea towel or the remainder of the couche. Leave the baguettes to rise at room temperature for 30 to 45 minutes. When ready, the baguettes will have plumped up to about 1½ times their original size.

BAKE. Baguettes get their signature, crusty "ears" from their oven spring (see page 61 for more on oven spring). To get them, the dough must be active (gaining volume and showing bubbles) when the baguettes go in.

Cut a sheet of parchment paper that will fit over the back side of a half sheet pan to use as a peel (or line a large cutting board with parchment). Then gently lift and transfer two baguettes to the parchment, flipping them over so they are seam-side down. Adjust them so they are straight and evenly spaced from each other. Re-cover the remaining baguettes with the couche or a tea towel. Working quickly, score each baguette three to five times with a few almost perfectly centered lines from end to end (see "Baguette scoring," page 60).

Quickly, but carefully, open your oven, pull the rack that you are baking on partway out, and move the hot hotel pan to the stovetop or side of the oven. Slide the parchment paper with the baguettes onto the stone. Still working quickly, but without burning yourself or smooshing the baguettes, rest one side of the hotel pan on the back of the stone, spray water into the pan, then set the pan onto the stone over the baguettes to trap steam. Close the oven and bake for 8 minutes. Remove the hotel pan completely and then rotate the loaves from side to side and front to back to ensure even color. At this point, the baguettes will be full size, and some spots will have turned golden in color. Ideally, you'll have a nice crisp ear on every cut, and those will color first, along with the ends. Bake (without the hotel pan) until the predominant color all over the baguettes is a light terra-cotta, slightly darker than the skin of butternut squash, an additional 8 to 10 minutes. Remove the baguettes to a rack to cool and repeat the scoring and baking with the remaining baguettes.

Try to eat them within 36 hours; baguettes are not for long keeping.

OPTIONS

If you're obsessed with baguettes, try the Sourdough Baguette (page 176).

To make **Pain di Epi (Wheat Stalk Bread)**, follow the "Epi scissor cutting" directions on page 60, as shown in the photo below.

RED ONION FOCACCIA

MAKES 1 HALF SHEET
PAN FOCACCIA,
18 BY 13 INCHES

Day 1 → 5 minutes
active time with an
overnight rest

Day 2 → 45 minutes
active time over 4 hours

This is not the infamous Vetri focaccia, that giant fluffy sponge made with durum flour and served with every pasta course. Check out that recipe in *Mastering Pizza*. This is a more traditional flatbread focaccia . . . about an inch thick, airy, light, and made ultra-simple by starting with a basic baguette dough. This recipe shows how some iconic breads like baguettes and focaccia differ mainly in the baking traditions from which they originate. While the shaping of baguettes and focaccia is quite different, the doughs themselves are very similar. —CKM

DOUGH

Ursa Baguette dough (full recipe, page 81)	1,360 g (2 quarts)	100%

TOPPING

¼ cup extra-virgin olive oil, plus some for shaping

2 teaspoons balsamic vinegar

1 small red onion, sliced lengthwise about ¼ inch thick

1 tablespoon coarse salt, such as Maldon

½ teaspoon freshly ground black pepper

DAY 1: MIX POOLISH. Follow the instructions for mixing the baguette dough poolish.

DAY 2: MIX DOUGH. Continue making the baguette dough through the bulk fermentation.

PRESHAPE. Drizzle a little water on your countertop and spread it around so the surface is wet but not puddled. Turn the dough out onto the countertop, then give it a loose preshape by folding all four edges in toward the center and rolling it over so it is seam-side down. Spread a teaspoon or two of oil on the top of the dough, cover with a tea towel, and leave to rest for 30 minutes.

MAKE TOPPING. While the dough rests, heat a sauté pan over medium-low heat. Add 2 tablespoons of the oil and the balsamic vinegar. Add the onion slices and sauté until they sweat down a bit and soften, 8 to 10 minutes, stirring occasionally. Transfer the onion to a plate and spread out to cool.

SHAPE. Now, I hope you don't mind a bit of a mess. Line a half sheet pan with parchment paper. Spread a couple tablespoons of olive oil over a section of your countertop and use a bench knife to pick up the dough and transfer it to the oiled area. Stretch the dough from left to right by lifting a section of it and letting it lengthen under its own weight, kind of like stretching a section of pizza dough. Coax it out farther by using your fingers to dock the dough, pressing your fingers deep in all over the dough. Try to work the edges first, then the center to get an even thickness throughout. You ultimately want a rectangular shape. Continue going all around the dough, lifting and tugging sections to work the dough to about the size of your half sheet pan. It is better to have the dough a little overstretched and crumpled in the pan than understretched and dull looking. Now carefully and quickly lift the dough under your hands and forearms and transfer it to the pan. This will stretch it farther. Coax and tug it gently to evenly fill the pan. Scatter the onion evenly over the focaccia so there are no large clumps. Leave the dough to rise in a draft-free place until it is puffy, about 1 hour.

BAKE. Place a large baking stone on the middle rack of the oven. Preheat the oven to 450°F. Drizzle the focaccia with the remaining 2 tablespoons olive oil. Dock it all over by poking your fingers deep into the dough. Sprinkle the top with the salt and pepper, then load the pan into the oven on the stone. Bake for 15 minutes, then rotate the pan and bake until lightly browned, another 5 to 10 minutes. Depan by sliding the focaccia to a rack to cool.

Focaccia tastes best on the day it is baked.

ARTICHOKE FOUGASSE

MAKES 4 FOUGASSES,
ABOUT 12-INCH DIAMETER

Day 1 → 5 minutes
active time with an
overnight rest

Day 2 → 60 minutes
active time over 4 hours

A Provençal variation of the leavened flatbreads found all over the Mediterranean region, fougasse is similar to Italian focaccia. I learned about it in my first job at Tall Grass Bakery in Seattle, Washington. It's fun to make, and the crazy shape makes fougasse wildly popular at farmers' markets. People call it "that giant pretzel thing" or "fugazi." Traditionally, fougasse is shaped like a pointy oval leaf or a sheaf of wheat. You cut the dough with scissors so the holes and strips of dough left by the cuts are like the veins of the leaf. I shape my fougasse to look like an upside-down peace sign. As with the Red Onion Foccacia (page 84), I like to start with the Ursa Baguette dough to simplify things—and also because the doughs are so similar. You can experiment with all kinds of inclusions here. Poached artichokes are one of my favorites. —CKM

Ursa Baguette dough (full recipe, page 81)	1,360 g (2 quarts)	100%
Poached Artichoke Hearts (page 256)	203 g (¾ cup)	35%
extra-virgin olive oil	23 g (1¾ tablespoons)	4%
salt	3 g (½ teaspoon)	0.5%
TOTAL	**1,589 g**	**139.5%**

DAY 1: MIX POOLISH. Follow the instructions for mixing the baguette dough poolish.

DAY 2: MIX DOUGH. Chop the artichoke hearts into pieces between ¼ and ½ inch.

Continue making the baguette dough through the mixing stage. After mixing on medium speed for 3 minutes, add the oil, artichokes, and salt and mix on low speed until mostly incorporated, just a minute or so.

BULK FERMENT. Transfer the dough to a lightly oiled bowl, cover with a tea towel, and rest in a draft-free place for 1½ hours total, giving the dough a four-fold (see page 28) after 30 and 60 minutes. With each fold, the dough should become increasingly active with bubbles of gas showing under the surface. It should also feel somewhat stretchy and smooth. Make sure the oil and artichokes are evenly incorporated.

PRESHAPE. Place a large baking stone on the middle rack of the oven. Preheat the oven to 500°F.

Turn the dough out onto a lightly floured countertop and gently pat it out. Divide the dough into four equal pieces, each about 400 grams. Loosely preshape each piece by patting it down and folding all four edges in toward the center. Set the pieces seam-side down on the countertop, cover with a tea towel, and let rest for 30 minutes.

SHAPE. You will shape and bake these one at a time, so be prepared to spend about an hour mostly in the kitchen. Cut a sheet of parchment paper that will fit over the back side of a half sheet pan to use as a peel. Have plenty of flour at hand to keep the fougasse from sticking. For each piece of dough, pat out to an oval about 1½ inches thick and dust with flour. Grab a pair of scissors. Starting and ending about an inch from the edge, make four slightly fanned cuts all the way

CONTINUED

through the fougasse (see the photos on the facing page). Immediately dust flour into the holes you cut to keep them from sticking. You could also make other shapes and decorative cuts if you prefer.

Either way, stretch the dough from the holes out to its final size by pulling and stretching from the thickest parts with your fingers in the holes. If your dough is stiff enough to pick up, you can lift it, allowing gravity to pull down the "branches" of dough between the holes, so each branch is about an inch in diameter. It's okay if some branches get slightly thinner but try to pull and work out the thickest ones. Stretch out the dough more than you might expect to: it will puff and partially fill the holes, and you don't want them to close completely. The final diameter of the whole fougasse should be about 12 inches. Slide the fougasse onto the parchment-lined peel, adjusting to ensure the shape is artful, with big spaces between the branches. The shape should be somewhat like a triangular leaf; my fougasse tends to have two larger holes on the bottom of the leaf and two slightly smaller holes on top, like a peace sign.

BAKE. Slide the fougasse and parchment paper directly onto the preheated stone. Bake for about 15 minutes. The fougasse is finished when the crust reaches a corn-flake color, ideally with some singed bubbles, like a good pizza crust. Unlike many breads in this book, when in doubt, err on the side of underbaking rather than overbaking. With such thin segments, the finished fougasse texture can go from crispy crust and chewy interior to thoroughly crunchy rather quickly. Repeat shaping and baking the remaining dough.

Like a baguette, fougasse tastes best eaten within a day or so.

OPTIONS

You can swap out the artichokes with other additions like pitted and chopped olives; caramelized onions; chopped mushrooms, nuts, or cheeses; and fresh herbs. Olive and rosemary makes a great combo.

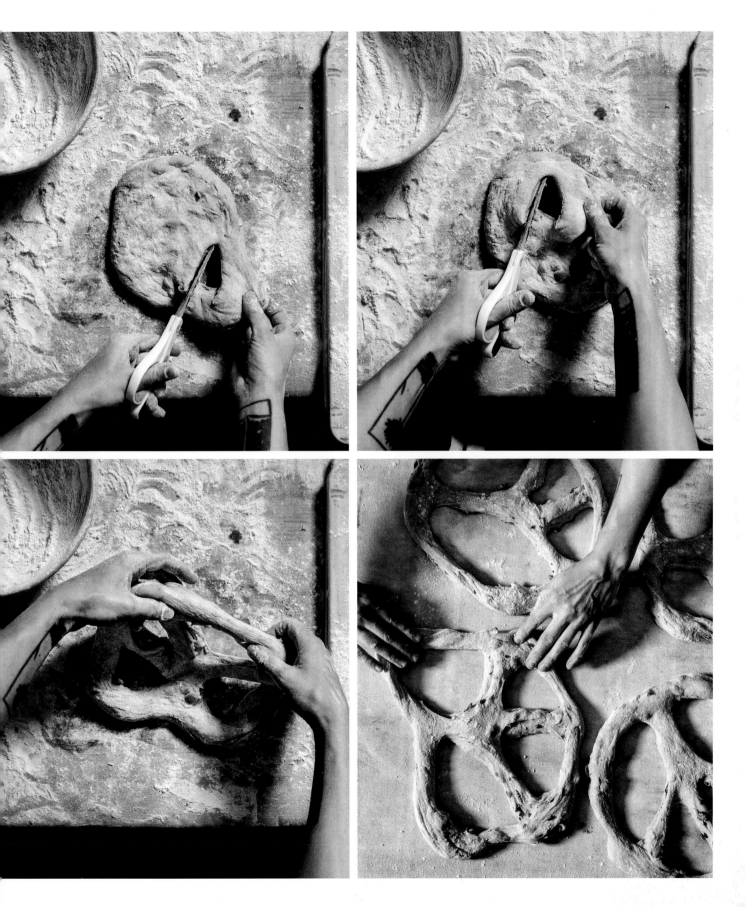

SPELT PRETZELS

MAKES 10 LARGE PRETZELS,
4- TO 5-INCH DIAMETER,
OR 30 MINI PRETZELS,
1½- TO 2-INCH DIAMETER

Day 1 → 5 minutes
active time with an
overnight rest

Day 2 → 50 minutes
active time over 5 hours

In the early summer of 2019, I left Vetri to work full-time at my own bakery, Ursa. Ariel Einhorn replaced me at the restaurant, and at the time, everyone was so busy that I didn't hear from them for a while. Then she started making these pretzels, and suddenly everyone was contacting me saying, "Thank you for sending us Ariel—she's so great," and specifically mentioning the soft pretzels. Now we can all thank Ariel for sharing her recipe in this book. Thanks, Ariel! Spelt flour is a great choice for pretzels because it makes the dough easy to stretch and shape. Spelt also gives them a gentle, almost sweet, wheat flavor. A quick dip in lye (a strong alkaline) helps create that classic dark, shiny crust on these Bavarian-style pretzels. Look for lye at baking supply retailers or online. Lye is caustic, so wear gloves and eye protection when handling it. —CKM

BIGA

bolted hard wheat flour	91 g (¾ cup)	100%
water	61 g (¼ cup)	60%
dry yeast	0.06 g (¹⁄₆₄ teaspoon)	0.06%
TOTAL	**152.06 g**	**160.06%**

DOUGH

bolted hard wheat flour	375 g (3 cups)	75%
whole-grain spelt flour	125 g (1 cup)	25%
water	300 g (1¼ cups)	60%
extra-virgin olive oil	30 g (2¼ tablespoons)	6%
dry yeast	5 g (1⅔ teaspoons)	1%
biga (from above)	150 g (¾ cup)	30%
barley malt flour or powder (see Option, page 156)	10 g (4 teaspoons)	2%
salt	11 g (1¾ teaspoons)	2.2%
TOTAL	**1,006 g**	**201.2%**

1½ tablespoons food-grade lye (sodium hydroxide) for lye solution

2¼ cups water for lye solution

Pretzel salt (coarse, large-grain white salt) for sprinkling

CONTINUED

DAY 1: MIX BIGA. Measure the flour and set aside. Combine the water, yeast, and flour in a container with a lid, stirring them together with a spoon. Cover and let sit at room temperature (65° to 75°F) to rest overnight, 12 to 16 hours.

DAY 2: MIX DOUGH. Measure the hard wheat and spelt flours and set aside. Combine the water, oil, yeast, biga, reserved flours, malt flour or powder, and salt in the bowl of a stand mixer. Mix with the dough hook on low speed for 3 minutes. Switch to medium speed and mix until the gluten develops and the dough comes together, another 3 minutes.

Transfer to an oiled bowl, cover with a tea towel, and let rest for 45 minutes. Give the dough a four-fold (see page 28), then cover and let rest for another 45 minutes.

PRESHAPE. Divide the dough into ten 100-gram pieces for large pretzels or about thirty 30-gram pieces for mini pretzels. Preshape each piece on a dry surface by folding and rolling it into a short log, then rolling with a little more pressure under your palm to make a fat log for large pretzels, about 1½ inches wide by 4 inches long. Make a thinner log for mini pretzels, about ½ inch wide by 2 inches long. Let the logs rest for 10 minutes.

SHAPE. Line two sheet pans with parchment and coat the parchment with cooking spray. Pat the dough with your palms to start lengthening the log. Then roll it out under your palms, from the center outward, lengthening the dough as you go, until the rope is about 16 inches long and ½ inch thick for large pretzels, or 6 inches long and ⅛ inch thick for mini pretzels. To make the classic Bavarian pretzel shape, pick up the ends of the rope, leaving a semicircle of dough on the countertop, then cross the strands of dough, twist them once, and press the two ends you are holding onto the semicircle of dough (see photos on the facing page). Carefully transfer the pretzels to the parchment. The dough will be soft.

After shaping, you can either cover and refrigerate the pretzels for at least 2 hours or freeze them for up to 3 days. Either way, they must be firm before dipping in the lye solution. If frozen, defrost the pretzels in the refrigerator for 1 hour before dipping.

DIP IN LYE. Preheat the oven to 375°F.

The lye solution is caustic, so put on gloves, eye protection, and a face mask or bandana. Protect your countertop with parchment paper and coat two cooling racks with cooking spray, placing them over the parchment. Line a sheet pan with parchment paper and coat the parchment with cooking spray. Then carefully mix the lye and water in a medium stainless-steel or glass mixing bowl until the lye dissolves.

Dip each pretzel into the solution for about 30 seconds, turning to coat it completely, then transfer to the cooling rack to dry a bit. The dough will be soft, so handle it carefully. When the pretzels appear dry on the surface, after about 1 minute, transfer back to the oiled, parchment-lined sheet. The lye solution can be stored in a covered container and reused up to four times. This quantity of solution can also be safely poured down the drain.

BAKE. Score the dough if you like: it helps the pretzels split in the oven, so they look nicer. Just give each one a straight score where the ends of the ropes meet the base of the pretzel. Then sprinkle the pretzels with the salt. Bake until the pretzels are dark brown and shiny. Mini ones will take 8 to 10 minutes, and large ones 20 to 25 minutes.

Pretzels are best eaten warm, but they will last a day or two in an airtight container at room temperature. They can also be frozen for a few weeks and thawed/rewarmed in a 350°F oven for 10 minutes.

HOAGIE ROLLS

MAKES 12 ROLLS, ABOUT
6 INCHES LONG

2½ hours active time
over 4 hours

Philadelphians are very talented in the hoagie arts. If you're not a Philadelphian, I just want you to know that the cheesesteak is not our only sandwich. I used to make these rolls for staff meal at Vetri pretty regularly, and we filled them with everything imaginable. The recipe is easy and adaptable. I like a little oil in here to give the rolls a softer texture. Feel free to switch some or all of the flour to all-purpose flour if you want—because, let's be honest, sandwich greatness is all about dancing the line between quality and trash. —CKM

bolted hard wheat flour	844 g (6¾ cups)	100%
water	558 g (2⅓ cups)	65%
extra-virgin olive oil	25 g (1¾ tablespoons)	3%
dry yeast	5 g (1⅔ teaspoons)	0.65%
salt	17 g (2¾ teaspoons)	2%
TOTAL	**1,449 g**	**170.65%**

MIX. Measure the flour and set aside. Combine the water, oil, yeast, flour, and salt in the bowl of a stand mixer. Mix with the dough hook on low speed for 4 minutes. Switch to medium speed and mix for another 5 minutes. After mixing, the dough should feel moderately developed—elastic and cohesive but still a little sticky.

BULK FERMENT. Transfer the dough to an oiled bowl and cover with a tea towel. Leave to rise at room temperature (65° to 75°F) for 45 minutes. Then give the dough a four-fold (see page 28). At this point, there should be definite signs of activity: the volume should have increased by about 30%, and there should be visible bubbles. If you do not see this level of activity, move the bowl to a warmer place and give it an extra 15 minutes before portioning and shaping. If everything is progressing as it ought to at the fold, then just leave it for another 45 minutes of bulk fermentation. Ideally, the total rising time will be about 1½ hours (plus 15 minutes if you need to goose up the activity).

SHAPE. Line two sheet pans with parchment paper. Turn the dough out onto a lightly floured countertop, then divide the dough into twelve equal pieces, each about 120 grams. To shape each piece, start on one of the short sides and roll/crimp the edge in toward the center. Keep rolling and crimping

until you have a cylinder about 3 inches long. Even out and extend the cylinder to about 6 inches by placing one palm in the center and gently compressing the cylinder, then starting to roll the piece of dough while moving your hand outward toward the end. Add your second hand once you have moved the first from the center and press/roll that hand in the opposite direction. For the ends, roll harder with the outside edge of your palm to round them off and blunt the point, enclosing the seal at the rounded end. Place the roll seam-side down on the parchment. You should be able to fit six rolls on each half sheet pan. Repeat with the remaining pieces and cover the rolls loosely with a plastic grocery bag, plastic wrap, or beeswax wrap. Leave to rise for about 1 hour at room temperature, until the rolls have almost doubled in diameter.

BAKE. Halfway into the rising time, preheat the oven without a stone to 400°F. You'll need two oven racks to bake all the rolls at once. Quickly score the rolls all the way down the center in a straight line, then load them into the oven. Bake for 10 minutes, then turn the pans and bake for an additional 5 minutes. When done, the rolls will be puffed but somewhat pale, like the color of straw.

Hoagie rolls don't keep particularly well. Eat or freeze them within a couple days.

OPTIONS

A coating of sesame seeds is a nice touch. Place a damp towel across half a sheet pan and pour a layer of sesame seeds over the other half. After shaping each roll, dampen the top (the nonseam side) of the roll by blotting it on the wet towel like a stamp and then dipping the top side into the seeds.

For filling, the sky's the limit. It's a sandwich roll that loves classic Italian sliced meats like mortadella, Genoa salami, and prosciutto with sliced provolone, tomatoes, and iceberg lettuce—maybe some roasted red peppers, a little olive oil, red wine vinegar, salt, pepper, and dried oregano. For a traditional hoagie or cheesesteak, scoop out some of the inside of the bread. That way, you'll get a cylindrical wad of filling and a great crust without an excessive amount of bread. Use what you scoop out to make Bread Crumbs (page 240).

To make pan loaves instead (and **Sliced Sandwich Bread**), divide the finished dough in half, then press each piece into a rough rectangle. Starting at a long side, roll the rectangle up to the other long side to make a blunt log of dough. Press the seam to seal and place the loaves seam-side down in oiled 9 by 5-inch loaf pans. Cover and let rise for 2 to 3 hours, then bake at 350°F for 20 to 25 minutes, rotating the pans after 15 minutes.

BAGELS

MAKES 12 SMALL BAGELS,
ABOUT 4-INCH DIAMETER

Day 1 → 40 minutes
active time over 1 hour,
40 minutes with
an overnight rest

Day 2 → Mostly active
for 2 hours

People have strong opinions about bagels, so the breads are a touchy thing to mess with. And yet here we are. They are a great bread to revisit because traditional bagels are made with 100% refined white flour, only lightly fermented, dense, and pretty huge. By tweaking just one factor—the flour—we can make something a bit more nourishing that still satisfies with great chew. For me, the trick to getting a good homemade bagel is constructing a simple wood-and-cloth bagel board (see page 99), a tip from top-notch baker Jeffrey Hamelman. You could bake your bagels without one, but they may rise less and burn on the bottom. —CKM

DOUGH

bolted hard wheat flour	756 g (6 cups)	100%
water	416 g (1¾ cups)	55%
dry yeast	4 g (1¼ teaspoons)	0.5%
barley malt flour or powder (see Option, page 156)	8 g (3¼ teaspoons)	1%
salt	17 g (2¾ teaspoons)	2.3%
TOTAL	1,201 g	158.8%

3 tablespoons malt syrup or honey for boiling

1 cup sesame seeds, poppy seeds, or other seeds (optional) for topping

½ cup coarse salt for topping (optional)

DAY 1: MIX. Measure the hard wheat flour and set aside. Combine the water, yeast, reserved flour, malt flour or powder, and salt in the bowl of a stand mixer, then mix with the dough hook on low speed for 6 minutes. Let the dough and machine rest for 10 minutes, then mix on low speed for another 3 minutes. The dough should come together in a smooth ball and feel elastic. Alternatively, or if you have a less-powerful mixer, this dough is a good candidate for good old-fashioned hand kneading. As you knead, the dough should go from dry and shaggy to smooth and elastic. It is a low-hydration dough, so expect it to be firmer and drier than just about every other dough in this book. Once it's looking smooth and feeling elastic, work the dough into a ball and set it in a lightly oiled bowl. Cover and let rest for 1 hour at room temperature (65° to 75°F).

SHAPE. After an hour, the dough should have risen by about 75%. If it hasn't, give it a little more time. Turn the dough out onto a dry countertop and press out the gas until the dough is about 1 inch thick. Cut a 2-inch-wide strip off the dough and then cut a 3-inch-wide piece off. Weigh the pieces and add or subtract dough so that each piece is 100 grams, your target weight for each bagel. Now that you know what 100 grams looks like, repeat with the remaining dough, making 100-gram pieces.

For each bagel, press a dough piece out nearly flat with your fingers, then fold and roll it up along the longer side to make a blunt rope. Roll the rope on the countertop, starting with your palms at the center and moving outward until the rope is about 9 inches long. Wrap the rope around your

CONTINUED

hand, overlap the ends in your palm to connect them (the bagel will be wrapped around your hand), then gently press and roll the connected ends on the countertop to smooth out the seam. The dough should have some elasticity and shrink back a bit. When you remove it from your hand, the bagel should be near its final diameter (about 4 inches) with a fairly big hole. The hole will fill in some as the bagels rise overnight.

BULK FERMENT. Set the bagels on a lightly floured baking sheet with about a ½-inch space between them. Cover loosely with a plastic grocery bag, plastic wrap, or beeswax wrap and let rest at room temperature for 20 minutes. Then transfer to the refrigerator to rest overnight.

DAY 2: BOIL, THEN BAKE. The next morning, the bagels should have risen slightly. Fill a wide, deep pan with water to a depth of 5 inches, then add the malt syrup or honey and bring everything to a boil. Meanwhile, place a large baking stone on the middle rack of the oven. A rectangular stone is clutch here but make do with what you have. Preheat the oven to 450°F. Soak two bagel boards in a pan of water.

If you haven't realized it yet, this operation is going to take over your kitchen, so make some space and get organized. If you are topping your bagels with seeds, fill the bottom of a wide shallow bowl with a generous layer of whatever flavoring you've chosen. For a mixed batch, have one bowl for each topping ready to go. Next to that, lay out a towel to briefly dry the bagels after their bath. And get out a spider or other skimming tool for pulling the bagels from their bath. Have a timer that measures seconds ready to go (most smartphones work fine). Nearby (or wherever you can find room!), set up a rack for cooling the bagels.

Once the oven and water are ready, pull the bagel boards out and set them on the cooling rack to drain a bit. Pull the pan of bagels from the fridge and set it somewhere near the pot of boiling water. Carefully drop the bagels into the pot, one at a time. You can avoid splashing yourself with scalding water by imagining you are dropping the bagel like an airplane drops a payload: swoop down over the pot, drop the bagel when it is close to the water's surface, then continue on the trajectory, pulling your hand back up and away. Drop as many bagels into the pot as will fit comfortably, then set a 45-second timer. Return the remaining bagels to the fridge, since you'll be boiling and baking in batches.

At the end of the 45-second timer, flip the bagels and boil for another 45 seconds. The bagels should have puffed a bit in the bath. Skim them out of the pot and set on the towel to dry briefly. Once all the bagels have been boiled and pulled, the first bagel out will probably be ready to transfer to the topping bowl or, if you're skipping the toppings, straight to your bagel board for baking. If topping, just lift and set each bagel into the seeds, then lift and set it seed-side down on the bagel board. For salted bagels, sprinkle with the coarse salt and then set salt-side down on the bagel boards with at least 1 inch between each. Once the bagel boards are full, transfer to the oven, setting them directly onto the baking stone.

Bake for 4 minutes, then use two towels or hot pads to lift and tip each board, inverting the bagels onto the stone and removing the bagel boards from the oven. Bake the bagels directly on the stone until they are slightly puffed, shiny, and a few shades darker than when they originally went in, an additional 11 to 14 minutes. Check the bottoms, too: they should be browned but not scorched. Meanwhile, resoak the boards for the next rounds of bagels. Transfer the baked bagels to the rack to cool. Then repeat the boil-drain-top-bake cycle, until all the bagels are finished.

Allow the bagels to cool for a few minutes before digging in. Bagels are best fresh but will keep in an airtight container at room temperature for up to 3 days.

Bagel Boards Help Prevent Burning

Bagels are baked at a pretty high temperature, and in home ovens—especially with strong bottom heat—they tend to burn on the bottom. Here's a useful trick from bread guru Jeffrey Hamelman: start the bagel bake on homemade boards. To make two bagel boards, you will need two thin pieces of wood about 3 by 12 by ¼ inch (shims from the hardware store may work well) and two strips of heavy canvas, linen, or spare couche material (about 6 by 12 inches). Wrap the fabric around the boards and then staple the fabric to the backs of the boards with a heavy-duty stapler. You could also stitch the fabric around the board to secure it. Starting the bake on these fabric-lined boards will help prevent the bagels from burning on the bottom.

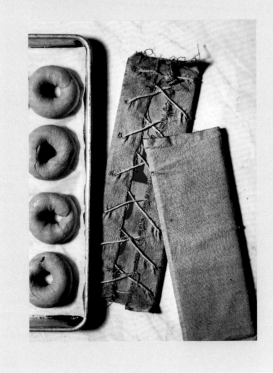

OLIVE FILONE

MAKES 3 NARROW
LOAVES, ABOUT
3 BY 12 INCHES

Day 1 → 15 minutes
active time over 1 hour
with an overnight rest

Day 2 → 10 minutes
active time over 2 hours

I think of this bread as a short, chunky baguette, or the little sister of a larger loaf of Italian bread. The name filone (fee-LONE-ay) comes from the Italian word *filo*, which means "line," and the bread usually has a single score down the center. It makes a good table bread, sandwich bread, and bruschetta base. Olives are a popular inclusion, adding some texture and a salty pop. Any olives will work, but stronger olives such as Gaeta and Kalamata are best because the olive flavor mellows as the bread bakes. —CKM

bolted hard wheat flour	577 g (4⅔ cups)	100%
water	404 g (1⅔ cups)	70%
extra-virgin olive oil	29 g (2 tablespoons)	5%
dry yeast	9 g (1 tablespoon)	1.5%
salt	9 g (1½ teaspoons)	1.5%
chopped briny olives	173 g (¾ cup)	30%
TOTAL	**1,201 g**	**208%**

DAY 1: MIX. Measure the flour and set aside. Combine the water, oil, yeast, flour, and salt in a medium mixing bowl. With clean hands, mix everything by hand until it comes together in a shaggy mass, then mix it in the bowl for a few minutes more, alternately breaking the dough up and folding it back onto itself. At this point, the dough will still look shaggy and feel sticky and weak. Cover the bowl with a tea towel and let rest for 15 minutes.

Repeat the hand-mixing process in the bowl. By now, you'll notice that the dough feels a bit firmer; it will stretch some instead of tearing, and while it's still shaggy, it will look somewhat smoother. Cover and let rest for 15 minutes more. Then add the olives and hand-mix it again. It will still be a little sticky, but more gluten should be developed; this will make the dough feel more supple and allow it to stretch more easily without tearing. The dough should also look shinier. Finally, give the dough another 15-minute rest, then transfer to an airtight container, cover, and refrigerate it overnight.

DAY 2: PRESHAPE. Pull the dough from the refrigerator and allow it to warm up for 30 minutes. By now, the dough should be elastic and strong, and you should see some bubbles in the dough: signs of fermentation. Place the dough on a lightly floured countertop and divide it into three pieces, each about 400 grams. For each piece, pat the dough down, then fold all four edges in toward the center, until the dough is somewhat rounded. Place the pieces seam-side down on the countertop and let rest for 15 minutes.

SHAPE. Dust the top of each dough piece lightly with flour. To shape each loaf, flip it over, pat it down a bit, and roll it under your palms from the center outward to a rough cylinder about 3 inches in diameter in the center and 11 to 12 inches long. Keep the edges blunt so the loaf looks like a pudgy baguette. Place the loaves seam-side up on a lightly floured couche or tea towel, with small folds between the loaves to give each some support. Cover with another tea towel and let rest for about 1 hour at room temperature (65° to 75°F).

BAKE. Place a large baking stone and hotel pan (see page 62) on the middle rack of the oven. Preheat the oven to 500°F. Have a spray bottle and razor within reach.

Cut a sheet of parchment paper that will fit over the back side of a half sheet pan to use as a peel, then place two loaves seam-side down on the parchment. Quickly score the top of each loaf in a single line down the center from end to end, less than ½ inch deep. Immediately slide the scored loaves and parchment onto the stone, cover with the hotel pan while spraying water into the top of the pan, and close the oven door.

Bake until the loaves are fully puffed and the score marks are filled in, about 9 minutes. This is not a baguette, so you won't get dramatic "ears" from the scoring. Remove the hotel pan and bake for an additional 10 to 12 minutes. These guys will color like baguettes, with a shade similar to corn flakes. Pull the loaves out and allow them to cool on a rack.

The loaves will last for about 3 days at room temperature in a paper bag, bread box, or cupboard.

OPTIONS

If you're making these loaves for sandwiches, you can skip the olives and roll the loaves in sesame seeds, as shown in Filone Sandwich with Roast Lamb and Horseradish (page 261).

To switch up the flavors, you can also replace the olives with sautéed or caramelized onions, finely cubed provolone cheese, Poached Artichoke Hearts (page 256), or other inclusions from elsewhere. Experiment!

OVEN-DRIED-TOMATO STECCA

MAKES 4 NARROW
LOAVES, ABOUT
3 BY 10 INCHES

Day 1 → 5 minutes
active time with an
overnight rest

Day 2 → 30 minutes
active time over 2 hours

Day 3 → 20 minutes
active time over 2 hours

When I was a kid, my mom used to sun-dry racks of tomatoes, fruits, and herbs on her car's dashboard. I was horrified to be seen in the car with all that going on. It worked, though. And it must have stuck with me because, later, I started mixing semi-dried tomatoes into bread. But I use a different tomato-drying method. This bread is ideal for deep summer when you're awash in fresh, local tomatoes. I made a version of it when I worked at Avance restaurant in Philadelphia. I had our local farmers send us B-grade heirloom tomatoes that were too imperfect to sell but still delicious: we saved money, reduced waste, and had an incredible bread to show for it. The tomato guts (juice, seeds and pulp) make a fun substitute for some of the water in the dough. —CKM

OVEN-DRIED TOMATOES

1 pound fresh tomatoes, any kind

POOLISH

bolted hard wheat flour	138 g (1⅛ cups)	100%
water	138 g (½ cup)	100%
dry yeast	0.19 g (1/16 teaspoon)	0.14%
TOTAL	**276.19 g**	**200.14%**

DOUGH

bolted hard wheat flour	413 g (3½ cups)	100%
tomato guts	165 g (1 cup)	40%
water	103 g (½ cup)	25%
extra-virgin olive oil	25 g (1¾ tablespoons)	6%
dry yeast	0.66 g (¼ teaspoon)	0.16%
poolish (from above)	276.19 g (1⅓ cups)	67%
salt	11 g (1¾ teaspoons)	2.7%
oven-dried tomatoes (from above)	206 g (1⅛ cups)	50%
TOTAL	**1,199.85 g**	**290.86%**

extra-virgin olive oil for drizzling	
coarse salt for topping	

CONTINUED

DAY 1: DRY TOMATOES. If your tomatoes are medium or large, cut away the stem, cut them in half, and scoop or squeeze out the juice and seeds, reserving the tomato guts for the dough. Then cut the tomatoes into bite-size pieces about ¼ inch thick. If you are using cherry tomatoes, you can just nick them to squeeze out the guts, then cut them in half. Drying is easiest with a dehydrator. If you have one, set it to medium (about 150°F) and dehydrate the tomatoes for several hours until semi-dry but still flexible. Or place the tomatoes on wire racks in an oven set as low as it goes and dry for several hours. You could also go old-school and place the tomatoes on a wire rack, cover them with cheese-cloth, then allow them to air-dry outside on a warm, sunny day or in a sunny window until ready to use. This method will take several days. You don't want them leathery like fully dehydrated tomatoes, just more concentrated and less watery than fresh tomatoes.

MIX POOLISH. Measure the flour and set aside. Combine the water, yeast, and flour in a container large enough for the poolish to triple in volume. Cover with a lid, plastic grocery bag, plastic wrap, or beeswax wrap and leave at room temperature (65° to 75°F) to rest overnight.

DAY 2: MIX DOUGH. Weigh the flour and the remaining ingredients, including the tomato guts. If you're short on tomato guts, make up the difference with water. We'll be hand-mixing (see page 27), so everything will go into a mixing bowl. If you prefer to mix the dough in a machine, follow the mixing instructions for Ursa Baguette (page 81), adding the oven-dried tomatoes with the salt.

Combine the tomato guts, water, oil, yeast, poolish, and flour in a large mixing bowl. Mix with a spoon, dough scraper, or your hands, scraping the bottom of the bowl to hydrate all the flour. Keep mixing by stirring, folding, and breaking up the dough for another 3 minutes. Cover with a tea towel and let rest for 15 minutes. Add the salt and repeat hand-mixing (breaking up and folding the dough) for 3 minutes. Cover and let rest for 15 minutes. Add the oven-dried tomatoes and mix again for 3 minutes. Cover the bowl and let the dough rest at room temperature for 1 hour. Transfer the dough to a lightly oiled container with a lid and room for the dough to double in volume. Put on the lid and refrigerate for 30 minutes. Then pull the dough and give it a four-fold (see page 28). Finally, return the container to the fridge for 8 to 24 hours. On the short end of that range, the dough will be bubbly and well risen, and on the long end, it may be more wobbly and on the brink of collapse. Try not to let it go too long.

DAY 3: SHAPE. Pull the dough from the fridge. At this point, it should be very bubbly and inflated. Place a large baking stone on a rack, preferably near the top of the oven. Preheat the oven to 400°F. Have a couche, sheet pan or large cutting board, and a bench knife ready. Dust a section of countertop liberally with flour and turn the dough out onto it. Dust the top of the dough with more flour. This is a sticky dough, so be prepared to handle it lightly. Coax the dough from an oval into a loose rectangle, then divide the dough in half, bisecting the long sides. Divide each piece again to make four strips of dough, about 3 by 10 inches. Dust all the cut edges with flour. Roll each strip over once to ensure it is evenly coated with flour, then gently lift it onto the couche. Leave about 1 inch of fabric between each strip, lifting the fabric so that each strip of dough supports the other with folds of fabric between them. Cover with a tea towel and leave to rest for 30 to 45 minutes.

Assemble your toppings, in this case, the olive oil and salt. Cut a sheet of parchment paper that will fit over the back side of a half sheet pan to use as a peel, then gently transfer two of the loaves to the parchment. If the dough has been very active, put the remaining two loaves in the fridge to slow the fermentation down a bit. Dock the stecca all over by poking your fingers down into the dough, almost all the way through. Drizzle the stecca with the oil, then sprinkle with the salt.

BAKE: Load the stecca into the oven by sliding the parchment paper onto the stone. Bake for 12 minutes. Rotate the loaves as necessary for even browning, then bake for an additional 5 minutes. When done, the crust color should be medium tan. Pull the stecca out and transfer to a rack to cool. Give the oven 5 minutes to rebound, then begin assembling your second round to bake.

Stecca are great fresh, but they'll keep all right for a few days in a paper bag or a bread box at room temperature. After day one, refresh them in a 350°F oven for a few minutes for the best flavor and texture.

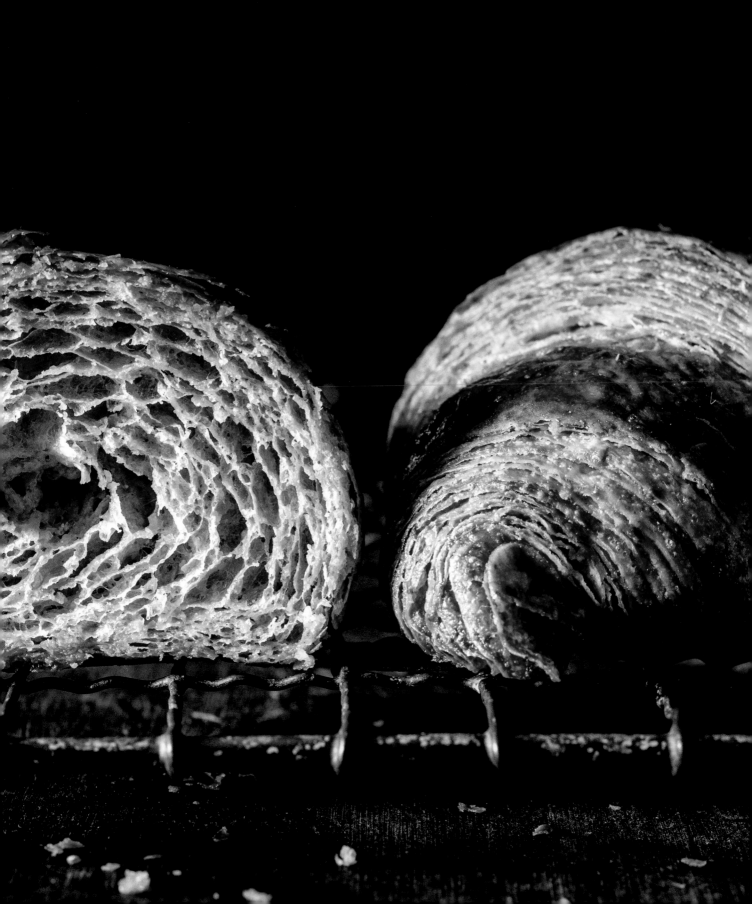

7

ENRICHED YEAST BREADS

WHENEVER I LAND IN ITALY, THE FIRST THING I DO IS GRAB SOME *MARMELLATA CORNETTI* AT AN AUTOGRILL REST STOP ON THE HIGHWAY. Cornetti are the Italian version of croissants, only better. I like them stuffed with marmalade (*marmellata*). The marmalade runs all over your hand and falls onto your plate. So good.

It's hard to explain why this first bite at an Italian rest stop is so very satisfying. It's like any one of those inexplicable moments that evoke special memories and feelings for you and you alone. For instance, my mom always left big red lipstick marks on clear drinking glasses, and when I saw them as a kid, I would freak out for some reason. Now, I still shiver when I see red lipstick on a drinking glass.

Or take American cheese: as a teenager, I was able to eat more slices of American cheese than any of my friends. It was a mark of pride. My tastes evolved when I grew up, but even now, when I eat crappy American cheese, it always tastes so good. And no matter how many times I eat meatballs, I still get that warm feeling of being at my grandparents' house on a Sunday for Sunday gravy. Landing in Italy and stopping at the Autogrill feels the same way. Italian rest stops are not like the ones in America. Yes, Autogrill is a chain. But when you walk into an Autogrill, you see whole legs of prosciutto hanging over a meat case filled with stacks of good-quality salumi. You see fresh mozzarella di bufala and a beautiful display of cheeses, great pizza al taglio with tons of different toppings, expensive wines and limoncello, local beers, and high-end chocolates and confections. This may be Italy's version of a 7-Eleven store, but it's more on the level of our gourmet markets. In Italy, eating well is a priority even on a road trip.

And you actually look forward to the coffee. There's no dishrag coffee in Italy! It's all on par with high-end craft coffee in America, and it comes out so fast and so good that you wonder what could possibly take 15 minutes to get a decent cup of coffee in the States. What's with the digital scales and exacting water pours in these little coffee shops? It's a fucking espresso! Do they wash the machine after every order? Truly maddening! In Italy, you order and it's up before they even hand you your change.

But it's those cornetti that really move me. There is something about the taste. And the texture. I don't crave them in America. I rarely order a croissant, even a good one. But when I land in Italy, I have to, I must . . . I simply cannot go on with life if I don't get a *marmellata e un cappuccino*. The buttery, flaky, crunchy sweet taste swirling around your mouth while you sip a cappuccino is just something you have to experience.

The difference between a cornetto and a croissant is subtle but important. Cornetti are more buttery and rich, while croissants are lighter and airier. That's why cornetti are better for dipping or having with coffee: they hold up. A croissant would almost melt away if you dipped it in anything. For me, a cornetto is the best of all worlds: it's light, flaky, buttery, *and* tender. When it's stuffed with something sweet or creamy, that just takes the whole thing to another level.

If you've never had a cornetto, go to Italy and stop at an Autogrill. Better yet, make your own Cornetti (page 137). They're a good introduction to laminated dough, a whole world of rich, flaky baked goods that includes Whole-Grain Rough Puff Pastry (page 229). Laminating just means you roll and fold the dough up with butter a bunch of times to make lots of layers of thin dough separated by layer after layer of butter. When it bakes, the butter melts, the layers puff up, and the bread gets flaky, crisp, and completely delicious.

Butter, oil, eggs, sugar, honey . . . basically any significant amount of something fatty or sweet is an enrichment to your standard flour-and-water dough. The olive oil in our Grissini (page 113) makes them richer and crisper. Even the potato in our Potato Bread (page 110) acts as an enrichment, making the dough softer (thank you, potato starch). That's a common theme in this chapter: the breads are richer, softer, and more tender than straight yeasted doughs. That softness means you can make lots of fun shapes, like crescents (*cornetti*) and braids for the Ursa Challah (page 119). These breads can also go in a savory or sweet direction. The Olive Oil Durum Rolls (page 121) are savory, while the Beignets (page 133) are sweet.

You don't have to worry about any unusual baking techniques here. Since the doughs are tender, the breads generally won't develop thick, chewy crusts. All of these breads are baked in or on pans. No baking stone. No steam. They are also baked at somewhat lower temperatures than straight yeasted doughs because enrichments make bread darken sooner.

Try a couple of these recipes to get a feel for enriched yeasted dough, then you can start playing around. You'll see that the Cinnamon Raisin Pan Loaf (page 129) is really just a variation on the Ursa Challah, with the inclusion of raisins, cinnamon, and a little more water to loosen up the dough. The challah itself could be baked in a loaf pan instead of braided if you prefer. And the Brioche (page 115) is baked in a loaf pan, but you could just as easily shape it into rolls. You could even add cinnamon and raisins to that brioche dough. Or dark chocolate and candied orange peel. But then you're starting to get into panettone territory. And that's another story altogether! **—MV**

STEVE SCOTT

Babettes Pizza & Pane | Longmont, Colorado

Steve Scott is the owner/baker at Babettes Pizza & Pane in Longmont, Colorado (formerly the award-winning Babettes Artisan Bread in Denver). After twelve years as a semipro bike racer, Steve worked for nearly two decades at bakeries such as Artisan Bakers, Della Fattoria, and Udi's. Babettes is now in its sixth year as a bakery, and first year as a restaurant. Steve specializes in handcrafted, high-hydration sourdough breads and laminated croissant and Danish-style doughs. Everything he makes is sourced from local farms.

"

I bake to bring the community together. I love finding out answers to the science of baking and pastry. But most of all, I love to feed people.

We mill our own grain, and the goal for me is freshness, nutrition, and knowing where my flour comes from.

Our local customers want to know what's on the plate and where it comes from. This inspires me to help them understand whom we purchase from and why.

Small-scale, handmade bread from high-quality grain that's fermented with levain and high hydration yields an almost pre-digested loaf of bread that is healthy for the gut and delicious.

"

POTATO BREAD

MAKES 12 HAMBURGER
BUNS OR 2 PAN LOAVES,
ABOUT 9 BY 5 INCHES

1½ hours active time
over 4 hours

This is my go-to hamburger bun recipe. It also works as a soft and mellow pan loaf. Potato is a great inclusion because it adds a cozy, warm flavor and starchy softness. —CKM

ROASTED AND MASHED POTATO
1 medium russet potato
2 tablespoons unsalted butter, melted

DOUGH

bolted hard wheat flour	638 g (5⅛ cups)	100%
roasted and mashed potato (from above)	159 g (¾ cup)	25%
water	287 g (1¼ cups)	45%
egg	64 g (¼ cup)	10%
dry yeast	10 g (3¼ teaspoons)	1.5%
sugar	51 g (4⅛ tablespoons)	8%
salt	16 g (2⅔ teaspoons)	2.5%
unsalted butter, cubed, at room temperature	96 g (6¾ tablespoons)	15%
TOTAL	1,321 g	207%

egg for egg wash
pinch of salt for egg wash
sesame seeds (optional) for topping

ROAST POTATO. Preheat the oven to 350ºF. Peel and cube the potato, then toss it with the melted butter and spread it on a sheet pan. Roast until the potato is very soft, 20 to 30 minutes. Pass the potato through a food mill or mash with a potato masher and let the mashed potato cool before mixing.

MIX. Measure the flour and set aside. Weigh 159 grams of the mashed potato and combine it with the water, egg, yeast, flour, sugar, and salt in the bowl of a stand mixer. Mix with the dough hook on low speed for 5 minutes, then leave the dough to rest for 5 minutes. Resume mixing on low speed and add the softened butter during the first minute. You may need to scrape down the bowl once or twice. Once the dough has softened from the incorporation of the butter, increase the speed to medium. Then mix until the dough is clearing the sides of the bowl, about 6 minutes more.

BULK FERMENT. Rest the dough at room temperature (65º to 75ºF) for 1 hour total with a four-fold (see page 28) at the 30-minute mark.

SHAPE. For burger buns, divide the dough into twelve 110-gram pieces. Then shape the pieces into rounds or small boules (see page 49) and divide evenly between two half sheet pans (if you only have one half sheet pan, the buns may touch each other when they bake, which is okay)."

For pan loaves, divide the dough in half so each piece is about 650 grams. Then press each piece into a rectangle-ish shape. Roll the rectangle-ish dough along one long side, until you have a blunt log of dough, and press the seam to seal. Oil two 9 by 5-inch loaf pans and place the dough in the pans, seam-side down.

Cover the trays or pans with a plastic grocery bag, plastic wrap, or beeswax wrap and leave to rise at room temperature until the buns or loaves have doubled in size. Depending on your room temperature, this could take 1 to 2 hours for buns and 2 to 3 hours for loaves.

BAKE. Preheat the oven to 350°F. When your buns or loaves are close to full size, beat together the egg and salt and brush the egg wash all over the dough. To make sesame seed buns, sprinkle sesame seeds evenly over the tops of the rolls. For a split-top loaf, score the dough once down the center immediately after egg washing it. Bake the rolls or loaves for 15 minutes, rotate the pans, then bake until the tops are reddish gold, almost copper in color, an additional 4 to 5 minutes for buns or 10 to 12 minutes for loaves.

This bread will last 2 to 3 days at room temperature in a paper bag, bread box, or cupboard. And it freezes well.

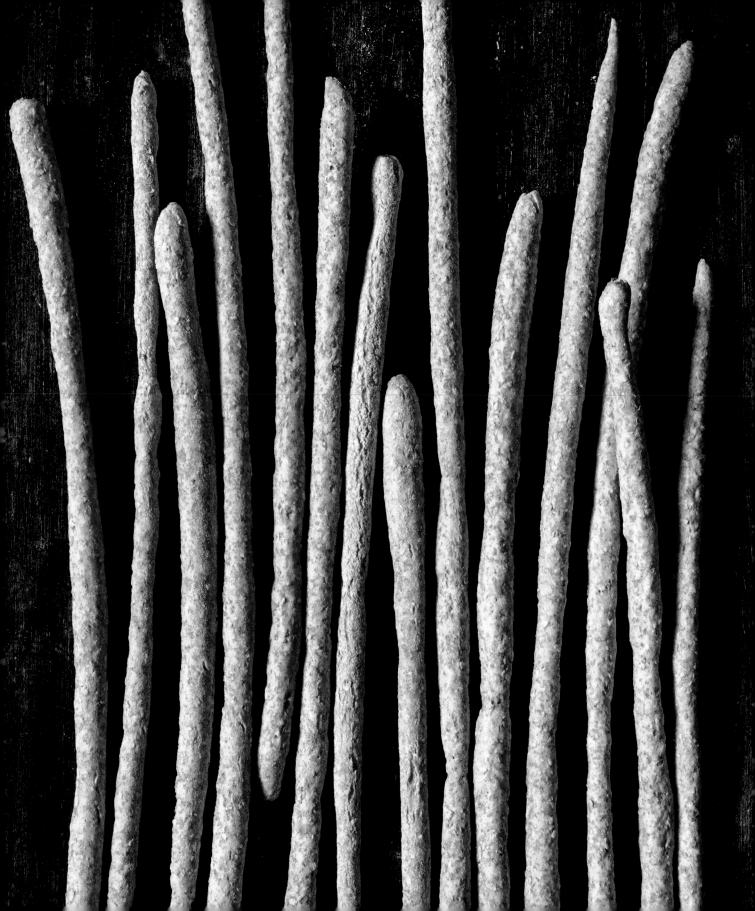

GRISSINI

MAKES ABOUT
36 GRISSINI, ABOUT
¼ BY 18 INCHES

1 hour active time
over 9 hours

You'll notice spelt in quite a few of our breads. It's one of the tastiest grains and has great extensibility, which is perfect for grissini because these Italian breadsticks are usually stretched out very long. You can shape these whole-grain grissini into anything from thick breadsticks to long, thin, crispy straws. Depending on your preferred shape, you can roll the dough by hand or use a fettuccine cutter (see Option, page 114). Either way, grissini are always welcome on the table when you're entertaining. Munch on them before the main dishes are served, either plain or wrapped in prosciutto. —CKM

whole-grain spelt flour	250 g (2⅛ cups)	100%
water	140 g (⅔ cup)	56%
dry yeast	4 g (1¼ teaspoons)	1.6%
salt	8 g (1⅓ teaspoons)	3.2%
extra-virgin olive oil	25 g (1¾ tablespoons)	10%
TOTAL	**427 g**	**170.8%**

MIX. Measure the flour and set aside. Combine the water, yeast, flour, salt, and oil in the bowl of a stand mixer. Mix with the dough hook on low speed for 4 minutes, then switch to medium speed and mix for 8 minutes more. If there's too little dough for your machine to mix effectively, you can hand-mix the dough on a countertop instead, for 10 to 12 minutes total. This mix is more intensive to get the gluten developed right away, so the dough can go directly into the fridge for some rest and hydration. Once finished mixing, put the dough into a lightly oiled container with a lid large enough for the dough to roughly double in size. Cover with the lid and leave the container in the refrigerator for about 8 hours. This isn't a firm time—feel free to go as short as 3 hours and as long as 24 hours, depending upon your baking schedule. This dough is very forgiving and holds well in the fridge.

SHAPE. Preheat the oven to 325°F. For long, thin, hand-crafted grissini, cut the dough into thirty-six pieces about 12 grams each and hand-roll each one into a thin rope the length of your sheet pan, about 18 inches. Roll the ropes on a lightly floured countertop under your palms from the center outward and try to make them as even as possible in diameter and length.

For quicker, more uniform grissini, you could turn all the dough out onto a lightly floured countertop. Flour the top of the dough, then use your hands to press the dough out to a rectangle about 4 by 8 inches. Grab a rolling pin and roll the dough out to a larger rectangle about 8 by 12 inches and ¼ inch thick. Use a hard-edged ruler and a pizza cutter or a long, sharp knife to cut the dough into strips ¼ inch wide and 12 inches long.

BAKE. Line two sheet pans with parchment paper and arrange the grissini on them. The grissini won't expand much, so you can get them pretty close to one another. Bake for 20 minutes, turning once during the last 5 to 8 minutes to ensure even browning. The grissini are done when they have just taken on a straw color. They should be crisp, and the snap will increase as they cool. Grissini taste best after fully cooling, so cool them completely.

They will keep for 1 to 2 weeks in an airtight container at room temperature.

CONTINUED

OPTION

You can use a pasta roller and fettuccine cutter to shape and cut the grissini. Use a rolling pin to roll out the dough on a lightly floured countertop so that it fits your pasta roller. The dough should be a bit under ½ inch thick. Flour it lightly, brush off the excess, and pass it once through the widest setting of the pasta roller. You should have a long strip of dough. The long sides should be reasonably straight and smooth, so you don't have a bunch of ragged off-cuts. If necessary, fold the strip in half widthwise and reroll to smooth it out. After rolling, the strip of dough should be about ¼ inch thick. Set up the fettuccine cutter and line a half sheet pan with parchment paper. Now, cut the strip of dough crosswise into shorter rectangles. This cut will determine the final length of the grissini. They will stretch a bit in the fettuccine cutter, so if you want plenty of short grissini, cut the dough into four pieces. If you want fewer but longer grissini, cut the dough into just two pieces. Three pieces is the middle road. Dust the pieces with flour and run through the fettuccine cutter, pausing after each one to arrange the grissini on the parchment-lined tray. You don't want to wait too long to separate the grissini, as they may begin to stick together. Repeat with the remaining rectangles and bake as directed in the recipe.

BRIOCHE

MAKES 1 PULLMAN LOAF,
ABOUT 13 BY 4 INCHES

Day 1 → 30 minutes
active time over 1½ hours
with an overnight rest
(optional)

Day 2 → 15 minutes
active time over 3½ hours

Traditional brioche is made with all-white flour because that was considered classy for a long time. This brioche is made from a blend of bolted and whole-wheat flours because that's classy now. It's a bread that's best made over two days for maximum flavor. After mixing, the dough can also be portioned and frozen to bake off later. I've written the recipe to make a long, rectangular Pullman loaf, but you could shape it into brioche rolls instead (see Options) and bake them on a sheet pan. I like brioche in a loaf because it makes extra-special tea sandwiches, cinnamon toast, and croutons. —CKM

bolted hard wheat flour	357 g (2¾ cups)	80%
whole-grain hard wheat flour	90 g (¾ cup)	20%
water	67 g (¼ cup)	15%
dry yeast	7 g (2¼ teaspoons)	1.5%
eggs	223 g (¾ cup, about 5 medium)	50%
sugar	45 g (¼ cup)	10%
salt	11 g (1¾ teaspoons)	2.5%
unsalted butter, cubed, at room temperature	200 g (1 cup)	45%
TOTAL	**1,000 g**	**224%**

DAY 1: MIX. Measure both flours and set aside. Combine the water and yeast in the bowl of a stand mixer, then mix with the dough hook on low speed, gradually adding the eggs, flours, and sugar. Mix on low speed for 5 minutes, scraping any dry ingredients from the bottom of the bowl as necessary. The dough will be stiff and sticky. Let it rest for 10 minutes.

Add the salt and mix on low speed again. Then add one-third of the butter cubes. Mix until the butter is almost fully incorporated, then add another third of the butter. When the butter is almost fully incorporated, add the final third and continue mixing until the dough is smooth and shiny and clings to the dough hook, 4 to 6 minutes after the final addition. Cover the bowl with a tea towel and let the dough rest for 1 hour.

PRESHAPE. Lightly flour a countertop and turn the dough out onto it. Pat it down a bit, then give it a four-fold (see page 28). Pat it down again, then tighten the dough into a

round by rolling, pressing, and shaping it on the countertop. Once you have a round shape, roll the dough back and forth on the countertop into a cylinder about 10 inches long and 2 inches wide. At this point, you can shape the dough right away or chill it for better texture and flavor. Wrap the dough loosely in a plastic grocery bag, plastic wrap, or beeswax wrap (it will expand) and place it in the refrigerator to rest overnight or in the freezer for up to 1 week. Defrost frozen dough overnight in the refrigerator before shaping it.

DAY 2: SHAPE. Butter a lidded Pullman pan (13 by 4 by 4 inches) and lightly flour a countertop.

Pull the dough from the refrigerator, unwrap it, and press it into a rough rectangle on your countertop. Starting from a long edge, fold the dough one-third of the way over itself, like folding a letter. Press down the fold to seal it. Then fold

CONTINUED

the opposite edge up and into the center and press again. Continue pressing the dough and evening it out to a uniform rectangle that matches the dimensions of the bottom of the pan (13 by 4 inches). Place the dough seam-side down in the pan, gently shaping it to fit the bottom. Slide on the lid and leave the pan in a warm (about 80°F), not hot, spot for about 3 hours. The dough is ready to be baked when it is very close to touching the lid. If you open the lid to check and feel the dough tugging, stop and close the lid. It's ready.

BAKE. About an hour before the dough is done rising, preheat the oven to 360°F. Place the pan in the oven and bake until golden to reddish brown, 30 to 35 minutes. The bread's internal temp should be about 195°F. After about 30 minutes of baking, slide back the lid to check the bread's doneness. Depan the loaf immediately and let it cool completely on a rack.

The brioche will keep well in an airtight container at room temperature for up to 1 week. It also freezes well. (We freeze brioche to get really clean, thin slices to serve with foie gras.)

OPTIONS

You could shape the brioche into rounds, braids, or other shapes. See pages 49 to 54 for options and bake the shaped dough on a sheet pan lined with parchment paper.

To make **Squid Ink Brioche**, substitute 8 grams of squid ink for 8 grams of the water. Squid ink, or more accurately cuttlefish ink, is a fun ingredient to keep in your freezer. Look for it in gourmet grocery stores or online at retailers such as La Tienda. This brioche variation comes out soft and close textured, like the regular brioche, but jet black and with a mild shellfish flavor. It makes dramatic bread crumbs and croutons for seafood dishes. Before digging in to this recipe, I recommend making the plain brioche. That will give you a sense of how long the loaf needs in *your* oven, since you won't be able to rely on crust color once you add squid ink to the dough.

URSA CHALLAH

MAKES 2 BRAIDED
OBLONG LOAVES,
ABOUT 8 BY 10 INCHES

I developed this versatile, tight-crumbed sweet dough for my bakery. While it can be baked day of, I prefer to shape the challah, then give it a long final proof in the refrigerator for more flavor and a more burnished mahogany crust. Warthog and Redeemer are good all-around hard wheat flours to use in this dough. —CKM

Day 1 → 45 minutes active time over 1¾ hours with an overnight rest (optional)

Day 2 → 5 minutes active time over 30 minutes

bolted hard wheat flour	510 g (4⅛ cups)	80%
whole-grain hard wheat flour	128 g (1⅛ cups)	20%
water	281 g (1¼ cups)	44%
eggs	137 g (½ cup, about 3 medium)	21.5%
canola oil	64 g (⅓ cup)	10%
dry yeast	4 g (1¼ teaspoons)	0.6%
sugar	64 g (⅓ cup)	10%
salt	13 g (2⅛ teaspoons)	2%
TOTAL	**1,201 g**	**188.1%**

egg for egg wash

pinch of salt for egg wash

1 tablespoon sesame or poppy seeds (optional) for topping

DAY 1: MIX. Measure both flours and set aside. Combine the water, eggs, oil, yeast, flours, sugar, and salt in the bowl of a stand mixer. Mix with the dough hook on low speed for 5 minutes. Switch to medium speed and mix for 4 minutes more. At this point, the dough should clear the sides of the bowl and be relatively firm and elastic. Transfer it to an oiled bowl, cover with a tea towel, and leave to rest at room temperature (65° to 75°F) for 1 hour. Line a half sheet pan with parchment paper.

PRESHAPE. Divide the dough into two 600-gram pieces. To begin creating braided oblong loaves, pat each piece out and divide each into four pieces, so you have eight even pieces. Tuck and roll each piece under your palms into a rope about 16 inches long and 1 inch thick. For each loaf, braid four pieces into an oblong loaf (see page 54).

Transfer the loaves to the parchment paper–lined sheet pan. Two loaves will fit on a true half sheet pan but stagger them so each has a bit of extra space. Cover the loaves with a tea towel and leave at room temperature, until they've risen to about double their original size, about 1½ hours. Or, if you are retarding the loaves, let them rise about halfway, 45 minutes to 1 hour, then transfer them to the refrigerator to rest overnight. I prefer to retard the loaves, which gives more time for enzymatic activity, creating a richer, tangier flavor and a more burnished crust. Plus, a fully risen cold loaf is more stable than a fully risen warm loaf, and that makes it easier to egg wash. Retarding the dough in the fridge overnight also allows you to bake the loaves in the morning.

At bake time, the loaves should be almost double their original size and look as if they can barely rise any more. They will still spring a small amount in the oven but not much. Baking too early will result in a greater oven spring that erases the contour of the braid, rounding out the whole loaf.

CONTINUED

DAY 2: BAKE. When the loaves are close to readiness, preheat the oven to 350°F. Beat together the egg and salt and paint the egg wash all over the loaves. If you like, sprinkle sesame or poppy seeds over the egg wash. Then load the sheet pan onto the middle rack of the oven.

Challah and other enriched doughs do not need steam or to be covered. They should be baked when there is not much rise left to gain, so it is fine to leave them uncovered and begin setting the crust early in the bake. Bake for 20 to 25 minutes, turning the pan after about 20 minutes to ensure even browning. When fully baked, challah should have a deep reddish brown color. When finished, transfer the loaves to a rack to cool.

This bread keeps moderately well in a paper bag, bread box, or cupboard for a few days and can always be revived as French toast.

OPTIONS

Challah can be shaped in infinite ways to make small, sweet dinner rolls similar to Parker House rolls, pan loaves that make amazing PB&J, or different braids. See pages 49 to 54 for some shaping options. You could even fold in some cinnamon and raisins to make Cinnamon Raisin Pan Loaf (page 129).

Spelt flour is a good candidate for the whole-grain portion of flour here, as its extensibility can help with rolling out ropes. Spelt is often less absorbent than other wheat flours, so it may be wise to decrease the hydration here a bit at first (maybe by 2%), then add more water as necessary.

OLIVE OIL DURUM ROLLS

MAKES 28 OVAL ROLLS,
ABOUT 2-INCH DIAMETER

Day 1 → 5 minutes
active time

Day 2 → 1 hour
active time over
4 hours, 15 minutes

It's uncommon to score a dinner roll, but it's a nice touch. I first made these little rolls as one of our table breads at Avance restaurant in Philly. They have a lot of olive oil, and that flavor shines through, so use your boldest oil. It's the durum flour that allows the dough to take up so much oil. Durum wheat is high enough in protein that you can mix long enough for all the oil to incorporate. Durum also gives the bread an attractive mellow yellow color. If you can't find whole-grain durum flour in your area, you can buy durum wheat berries and flour online. —CKM

POOLISH

whole-grain durum flour	194 g (1⅔ cups)	100%
water	194 g (¾ cup)	100%
dry yeast	0.05 g (¹⁄₆₄ teaspoon)	0.025%
TOTAL	**388.05 g**	**200.025%**

DOUGH

bolted hard wheat flour	323 g (2⅔ cups)	100%
water	81 g (⅓ cup)	25%
dry yeast	1 g (⅓ teaspoon)	0.4%
poolish (from above)	387 g (2½ cups)	120%
sugar	81 g (6½ tablespoons)	25%
salt	11 g (1¾ teaspoons)	3.4%
extra-virgin olive oil, plus more for brushing	116 g (8½ tablespoons)	36%
TOTAL	**1,000 g**	**309.8%**

DAY 1: MIX POOLISH. Measure the flour and set aside. Choose a container with a tight-fitting lid and enough space for the poolish to triple in volume. Pour in the water and sprinkle in the yeast. Then mix in the flour, stirring just long enough to make sure all the flour is wet. Scrape the bottom of the container to get any stray clumps. Cover with the lid and leave at room temperature (65° to 75°F) to rest for 8 to 16 hours (overnight works well). On the short end of that time, you may get a very stiff dough. On the long end, you may get a very extensible dough due to the extra enzyme activity.

DAY 2: MIX DOUGH. Measure the flour and set aside. Combine the water, yeast, poolish, flour, and sugar in the bowl of a stand mixer. Mix with the dough hook on low speed for 6 minutes. Cover the bowl with a tea towel and leave to rest at room temperature for 15 minutes. Add the salt and about half of the olive oil, then mix on low speed until the oil is absorbed, 5 to 10 minutes. Keep an eye on this process; you may end up with dough circling the bowl

CONTINUED

without the oil mixing in. In that case, stop and manually break up the dough to help mix in the oil, then continue mixing; once enough oil is absorbed to keep the mixture from splashing, switch the mixer to medium speed to help work the oil into the dough. After the first addition of oil is absorbed, return to low speed and add the remaining oil. Continue mixing, stopping, and breaking up the dough as necessary, until all the oil is absorbed and the dough feels silky and elastic when tugged. The total mixing time here could be as much as 15 minutes.

Place the dough in an oiled bowl, cover with a tea towel, and let rest for 2¼ hours with two folds during that time: give it a four-fold (see page 28) after 45 minutes, then another four-fold after another 45 minutes. Finally, let the dough rest for 45 minutes.

SHAPE. Line two half sheet pans with parchment paper. Turn the dough out onto a lightly floured countertop and cut into twenty-eight 35-gram pieces. For each piece, first shape it into a round by rolling it in a circle on your countertop, cupping your hands around the dough to increase the surface tension all around it as you form it into a ball. Then make the ball an oval egg shape by pressing one side against the counter and pulling it taut to increase the tension on the other side. Place the ovals on the parchment paper–lined half sheet pans with at least a 1-inch space between each. Cover with a tea towel and allow to rest until the dough nearly doubles in size, about 1 hour if the room is warm.

BAKE. Preheat the oven to 350°F. I like to score a little wheat-stalk pattern into the tops by taking a sharp knife and nicking one vertical and four angled, staggered cuts (see "Wheat-stalk scoring" illustration on page 60). Load the sheet pans into the oven and bake until the rolls have turned a nice deep golden color, about 16 minutes. After pulling the trays, I also like to accentuate the olive oil flavor by brushing the rolls with a little more oil while still hot on the pan. Serve warm if possible.

These rolls will last about 2 days in an airtight container at room temperature, but they're better reheated in a 350°F oven for 10 minutes before serving.

ENGLISH MUFFINS

MAKES 9 MUFFINS, ABOUT
3-INCH DIAMETER

1 hour active time
over 3 hours (or overnight)

I came up with these muffins because I wanted to use up some buttermilk after making Cultured Butter (page 264). I love the tanginess the buttermilk brings to the dough, and the butter is ideal for melting into the nooks and crannies after you split and toast the muffins. —CKM

bolted hard wheat flour	250 g (2⅛ cups)	50%
whole-grain hard wheat flour	250 g (2⅛ cups)	50%
water	150 g (⅔ cup)	30%
buttermilk	225 g (1 cup)	45%
honey	25 g (3½ teaspoons)	5%
dry yeast	10 g (3¼ teaspoons)	2%
salt	13 g (2⅛ teaspoons)	2.6%
unsalted butter, at room temperature	20 g (4¼ teaspoons)	4%
TOTAL	**943 g**	**188.6%**

semolina or cornmeal for dusting

MIX. For this dough, I favor a quick, aggressive mix. Measure both flours and set aside. Combine the water, buttermilk, honey, yeast, flours, salt, and butter in the bowl of a stand mixer. Mix with the dough hook on low speed for 1 minute, then bump it up to medium speed for 7 minutes. At the end, the dough should be on the firmer side but pliable. Transfer to a lightly oiled container with a lid and enough space for the dough to rise. English muffins are a breakfast bread, and while you could wake up crazy early to do all the work hours before breakfast, most people like to do the prep the night before, then retard the dough so it's ready in the morning. Plus, whenever you retard a dough, you get a tangier, richer taste.

To make English muffins the next morning, leave the dough at room temperature (65° to 75°F) for 45 minutes, then transfer it to the refrigerator to rest overnight. The dough should balloon to 1½ times its original size. If you're set on making English muffins in one day, transfer the dough to an oiled bowl, cover with a tea towel, and let rest at warm room temperature (75° to 85°F) for 90 minutes. The dough should still reach 1½ times its original size—even over the shorter time—due to the warmer temperature.

SHAPE. Dust a baking sheet with semolina or cornmeal. Turn the dough out onto a generously floured countertop and dust more flour on top. Using a rolling pin, roll the dough out to about ¾ inch thick. Punch out muffins with a 3-inch round cookie cutter. If you don't have a cookie cutter, you can use a tin can or a glass but be careful to push the glass down gently, and try to lift straight up after punching. Otherwise, the muffins may be uneven and rise awkwardly in the pan. You can punch the muffins very close to one another and get seven muffins from the first pass over the dough. Set the muffins on the prepared baking sheet. Then push the scraps together to make two more wonky full-size muffins or you

CONTINUED

can cut up the dough into bite-size snacks and cook them off to keep any roving scavengers at bay. Cover the muffins with lightly oiled plastic wrap and leave to rise at room temperature for 45 minutes, or for 1 hour if the dough has come from the fridge.

BAKE. My preferred method for cooking English muffins is in a 10-inch cast-iron pan over low heat with a toaster oven to finish them off. If you don't have a toaster oven, it seems silly to me to preheat a full-size oven. I would personally just cook the muffins in the pan for an additional minute or two on each side. But you do you. Set the toaster oven to 350°F and thoroughly preheat your cast-iron pan over low heat for a good 5 minutes. Set four muffins in the pan and cook for 6 minutes on each side. Transfer the first batch to the toaster oven for 6 minutes while starting the second batch in the pan.

When finished, transfer the muffins to a rack to cool. Let them cool at least halfway: I promise they will taste better once they've cooled a bit. As everyone knows, the best preparation is to split them with a fork to get a nice ragged surface, then retoast and slather with butter and jam or top with egg and cheese.

English muffins are best eaten the same day, but they can be kept in an airtight container at room temperature for about 2 days.

CINNAMON RAISIN PAN LOAF

MAKES 2 PAN LOAVES,
9 BY 5 INCHES

30 minutes active time
over 6½ hours

At Ursa, I try to make at least two different breads from every dough that I mix. Here's a good example. Just by adding a little water, cinnamon, and raisins to the challah dough, then baking the dough in pans, you get cinnamon raisin bread, a reasonably different kind of loaf. The cinnamon makes it feel as if you're eating something sweet, but the bread itself doesn't actually have much sugar in it. And who doesn't love cinnamon raisin bread? —CKM

Ursa Challah dough (full recipe, page 119)	1,200 g (7 cups)	100%
water	120 g (½ cup)	10%
ground cinnamon	2 g (¾ teaspoon)	0.2%
raisins	168 g (1 cup)	14%
TOTAL	1,490 g	124.2%

egg for egg wash
pinch of salt for egg wash

MIX. Follow the recipe for making the challah dough but add the amount of water called for here (120 grams) to the water called for there (281 grams) for a total of 401 grams water. Follow the challah dough recipe through the mixing stage. Once fully mixed, add the cinnamon and raisins and mix until fully incorporated, about 1 minute on low speed. Transfer to an oiled bowl, cover with a tea towel, and leave to rest at room temperature (65° to 75°F) for 1½ hours.

SHAPE. Oil two 9 by 5-inch loaf pans. Turn the dough out onto a lightly floured countertop and divide it into two pieces, about 745 grams each. Press each piece out thoroughly, coaxing it into something resembling a rectangle, with the short side about 6 inches wide. Fold the dough into thirds like a letter, sealing the seams well, then roll in the same direction to create a tube 8 to 9 inches long and 4 to 5 inches wide. Press the dough into the oiled pans and cover with a tea towel. Leave to rise in a warm place until the dough has fully risen and is cresting about 1 inch over the rim of the pan, about 4 hours. If the dough is moving slowly and seems to be stuck under a skin of dry dough, you can help speed up the rise by scoring the loaves in a decorative pattern and then leave them to finish rising.

BAKE. Preheat the oven to 350°F with a rack in the center. Beat together the egg and salt, brush the egg wash over the loaves, then score a decorative pattern lightly onto the tops of the loaves. Bake for about 30 minutes overall, turning once during the last 15 minutes to ensure even browning. If the loaves take color quickly, you can tent them with aluminum foil to prevent burning. The finished loaves will be dark and shiny like chestnuts. Carefully depan and allow to cool on a rack.

This bread will keep well in a paper bag, bread box, or cupboard at room temperature for about 4 days. If you will be eating it more slowly, slice and freeze the loaves so that portions can be pulled as needed.

OPTION

If you don't have two loaf pans, you can bake half in a loaf pan and braid the other loaf as shown on page 54.

PANE ALLA ZUCCA

MAKES 4 SMALL BOULES,
ABOUT 6-INCH DIAMETER

40 minutes active time
over 4 hours

Soft, lightly sweet, and bright gold in color, these pane alla zucca (pumpkin breads) make fantastic breads for the holiday table. A simple scoring technique makes the finished bread reminiscent of a pumpkin. Any winter squash will do, especially a deeply pigmented one like butternut, red kuri, or kabocha. Using 20% whole-wheat flour gives the bread a satisfying texture. —CKM

ROASTED SQUASH

1 small (1 pound) winter squash

1 tablespoon extra-virgin olive oil

½ teaspoon salt

DOUGH

bolted hard wheat flour	559 g (4½ cups)	80%
whole-grain hard wheat flour	140 g (1⅛ cups)	20%
whole milk	105 g (½ cup)	15%
unsalted butter, cubed, at room temperature	210 g (15 tablespoons)	30%
dry yeast	10 g (3¼ teaspoons)	1.5%
eggs	210 g (¾ cup, about 4 medium)	30%
sugar	70 g (⅓ cup)	10%
salt	17 g (2¾ teaspoons)	2.5%
roasted squash (from above), cooled	279 g (⅔ cup)	40%
TOTAL	**1,600 g**	**229%**

egg for egg wash

pinch of salt for egg wash

ROAST SQUASH. Preheat the oven to 400°F. Cut the squash in half lengthwise and discard the seeds and strings. Rub the cut sides with the oil and sprinkle with the salt. Set the squash on a sheet pan, cut-sides up, and roast until the flesh is very soft, 45 minutes to 1 hour. Set aside and when cool enough to handle, scoop 279 grams of the squash from its shell and mash it in a bowl. Let cool. Save the rest of the squash for another use (mashed with butter and salt always works).

MIX. Measure both flours and set aside. Scald the milk by bringing it to a bare simmer, then turn off the heat. Let cool. Weigh the butter so it will temper by the time it is needed. Then combine the milk, yeast, flours, eggs, and sugar in the bowl of a stand mixer. Mix with the dough hook on low speed until the dough develops enough strength to cling to the hook and clear the sides of the bowl, about 8 minutes. You will probably have to stop the mixer and scrape down the bowl and hook one or two times during this mix. Add the butter and salt and continue mixing on low speed, until the butter is mostly incorporated, about 4 minutes. Add the squash and mix until partly incorporated, about 1 minute, then switch to medium speed and mix until the ingredients are fully incorporated and the dough is smooth, shiny, and feels fairly extensible, another 3 to 4 minutes. Cover the bowl with a tea towel and leave to rest at room temperature (65° to 75°F) for 1 hour with a four-fold (see page 28) at the halfway point.

SHAPE. Line two half sheet pans with parchment paper. Lightly dust the countertop with flour. Divide the dough into four pieces, each about 400 grams, then shape them into balls. You can shape this dough pretty aggressively: just smash a piece down and roll it into a tight ball, pressing your hands around the outsides of the dough to increase the surface tension all around it. (At this point, you can wrap and refrigerate the dough balls for a day or two or freeze them for up to a month. If you freeze the dough, pull a wrapped portion from the freezer to the refrigerator the day before using it so it has time to thaw.)

Put the dough balls on the parchment paper–lined half sheet pans. Cover with a plastic grocery bag, plastic wrap, or beeswax wrap and allow to rise until doubled in size, about 1½ hours (or 2 hours if you're pulling the dough from the fridge).

BAKE. Preheat the oven to 350°F. Beat the egg with the salt, then brush the egg wash all over the loaves, being careful to go all over the sides and a little underneath. To get a shape that's reminiscent of a pumpkin for each loaf, hold scissors vertically over the top of the dough and make a big snip across the center about a third of the way down into the dough. Turn the dough a third and snip again, then turn a third and snip again, so you have a score that looks like an asterisk. Load the sheet pans with the loaves into the oven and bake until the crust is a two-toned orange-brown pumpkin color, 20 to 25 minutes. The internal temperature of the loaves should be around 210°F. Remove the pans from the oven and let cool on a rack.

These guys will last for 3 to 4 days in a paper bag, bread box, or cupboard at room temperature.

HONEY DURUM BATARD

MAKES 3 BATARDS,
ABOUT 9 BY 5 INCHES

Day 1 → 5 minutes
active time with an
overnight rest

Day 2 → 30 minutes
active time over 5 hours

Durum flour is usually used for pasta, but it gives bread an amazing chew. And I love how adding honey to the dough sweetens it up a little. We use both dry yeast and a biga preferment here to create more complex flavors in the bread and to give it a more airy crumb. The biga called for in Spelt Pretzels makes exactly the right amount. —MV

152 g (¾ cup) biga (page 91)		
DOUGH		
bolted hard wheat flour	700 g (5⅔ cups)	70%
whole-grain durum flour	300 g (2½ cups)	30%
water	625 g (2⅔ cups)	62.5%
dry yeast	3 g (1 teaspoon)	0.3%
biga (from above)	152 g (¾ cup)	15%
honey	254 g (¾ cup)	25.4%
salt	22 g (3⅔ teaspoons)	2.2%
TOTAL	**2,056 g**	**205.4%**

DAY 1: MIX BIGA. Make the biga as instructed in the Spelt Pretzels and let sit overnight.

DAY 2: MIX DOUGH. Measure both flours and set aside. Combine the water, yeast, biga, flours, and honey in the bowl of a stand mixer. Mix with the dough hook on low speed for 8 minutes. Switch to medium speed, add the salt, and mix until the dough clings to the hook and clears the sides of the bowl, another 2 to 4 minutes. Transfer the dough to an oiled bowl, cover with a tea towel, and leave to rest at room temperature (65° to 75°F) for 2 hours.

SHAPE. Cut the dough into three pieces, each about 685 grams, and let rest for 5 minutes.

Shape the loaves into batards (see page 50). Flour three medium oval bannetons or towel-lined bowls (you'll get round loaves if using the latter). Transfer the loaves to the bannetons; loosely cover with plastic grocery bags, plastic wrap, or beeswax wrap; then leave to rest at room temperature until the loaves are roughly doubled in size, about 2 hours. Or, to bake the loaves the next morning, place the wrapped bannetons of dough in the refrigerator to rest overnight. Remove them from the fridge about 1 hour before baking.

BAKE. Place a large baking stone and hotel pan (see page 62) on the highest rack of the oven they will fit on. Preheat the oven to 460°F. Have two towels or hot pads, a spray bottle of water, and a razor within reach.

Quickly but carefully open your oven, pull the rack that you are baking on partway out, and move the hot hotel pan to the stovetop. Invert the loaves onto the stone and score the tops (I like four or five parallel lines on a slight angle across the loaves). Cover with the hotel pan, spraying water into the pan before setting it onto the stone to trap steam.

Bake for 10 minutes, turn the heat to 400°F, and bake for 10 minutes more. Remove the hotel pan, rotate the loaves for even browning, and bake until the crusts are dark golden brown, another 20 minutes. Remove to a rack to cool.

This bread can be kept in a paper bag, bread box, or cupboard at room temperature for 4 to 5 days.

BEIGNETS

MAKES ABOUT
20 BEIGNETS,
2 BY 3 INCHES

30 minutes active time
over 2 hours

After a great beignet breakfast one morning in New Orleans, we decided we needed a beignet recipe for this book. Some versions call for vegetable shortening and/or evaporated milk, but those are not ingredients I want to encourage folks to buy. However, I felt okay about using sweetened condensed milk. Why? I don't know. I think Vietnamese coffee has influenced me. —CKM

bolted hard or soft wheat flour	194 g (1½ cups)	100%
whole milk	163 g (⅔ cup)	84%
sweetened condensed milk	23 g (1¼ tablespoons)	12%
unsalted butter	15 g (1 tablespoon)	8%
dry yeast	1 g (⅓ teaspoon)	0.6%
baking powder	1 g (¼ teaspoon)	0.6%
salt	4 g (⅔ teaspoon)	2%
TOTAL	**401 g**	**207.2%**

canola oil for deep-frying
confectioners' sugar for dusting

MIX. Measure the flour and set aside. Take the chill off the milk, condensed milk, and butter by warming them gently in a small saucepan over low heat until the butter melts. Let cool a bit, then pour the mixture into the bowl of a stand mixer. Add the yeast, flour, baking powder, and salt and mix with the dough hook on low speed for about 8 minutes. This is a small amount of dough, so you may need to scrape down the bowl during the mix. The dough will have only low to moderate gluten development and won't totally clear the sides of the bowl, but that's okay. Transfer the dough to an oiled bowl, cover with a tea towel, and leave to rise at room temperature (65° to 75°F) for 90 minutes. When ready, the dough will be puffy but not necessarily doubled in size.

SHAPE. About 15 minutes before the dough is ready, fill a heavy-bottomed saucepan with frying oil to a depth of about 3 inches. I like to use expeller-pressed, non-GMO canola oil. Begin heating the oil to 360° to 380°F, checking the temperature with a frying thermometer. Keep in mind

that once the oil hits the desired temperature, you'll want to adjust the heat to maintain that frying temperature. Check the temp often. Also, I hope you have a hood. If not, open a window.

Turn the dough out onto a floured countertop and flour the top of the dough. With a rolling pin, roll the dough out to a thickness of ¼ to ½ inch. Thicker dough will give a breadier interior, and thinner dough will make more hollow beignets. Cut the dough into 1½-inch strips, then cut the strips into 2-inch pieces. Your dough was probably round to begin with, and now you're making rectangles, so you will have many irregular cuts. That's okay; just get approximately similar sizes and don't fuss with it. You have about 30 minutes to fry these off. If you need more time or the room is really warm, place the pieces on a floured sheet pan and set it in the fridge to hold them.

CONTINUED

FRY. Prepare yourself with a timer set to 3 minutes, a plate lined with a not-too-nice tea towel or paper towels, a metal slotted spoon or spider strainer, a platter, and a method for dusting the beignets copiously with the confectioners' sugar (a small sifter or cheesecloth sachet both work well).

Gently drop two beignets into the oil, being careful not to splash yourself. Start the timer and begin checking the beignets after 1 minute to see if they're browned on the bottom. At 1 to 2 minutes, flip the beignets and fry until evenly browned, 1 to 2 minutes more. Use the slotted spoon or spider to transfer the beignets to the towel. Wait a couple minutes, then cut into a beignet. If it didn't puff and float quickly, the oil probably wasn't hot enough. (Are you winging it without a thermometer? You're a nut—I love it.) Turn up the heat slightly and wait a minute. If the beignets got too dark but are cooked through nicely, the oil is too hot. Turn down the temperature slightly and wait a minute. If they're the right color but doughy, turn it down slightly and add a few seconds to the cook time. If they're light colored and doughy, just fry them a few seconds longer on each side. If they're perfect, you're perfect.

After adjusting your process according to the test batch, gently drop as many beignets as you can fit, uncrowded, into your oil—probably three to five. Cook in batches until they're all fried off, transferring the cooked and drained beignets to a platter.

Dust aggressively with the confectioners' sugar. Envision how much confectioners' sugar you consume in an average year, and then apply that much confectioners' sugar to these babies. Eat immediately. They do not keep well.

OPTION

If you want to make the beignets the next day, cover the bowl of mixed dough with a plastic grocery bag, plastic wrap, or beeswax wrap and move it to the refrigerator to rise overnight.

CORNETTI

MAKES 10 CORNETTI,
ABOUT 3 BY 5 INCHES

Day 1 → 1 hour
active time over 12 hours
(or overnight)

Day 2 → 5 minutes
active time over 1¼ hours

Essentially Italian croissants, cornetti have just a few less layers than croissants, so they're easier to make. They're also a bit richer and sweeter than croissants, and they're traditionally filled with marmalade or chocolate to go with your morning cappuccino. At Vetri, we wanted a more savory version to serve with appetizers, so I came up with these cornetti, based on a recipe from dough guru Jim Lahey. —CKM

DOUGH

bolted hard wheat flour	383 g (3⅛ cups)	70%
whole-grain spelt flour	164 g (1⅓ cups)	30%
whole milk	262 g (1⅛ cups)	48%
dry yeast	4 g (1¼ teaspoons)	0.8%
salt	12 g (2 teaspoons)	2.2%
sugar	38 g (3 tablespoons)	7%
eggs	82 g (⅓ cup, about 1½ medium)	15%
unsalted butter	55 g (¼ cup)	10%
TOTAL	**1,000 g**	**183%**

330 g (1½ cups) unsalted butter for butter block

egg for egg wash

pinch of salt for egg wash

DAY 1: MIX. I've timed this dough for freshly baked cornetti on the morning of day 2. But you can adjust the timing to suit your schedule.

In the morning, measure both flours and set aside. Combine the milk, yeast, flours, salt, sugar, eggs, and butter in the bowl of a stand mixer. Mix with the dough hook on low speed for 5 minutes. You're not looking for much gluten development here because the dough will be worked extensively during the folding and laminating process.

Cover the bowl with a tea towel and let the dough rest at room temperature (65° to 75°F) for 1 hour. Then give it an aggressive four-fold (see page 28), pressing the sides into the center as you fold. Wrap the dough securely in plastic wrap and retard the dough in the refrigerator for 8 hours so you can laminate it later that day. Or, if you want to bake the cornetti

later in the afternoon or on the evening of day 2, you can retard the dough overnight instead.

PREPARE BUTTER BLOCK. Make a parchment packet by cutting a large rectangular piece of parchment paper, about 1½ feet long. Position the rectangle on your countertop with the short sides to the left and right, fold the left and right sides in about a third of the way, then fold the top and bottom in to make a 6-inch square packet. Set aside.

After retarding the dough, slice the butter into slabs ½ inch thick. Stack the pieces back up, then put the stack on half of a large sheet of parchment paper (not the parchment packet) and fold the other half of the parchment over the butter. Now, beat the hell out of the butter with a rolling pin. You

CONTINUED

want to smash it flat; this may take a minute. Then use the parchment to fold the butter back up into a thick wad and smash it again. You may need to do this two or three times to make the butter pliable. Smashing the butter quickly makes it pliable while maintaining its cold temperature, so you can roll and fold with the dough without the butter cracking or melting. Don't dawdle because you don't want the butter to melt. Once the butter is pliable but still cold, fold the butter back up into a wad about 4 inches square.

Open the parchment packet, place the butter into the parchment square, and fold the paper back over it so the parchment is back into a 6-inch square. Roll the butter out to fill the parchment. Try to create a perfectly even 6-inch square of butter inside the parchment. Place the butter package in the fridge.

LAMINATE. Now take the dough out of the fridge, unwrap it, and position it on a lightly floured countertop with the short sides to the left and right. Roll it out to a rectangle about 8 by 14 inches, just large enough to envelop the 6-inch square of butter. Reserve the plastic wrap to re-wrap the dough later. While you are rolling, dust the countertop and the dough with just enough flour to prevent sticking, brushing excess flour off the dough.

Take the butter package out of the fridge, unwrap it, and place the square of butter in the center of the dough rectangle, then fold the left and right sides of the dough over the butter so they meet in the center, gently pulling the corners of the dough if necessary and pressing gently to seal. You should have a rectangular packet of dough with butter in the center, about 7 by 8 by 1½ inches. Roll out this butter-and-dough packet to a long rectangle, about 8 by 24 inches. Now you want to square off the edges and remove portions of dough that do not contain butter. You can probably see the butter within the dough; it may be as much as 2 inches in from the edge on each side. A pizza wheel is handy for cutting here,

but a knife works, too. Trim off the dough to expose the butter and save the trim (you'll be trimming more later—you can bake off all the trim as a snack if you like). Brush off any excess flour from the top side and lightly mist with a spray bottle of water. Fold the short edges of the rectangle in so they nearly meet in the center but leave about a ½-inch gap. Line up the edges neatly. Brush off any excess flour from the folded sides and mist again. Now fold the dough in half again in the same direction over the gap in the center. This is called a book fold. Rewrap the book in plastic, give it a light press, then roll very gently with the rolling pin to seal the layers of butter and dough. Return to the refrigerator for 1 hour.

Let the dough rest at room temperature for 10 to 15 minutes (if it's blazing hot in your kitchen, shorten the rest to 5 minutes and work quickly to keep the butter from melting). For the next roll, you want to roll the dough in the opposite direction from the last roll. Alternating directions works the dough evenly and helps prevent irregular shrinkage during baking. To alternate directions, position the book so the sides that have four layers showing are the short sides, and the sides with one and two layers showing are the long sides. Roll again to 8 by 24 inches, essentially enlarging the rectangle. Cut off the ends again (you should see about four layers of butter at this point). Then repeat the book fold as for the last step: fold the short sides in toward the center, leaving a gap, then fold in the same direction into a book. Wrap the book in plastic again and refrigerate for 1 hour. The rests between rolling and folding help to reduce shrinkage overall, although you should still expect some shrinkage.

Let the dough rest for 10 minutes or so at room temperature to take the chill off, then for the last time, reverse the orientation and roll the dough out to a rectangle, about 8 by 27 inches. Trim a little off all four sides to make a nice rectangle that's about 7 by 25 inches. If you pick up the dough

CONTINUED

and look at the trim, you should see sixteen very faint lines of lamination.

SHAPE. Line two sheet pans with parchment paper. Cut the dough crosswise into five 5 by 7-inch strips. Then slice each strip diagonally to make ten triangles. Dust off any excess flour. Cut a ½-inch nick in the center of the short side of each triangle; this will help make wider, better-looking cornetti. Now take the triangle by the corners along the short side and gently tug it outward to make the nick about 1 inch wide. Finally, roll the cornetti up from the nicked side to the point, gently pressing the point onto the dough, and turn the cornetti over, so the point/seam is down. Repeat with each triangle and set the cornetti on the parchment paper–lined sheet pans with the point/seam-side down and with at least 1 inch between each cornetti. Wrap loosely with plastic wrap and refrigerate until chilled through. (This chilling step is mostly intended to buy you time so the cornetti can have a long, slow rise at room temperature while you sleep, and you can bake the cornetti in the morning.) After chilling for at least an hour or up to 2 hours, pull the cornetti out and leave to rise, still loosely covered, at cool room temperature (50° to 65°F), for 6 to 12 hours total. Avoid putting them on a sunny windowsill.

DAY 2: BAKE. Preheat the oven to 400°F. The timing here depends on factors like the temperature and humidity of your room and the temperature of your dough during the mix. While 9 hours of rising is a very reasonable prediction, it could easily be longer or shorter. Try to check the progress around the 8-hour mark. If the cornetti seem fully puffed, jiggly, and on the brink of collapse, get that oven heated. If they haven't puffed much, switch them to a slightly warmer place but not so warm that the butter will melt. Melted butter is a laminated-dough killer. And if they haven't been well covered or were in a drafty spot, they will likely have a skin that's preventing them from rising nicely. In that case, mist them with water and cover again.

The measure for readiness is that the cornetti have risen as far as the yeast can take them. If fermentation goes too far, the cornetti will collapse (you can still bake them anyway; you just won't get nice big airy layers). If you bake them before they are fully proofed, the oven spring caused by increased fermentation activity will squeeze the butter out of the cornetti, and that also means you won't get nice airy layers. When properly timed, the oven spring will come almost entirely from the butter melting and steaming, not from fermentation activity. While I'm generally not a follower of the poke test, it is absolutely helpful here. Gently press a cornetti. If the dough is very puffy and soft and does not immediately refill the depression from your fingertip, it is ready to bake. If you see even one cornetti that is leaking butter on the baking sheet (meaning the butter is melting), bake them right away.

Beat the egg with the salt, then lightly brush the egg wash over the cornetti. You'll get better oven spring if the egg doesn't get brushed onto the laminated portions of dough. Load the cornetti into the oven and bake until dark golden brown, 12 to 15 minutes. If they brown too much, cover them with aluminum foil (you may want to lower the oven temperature to 385°F the next time around). Let the cornetti cool at least partway before digging in.

They're best eaten immediately upon cooling, but they can be kept in a paper bag, bread box, or cupboard at room temperature for 2 to 3 days.

OPTIONS

To make **Rosemary Cornetti**, add about 2 tablespoons of chopped fresh rosemary to the mixer along with the flours.

To make **Sweet Cornetti**, let the baked cornetti cool completely, then slice and fill them with Apple or Peach Butter (page 266), marmalade, lemon mascarpone, or Nutella.

8

SOURDOUGH BREADS

COOKING HAS ALWAYS TOUCHED MY SOUL. Even as a kid, cooking with my Sicilian grandparents, it was much more than just putting together ingredients and making something delicious to eat. Food has always been a vital part of who I am and something that connects me to the world in a bigger way.

I think the food you cook and eat becomes a part of you, and you become a part of it. If I make a ragu or a noodle shape and someone else makes the same thing using the same recipe, no matter what they do, it never comes out the same. I'm not saying I have a magical touch or anything. It's just that when a person is cooking, their hands and their intentions are guiding the food every step of the way. Koreans have a word for it: *son-mat*. It literally means "the taste of one's hands." It's a compliment given to good cooks, and it's what makes your food taste like yours and no one else's.

JOSEY BAKER

Josey Baker Bread and The Mill
San Francisco, California

———————

Josey Baker (yes, that's his real last name) was born in New York, raised in Vermont, and moved to San Francisco in 2005. He is the owner of Josey Baker Bread and co-owner of The Mill, a café/bakery, both in San Francisco. The bakeries include a team of sixteen bakers and pizza makers specializing in freshly milled whole-grain sourdoughs. They source organic wheat from California and stone mill all of their whole-grain flours daily, providing bread, pizza, and flour to markets, restaurants, and bread lovers throughout the Bay Area.

"

I started out just trying to bake the best bread I could. I fell in love with the process . . . the patience required, the blend of art and science, the combination of handwork and technical understanding, the wildness and unpredictability of working with sourdough . . . it all spoke to me on a deep level.

Bread connects people and brings them together. It always has. It is this power that keeps me in love with it.

I think we're going to see a lot more of what's happening in pockets of the country right now: farmers growing high-quality grains with methods that benefit the environment; millers taking care to preserve the identity and integrity of these grains in their transition to flour; and bakers doing their best to coax the most potential out of these flours through sourdough fermentation.

I am hopeful that as the general public gains greater awareness of the importance of all these things, they will place higher value on artisan grain farming, milling, and bread baking.

"

The concept of *son-mat* is especially true in bread baking. When you bake a lot of bread, the bread develops your signature touch. It becomes *your* bread. And not just on the surface. It turns out that the microorganisms—the wild yeast and bacteria—that make sourdough bread what it is also exist on a baker's hands. That means the bread you bake will always be slightly different from the bread someone else bakes—even if they use the same recipe.

A biologist named Rob Dunn actually conducted experiments to illustrate this point. Dunn gathered fifteen bakers from around the world and took a bacterial swab of their hands. Then he had them all make fresh sourdough starters with the same ingredients. When all the starters were built up, he analyzed them, and it turned out that each starter had a different mix of yeasts and bacteria in it. And because of that, each starter made a different kind of bread. The bacterial swab showed that each baker's hands had a unique set of yeasts and bacteria, a distinctive microbiome.

Dunn also found that, in terms of microbes, bakers' hands more closely resemble a sourdough culture than they resemble other human hands. It's true! In sourdough, the most common beneficial bacteria are *Lactobacillus* and its relatives (the lactic acid bacteria). And the most common yeast is *Saccharomyces cerevisiae* and its relatives (baker's yeast). But on average, these microorganisms only account for about 3% of the total microbes on human hands. In Dunn's tests on the bakers' hands, they accounted for up to 60%.

I guess the more you bake sourdough bread, the more you resemble the sourdough itself. Dunn's experiments also help explain why people develop personal relationships with their starters. If you've ever kept a starter, you know what I'm talking about. You end up caring for it like a cherished family member. You feed it when it's hungry, and when it's cold, you put it near a sunny windowsill. Maybe you even give it a name. You care for it because you and the starter are actually related!

At least on a microbial level, you really do become part of the bread you bake. And the bread becomes a part of you. That's one reason why we think this is the best chapter in the book. These are the breads that you can really make your own. It's a beautiful thing.

These are also the breads that have the potential to develop the most complex flavors and textures. The natural wild yeasts and bacteria and the slow, cool fermentations bring out the best in the wheat, spelt, rye, durum, and einkorn grains called for in this chapter. You can really taste the subtle nuances of flavor. Some of these doughs also include "soakers," grains and/or seeds soaked or cooked in water to soften them up, adding even more flavor and texture to the bread.

Yes, these breads can be a little more advanced. But Pane di Genzano (page 155), Buckwheat Buttermilk Bread (page 167), and Omni Bread (page 169) . . . these are what we think of as real breads. They're big romantic loaves made with a high percentage of whole grains. In these breads, the crust and crumb have obviously different textures. And each bread has tons of flavor that comes from the dough itself.

Keep in mind that when you become a sourdough baker, you do have to incorporate it into your life. You have to maintain Sourdough Starter (page 147), or it will die. Don't worry; it's not hard or time-consuming.

The whole process of making sourdough can be very gratifying. Just allow some time in your schedule to ripen your starter before baking with it. A lot of these breads are mixed by hand, too. Why? Because that allows for *son-mat*. The dough picks up different kinds of yeasts and beneficial bacteria—and different flavors—from your hands. Of course, you can use a machine if you prefer. Choose your own adventure.

If you're experienced with sourdough breads, keep in mind that these doughs may feel stickier and weaker to you thanks to the fresh milled and whole-grain flours. It's okay. Shape them with water instead of flour. Wet your hands to prevent sticking. Handle the doughs gently. Everything will be fine.

I'm dreaming of those thick, tangy crusts just writing about them! These breads are generally baked in a hot oven for a slightly longer time, so you get big, sexy loaves with dark crusts and deep, savory flavors. They're pretty versatile, too. Any one of them could stand on its own as a table bread served with Cultured Butter (page 264). They also make great grilled cheese, PB&J, and Panzanella (page 246). If it's your first sourdough adventure, make the Simple Sourdough Table Bread (page 149) to start, then move on from there. Have fun! **—MV**

SOURDOUGH STARTER

MAKES ABOUT
250 GRAMS

15 minutes active time
over 10 to 14 days (plus at
least 5 minutes a week for
long-term maintenance)

It is pretty magical how flour and water can just start teeming with life when mixed together. When you add fresh flour and water, or "feed" it, the starter gradually becomes more established and stable. Then you can feed the starter simply to maintain it, or you can feed it to build it up and bake with it. Some bakers like to establish their own starters from scratch, and power to them. But as you will see below, starter maintenance involves a lot of discarding, so find a fellow baker in your area and ask them to share the wealth. They won't mind, and now you'll have a baking buddy. —CKM

INITIAL MIX

whole-grain rye flour	100 g (1 cup)	100%
water	100 g (½ cup)	100%
TOTAL	**200 g**	**200%**

REGULAR FEEDING

whole-grain rye flour	100 g (1 cup)	100%
water	100 g (½ cup)	100%
old starter	50 g (¼ cup)	50%
TOTAL	**250 g**	**250%**

MIX. Choose a 1-quart container, preferably clear and with a lid. For the initial mix, measure the rye flour and water into the container and stir it up. Cover with a cloth (not the lid) and leave it alone for 24 to 36 hours at room temperature (65° to 75°F). It's not strictly necessary to use rye flour, but rye's high starch and enzyme levels help to establish a starter culture from scratch. If you use another flour, it will still work, but it may take more time to obtain vigorous activity.

ESTABLISH. To help establish the starter, use the "Regular Feeding" amounts listed above: Discard all but 50 grams of the starter, leaving that amount in the same unwashed container. Then add 100 grams each of fresh flour and water to the container and stir it up. Give the starter this regular feeding twice a day, covering it with a cloth and keeping it at room temperature. When establishing a starter, it helps to reuse the same container because it gives you the best chance of capturing lots of the target microorganisms. Just wipe any messes from the outside of the container.

After 4 to 8 days of regular feeding twice a day, you should see signs of activity such as bubbles at the top or through the sides of the container and catch an aroma just before feeding that could range from a yogurtlike tang to a whiff from a vodka bottle. The starter should also begin to visibly rise in the container. At this point, the concentration of yeast and bacteria in the starter is sufficient to change containers and start using a lid.

After 7 to 14 days of regular feeding twice a day, the starter should approximately double in volume, bubble, and develop a tart tang between feedings. These are signs that the starter is ready to build up for baking. Congratulations, you did it!

MAINTAIN. Once your starter is established, or you were smart and acquired one from someone else, you need to maintain it to keep it alive. Once a day, give it a regular feeding, mixing 50 grams of old starter with 100 grams each of

CONTINUED

fresh flour and water. At this point, you can use any flour you want. A vigorous starter kept at room temperature (65° to 75°F) needs to be fed only once a day to keep it healthy. And if you bake often, you will never be more than a few hours away from starting any recipe. But if you plan on baking only once a week or less, you can keep your starter in the refrigerator so it doesn't need to be fed as often. In that case, to keep it alive, remove the starter from the fridge at least once a week, give it a regular feeding, and leave it out for a few hours before putting it back. There should be definite signs of activity, such as bubbles on the surface, before you return the starter to the fridge. If the starter appears to be flagging and doesn't show signs of activity, leave it out for a day at room temperature, then feed it again to help it get going.

BUILD AND RIPEN. Building your starter is similar to feeding it, but now you are feeding it for a specific baking recipe. This feeding may involve increasing the starter's total amount, changing its base flour, and/or changing its hydration. When you build a starter, you are also controlling its ripeness, or readiness for baking. To build up an established starter, about 3 hours before you plan to bake with it, give the starter a regular feeding at room temperature (65° to 75°F), using the flour specified in your recipe. After 3 hours or so, the starter should be on the upswing of fermentation activity, gaining in volume, and developing a lightly tangy aroma. It may not be fully aerated with bubbles everywhere, but it should have some bubbles. That's what we mean by "ripe sourdough starter," which is called for in most of our recipes. Although some of our recipes have different instructions for building the starter, including Pain Normand (page 162), Ciabatta Grano Arso with Einkorn (page 173), and Malted Grain Sourdough (page 204). For those recipes, establish and maintain your starter as described here and then follow the instructions in the recipe to build and ripen it. In this book, we wanted to show you several different starter styles, so that as you grow as a baker, you can choose the starters that best fit your palate and your baking schedule.

OPTION

Lievito madre: We use this very stiff, very yeasty, and not very acidic Italian-style sourdough starter to make Panettone alla Vetri (page 275). To convert your established sourdough starter to lievito madre (which literally means "mother yeast" in Italian), start about two weeks before you plan to bake with it. Begin by feeding 10 grams of your starter with 50 grams warm water and 100 grams bread flour (King Arthur is our benchmark). Hand-mix this stiff ball of dough for a few minutes, then ball it up and cut a deep X into the top. Put it into a covered container with space to triple in volume. Leave it to rise all day in a very warm (88° to 90°F) spot. Then, before bed, feed 100 grams of the starter with 50 grams warm water and 100 grams bread flour, hand-mixing it into a ball as before. This time, though, bind the starter by wrapping it in a piece of cloth like a close-weave tea towel or a large cloth napkin and tie it tight with string, like a gift. Then repeat the feeding every morning and every night, feeding 100 grams of the starter with 50 grams water and 100 grams bread flour, mixing it by hand, leaving it to rise, ideally for about 8 hours during the day, then binding it up after feeding it at night. When you have time, give it extra feedings midday. This schedule of feeding and binding at night in a very warm spot will favor your yeasts over bacteria, resulting in a very active, very stiff lievito madre that has little acidity.

SIMPLE SOURDOUGH TABLE BREAD

**MAKES 2 BATARDS,
ABOUT 8 BY 10 INCHES**

**Day 1 → 15 minutes
active time over 4 hours
with an overnight rest**

**Day 2 → 10 minutes
active time over 2 hours**

I teach this essential bread in every class. We use the Dutch oven baking method here, but you could just as easily use our baking stone–hotel pan method (see page 62). Although the bread is made over a couple days, the dough simply requires 10 to 15 minutes of hands-on time. Use whatever flour you want! That is not to say that every flour behaves the same, but there is no one right way to make this bread. Good options include 100% whole-wheat flour, bolted wheat flour, or half whole-wheat and half bolted. You can also add other grains in smaller amounts: try subbing in 10% rye flour, cornmeal, or oat flour. —CKM

bolted hard wheat flour	710 g (5⅔ cups)	100%
water	532 g (2¼ cups)	75%
ripe whole-wheat Sourdough Starter (page 147)	142 g (¾ cup)	20%
salt	16 g (2⅔ teaspoons)	2.3%
TOTAL	**1,400 g**	**197.3%**

DAY 1: MIX. Measure the flour and set aside. Combine the water, starter, flour, and salt in a mixing bowl. With clean hands, mix until it comes together in a shaggy mass, then mix it in the bowl for a few minutes more, alternately breaking the dough up and folding it back onto itself. At this point, the dough will still look shaggy and feel sticky and weak. Get as much dough from your hands back into the bowl as possible, scraping down your hands and the bowl. A dough scraper is handy here. Cover the bowl with a tea towel and leave to rise at room temperature (65° to 75°F) for 3 hours, giving the dough a four-fold (see page 28) every 30 minutes.

PRESHAPE. After the final 30-minute rest, dampen your countertop with water. Pour the dough out onto the damp countertop and divide it into two 700-gram pieces. For each loaf, give it a four-fold, then turn it over, so it is seam-side down. The loaves will look like square-ish pouches. Cover them with a tea towel and leave them to rest at room temperature for 20 to 30 minutes.

SHAPE. Generously flour the bottom and sides of two medium oval bannetons or towel-lined bowls (you'll get round loaves if using the latter). Drizzle a little more water on your countertop and spread it around so the surface is wet but not puddled. Use a bench knife to flip a loaf over onto the wet surface, then stretch and fold the left and right sides in toward the center, patting them into place. Now you should have a somewhat rectangular piece of dough. Starting from one of the short sides, roll the dough up, increasing the surface tension as you go. Roll firmly but try not to knock all of the gas out of the dough. Repeat with the other loaf, then let the loaves rest seam-side down on the countertop for a minute or two to help seal the seam shut. Lightly dust the loaves with flour, then gently slip your hand beneath each loaf, pick it up, and invert it into the floured banneton, seam-side up. (The seam will eventually become the bottom of the bread.)

Place the filled bannetons in plastic grocery bags or loosely cover with plastic wrap or beeswax wrap and leave at room temperature for 30 minutes. Then move the covered loaves to the refrigerator to rest overnight.

CONTINUED

DAY 2: BAKE. Place a 6-quart or larger Dutch oven (a round or oval Dutch oven will do) and its lid into the oven. Preheat the oven to 475°F. Have kitchen towels or hot pads, dusting flour, and a razor within reach, as well as space to place the hot Dutch oven and its lid.

When the oven is hot, pull one loaf from the refrigerator and dust the side facing up with flour. Using towels or hot pads, pull out the hot Dutch oven and place it on the stovetop or a trivet. Carefully remove the lid, setting it down on the stovetop or another trivet. Gently but confidently invert the banneton over the Dutch oven to set the loaf inside. Score the top of the loaf (I like one straight line down the center), quickly replace the lid, and return the Dutch oven to the oven shelf.

Bake for 20 minutes. Then remove the lid (leave the lid in the oven if there is space) and bake for an additional 10 minutes. When the loaf is deeply browned and singed in spots, carefully pull out the Dutch oven, then remove the loaf with kitchen towels or hot pads, or tip it out. Cool the loaf on a rack. Carefully replace the lid on the Dutch oven and return it to the oven shelf to reheat for 5 to 10 minutes. Repeat with the second loaf.

This bread keeps for almost a week in a paper bag, bread box, or cupboard at room temperature.

SESAME DURUM BREAD

MAKES 2 SKINNY
BATARDS, ABOUT
4 BY 10 INCHES

Day 1 → 15 minutes
active time over 2¼ hours
with an overnight rest

Day 2 → 30 minutes
active time over 2½ hours

Soon after I started building the bread program at Vetri, I developed this bread. It became a favorite, and I return to it often with small variations to the grain varieties. Whole-grain durum flour (coarse durum flour) adds the mellow, comforting flavor of pasta. This bread is great just dipped in olive oil. Or with antipasti. As a sandwich bread. Really, with anything. It's just a good-tasting, versatile bread. —CKM

bolted hard wheat flour	401 g (3¼ cups)	75%
whole-grain durum flour	134 g (¾ cup)	25%
water	401 g (1⅔ cups)	75%
ripe whole durum Sourdough Starter (page 147)	107 g (½ cup)	20%
salt	11 g (1¾ teaspoons)	2%
TOTAL	**1,054 g**	**197%**

sesame seeds for coating	

DAY 1: MIX. Measure both flours and and set aside. Combine the water, starter, flours, and salt in a medium mixing bowl. With clean hands, mix until it comes together in a shaggy mass, then mix it in the bowl for 3 to 5 minutes more, alternately breaking the dough up and folding it back onto itself. At this point, the dough will still look shaggy and feel sticky and weak. Get as much dough from your hands back into the bowl as possible, scraping down your hands and the bowl. Cover the bowl with a tea towel and let rest at room temperature (65° to 75°F) for 2 hours, giving the dough a four-fold (see page 28) every 30 minutes. During the first hour, the folds can be aggressive, but fold more gently during the second hour. After the 2 hours, transfer the dough to a lightly oiled container, cover with a lid, and move to the refrigerator to rest overnight.

DAY 2: PRESHAPE. Pull the dough from the fridge, then cover and rest at room temperature for 30 minutes.

Drizzle a little water on your countertop and spread it around, so the surface is wet but not puddled. Turn the dough out onto the damp countertop and divide it into two 500-gram pieces. Preshape each piece by giving it a four-fold, then turn it over, so it is seam-side down. The loaves will look like square-ish pouches. Cover with a tea towel and leave them to rest at room temperature for 45 minutes.

SHAPE. Place a large baking stone and hotel pan (see page 62) on the highest rack in your oven they will fit on. Preheat the oven to 475°F. Have ready a spray bottle of water and a linen couche. Dust the couche with flour.

Pour the sesame seeds into a large shallow dish or a quarter sheet pan. Lightly flour the countertop, then one at a time, flip each loaf over, pat it down a bit, and roll it under your palms into a fat cylinder about 4 by 10 inches that is pointed at the ends. To seed each loaf, spray it with water and slip your hand beneath it, pick it up, and roll the wet top side in the sesame seeds. Then place each loaf seeded-side down on the floured couche, gently peeling your hand from the loaf. Make little folds in the couche between the rows to support the loaves. Fold the excess couche over the loaves (or cover with a tea towel) and set aside to rest at room temperature for 1 hour.

BAKE. The loaves should be about 1½ times their original size. Cut a sheet of parchment paper that will fit over the back side of a half sheet pan to use as a peel. Have two towels or hot pads, a spray bottle of water, and a razor within reach.

Flip the loaves over onto the parchment paper, so they are seed-side up. Score with two cuts, similar to a baguette, with each cut a little over half the length of the loaf and parallel slightly in the center (see "Batard double score," page 60). Quickly but carefully open your oven, pull the rack that you are baking on partway out, and move the hot hotel pan to the stovetop. Slide the loaves and parchment paper onto the stone and cover with the hotel pan, spraying water into the pan before setting it onto the stone to trap steam.

Bake for 15 minutes. Then remove the hot hotel pan and rotate the loaves for even browning. Bake, uncovered, until the seeds are browned but not charred, like the skin of a russet potato, and the raised edges along the score marks are dark brown to black, another 5 to 10 minutes. Remove the loaves to racks to cool.

The loaves will keep in a paper bag, bread box, or cupboard at room temperature for about 4 days.

PANE DI GENZANO

MAKES 2 BATARDS,
ABOUT 8 BY 10 INCHES

Day 1 → 30 minutes
active time over 3½ hours
with an overnight rest

Day 2 → 10 minutes
active time over 2 hours

Pane di Genzano is a very specific name for a very broad category of bread. This bread is the Italian town of Genzano's claim to fame. But it's also a classic table bread and the ultimate country-style sourdough. A little rye brings a sweet floral aroma, some acidity, and bite, and wheat flour gives it backbone. With due respect, this is an IGP (*Indicazione Geografica Protetta*, or geographically protected) bread in Italy, so we're really just borrowing the Genzano name here as the textbook example of a beloved country bread. —CKM

bolted hard wheat flour	666 g (5⅓ cups)	90%
whole rye flour	74 g (¾ cup)	10%
water	592 g (2½ cups)	80%
ripe rye Sourdough Starter (page 147)	150 g (¾ cup)	20%
barley malt flour or powder (see Option, page 156)	4 g (1⅔ teaspoons)	0.5%
salt	14 g (2⅓ teaspoons)	2%
TOTAL	**1,500 g**	**202.5%**
wheat bran for dusting		

DAY 1: MIX. Measure the wheat flour and rye flour and set aside. Combine the water, starter, reserved flours, malt flour or powder, and salt in the bowl of a stand mixer. Mix with the dough hook on low speed for 10 minutes. Transfer the dough to a lightly oiled container, cover with a tea towel, and allow to rest at room temperature (65° to 75°F) for 2 hours, giving the dough a four-fold (see page 28) every 30 minutes.

PRESHAPE. Drizzle a little water on your countertop and spread it around, so the surface is wet but not puddled. Turn the dough out onto the countertop and cut it into two 750-gram pieces. For each loaf, fold the four edges in toward the center of the dough, then turn it over, so it is seam-side down. Cover with a tea towel and allow to rest on the countertop for 20 minutes.

SHAPE. Generously flour the bottom and sides of two medium oval bannetons or towel-lined bowls (you'll get round loaves if using the latter). Dampen your countertop again and flip each loaf over on the countertop. Fold the left and right sides in on an angle toward the center, forming a cone shape. Now roll up from the narrow bottom of the cone, forming a football shape. Set the loaves seam-side down on the countertop. Dust the tops with flour, then slip your hand beneath each loaf and gently invert it into the banneton, so it is seam-side up. Place the filled bannetons in plastic grocery bags or loosely cover with plastic wrap or beeswax wrap and leave at room temperature for 1 hour. Then move the covered loaves to the refrigerator to rest overnight.

DAY 2: BAKE. Place a large baking stone and hotel pan (see page 62) on the highest rack in your oven they will fit on. Preheat the oven to 475°F. Remove the bannetons from the fridge and let rest at room temperature for 1 hour. Have two towels or hot pads, a spray bottle of water, and a razor within reach.

CONTINUED

Dust a peel or flat board with wheat bran, then flip the loaves out onto the board, lining them up so you can easily slip them from the board to the stone. I like to score this loaf once from end to end down the center. But this bread won't have an incredible amount of oven spring, so it's a good candidate for a more elaborate scoring pattern without worrying about the loaf blowing out. If you like, get fancy and make lots of little score marks.

Quickly but carefully open your oven, pull the rack that you are baking on partway out, and move the hot hotel pan to the stovetop. Lay the back side of your peel or board toward the back of the stone, then tilt, shake, and slide the loaves onto the stone, quickly removing the peel. Cover the loaves with the hot hotel pan, spraying water into the pan before setting it onto the stone to trap steam.

Bake for 20 minutes. Then remove the hot hotel pan and rotate the loaves for even browning. Bake, uncovered, until the crust is very dark, another 15 to 20 minutes. To the untrained eye, the crust may look burnt when properly done. You want a bit of charring here and there. Don't worry; it will be delicious. Remove the loaves to a rack to cool.

This bread will last a good 5 to 7 days in a paper bag, bread box, or cupboard at room temperature.

OPTION

For the barley malt flour or powder, we like to use whole malted grains from craft maltsters, then mill them into flour. Find maltsters in your area at the Craft Maltsters Guild website. Diastatic malt is an easy alternative, and you can find it wherever baking supplies are sold. It's dried at low temperatures to preserve the enzymatic activity in the flour. Do not use non-diastatic malt powder because it is not enzymatically active. That type is used mostly as a coloring agent and sweetener.

SPELT SOURDOUGH BOULE

MAKES 2 BOULES, ABOUT
8-INCH DIAMETER

Day 1 → 15 minutes
active time over 4 hours
with an overnight rest

Day 2 → 5 minutes
active time over 1½ hours

If you've been baking through this book, by now you know that I have a crush on spelt flour. In this bread, I go all in with spelt. This dough will feel looser than most, similar to a higher-hydration dough, due to the high percentage of spelt flour. The folding process here is a bit more intensive to help build strength in the dough, and there's an additional round of shaping to make it cohesive and taut. The reward for this extra bit of handwork is a beautiful balance of sweet and sharp flavors, a somewhat open crumb, and a satisfying chewy crust. —CKM

whole-grain spelt flour	427 g (3½ cups)	60%
bolted hard wheat flour	284 g (2¼ cups)	40%
water	569 g (2⅓ cups)	80%
ripe spelt Sourdough Starter (page 147)	107 g (½ cup)	15%
salt	14 g (2⅓ teaspoons)	2%
TOTAL	1,401 g	197%

wheat or spelt bran for dusting	

DAY 1: MIX. Measure both flours and set aside. Combine the water, starter, and flours in the bowl of a stand mixer. Mix with the dough hook on low speed for 8 minutes. Early in this mix, the dough should be very slack and stick to the sides of the bowl. It should take some time for it to gather enough strength to grab the hook and clear the sides of the bowl. If it builds strength too quickly in the first 8 minutes of mixing, you can add up to 10% of the flour weight in water (up to about 75 grams of water). Add this additional water incrementally, in thirds (25 grams at a time), and continue mixing after each addition.

After mixing for 8 minutes, cover the dough with a tea towel and allow to rest for about 20 minutes. Add the salt and resume mixing on low speed for another 8 minutes. Cover the dough with a tea towel and leave to rest at room temperature (65° to 75°F) until the dough shows some signs of fermentation (such as bubbles under the surface), 2 to 3 hours, depending on the ambient temperature. About halfway through that time, give the dough a four-fold (see page 28).

PRESHAPE. Once the dough shows signs of fermentation, drizzle some water on your countertop and spread it around, so the surface is wet but not puddled. Turn the dough out onto the counter and divide it into two 700-gram pieces. Give each piece a little shape: fold the four edges in toward the center of the dough, then roll it over, so it is seam-side down. Cover and allow to rest on the countertop for 20 minutes.

SHAPE. Generously flour the bottom and sides of two medium round bannetons or towel-lined bowls. Set up a bowl of flour for dusting the loaves. Dampen your counter-top again and shape each loaf into a boule (see page 49): roll the dough in a circle on your countertop, pressing down and cupping your hands around the dough to increase the surface tension all around it as you shape it into a nice taut ball. As you roll, the seam will seal and smooth out on the bottom. Dust the tops of the loaves with flour, then slip your

CONTINUED

hand beneath each loaf and invert it into the banneton, so the floured side is down, peeling your hand away from the loaf. Place the filled bannetons in plastic grocery bags or loosely cover with plastic wrap or beeswax wrap, then move the covered bannetons to the refrigerator to rest overnight.

DAY 2: BAKE. Place a large baking stone and hotel pan (see page 62) on the highest rack they will fit on. Preheat the oven to 500°F. Have two towels or hot pads, a spray bottle of water, and a razor within reach.

Dust the loaves with bran (the loaves will be inverted, so the bran will end up on the bottom). Moving quickly but carefully, open the oven and pull the rack that you are baking on partway out and move the hot hotel pan to the stovetop or side of the oven. Invert the loaves one at a time onto the stone and score each loaf with four slashes to make a square on top. Cover the loaves with the hot hotel pan, spraying water into the pan before setting it onto the stone to trap steam. Close the oven and lower the temperature to 475°F. Bake for 20 minutes. Then, remove the hot hotel pan and rotate the loaves for even browning. Bake, uncovered, until the loaves are evenly browned and the raised edge along the score mark has scorched lightly, 15 to 20 minutes more. Remove to racks to cool.

These boules can be kept in a paper bag, bread box, or cupboard at room temperature for 5 to 6 days.

EINKORN PAN LOAF

MAKES 1 PAN LOAF, ABOUT 9 BY 5 INCHES

30 minutes active time over 10 hours

I retested this recipe more than most in the book, enjoying several iterations with Cultured Butter (page 264). It's a dense, chewy, whole-grain loaf that's fermented for a relatively short time at room temperature, which highlights the grain's beautiful flavor. Einkorn reminds me of mild-tasting miso: earthy, nutty, salty, and sweet. —CKM

SOAKER

whole einkorn berries	147 g (¾ cup)	100%
water	500 g (2⅛ cups)	340%
TOTAL	**647 g**	**440%**

DOUGH

whole-grain einkorn flour	491 g (4⅛ cups)	100%
water	403 g (1⅔ cups)	82%
ripe einkorn Sourdough Starter (page 147)	147 g (¾ cup)	30%
salt	12 g (2 teaspoons)	2.4%
soaker (from above)	147 g (1½ cups)	30%
TOTAL	**1,200 g**	**244.4%**

MAKE SOAKER. Place the einkorn berries and water in a small saucepan and bring to a boil. Turn down the heat to low, cover, and simmer until the berries are soft and plump, about 45 minutes. Turn off the heat and leave them to cool. Then drain and weigh the berries needed for the dough. Enjoy the excess berries seasoned or as part of another dish.

MIX. Measure the flour and set aside. Combine the water, starter, flour, and salt in a medium mixing bowl and hand-mix for about 3 minutes. Fold in the soaker, then cover with a tea towel and leave to ferment at room temperature (65° to 75°F) for 1 hour. Give the dough two back-to-back four-folds (see page 28), then cover again and ferment for 1 hour more. The dough will have an extremely extensible, almost taffylike texture.

SHAPE. Grease a 9 by 5-inch loaf pan. Drizzle a little water on your countertop and spread it around so the surface is wet but not puddled. Turn the dough out onto the wet counter-top, then fold the top half over the bottom half. Fold each side in toward the center, then fold the bottom edge up and roll away from you to finish the loaf. Place seam-side down in the pan, loosely cover with a tea towel, and leave to rise at room temperature until the loaf has risen by about 40%, about 2½ hours. It will still be somewhat flat, which is fine.

BAKE. Preheat the oven to 400°F with a rack in the middle of the oven. Load the pan into the oven and bake for a total of 50 minutes, rotating the pan after 30 minutes for even brown-ing. When finished, depan the loaf immediately and let cool on a rack for several hours. Put the loaf in a paper bag, bread box, or cupboard to finish cooling completely overnight. Do not cut this bread early, or it will be gummy.

It will keep in a paper bag, bread box, or cupboard at room temperature for 5 to 6 days.

100% SONORA SLAB

MAKES 2 FREE-FORM
LOAVES, ABOUT
8 BY 10 INCHES

The first bread I made from truly freshly milled flour was a 100% whole-grain Sonora sourdough. That exact recipe is lost to history, but this loaf is a tribute to that one. A relatively short fermentation time showcases the agreeable, nutty flavor of the flour. —CKM

30 minutes active time
over 6 hours

whole-grain Sonora flour	505 g (4¼ cups)	100%
ripe Sonora Sourdough Starter (page 147)	177 g (1 cup)	35%
water	505 g (2⅛ cups)	100%
salt	13 g (2⅛ teaspoons)	2.5%
TOTAL	1,200 g	237.5%

MIX. Measure the flour and set aside. About 1 hour before your starter is ready, mix the flour and water by hand in a medium bowl for about 3 minutes. Cover and leave to hydrate at room temperature (65° to 75°F) until the starter is ripe. When ready, add the starter and salt and mix again by hand for about 3 minutes, alternately breaking the dough up and folding it back onto itself. At this point, the dough will still look shaggy and feel sticky and weak. Get as much dough from your hands back into the bowl as possible, scraping down your hands and the bowl. Cover the bowl with a tea towel and leave to rise at room temperature for 3 hours, giving the dough a four-fold (see page 28) every 30 minutes.

SHAPE. After 3 hours, the dough should be showing clear signs of fermentation, such as bubbles under the surface. Lay out a couche or large tea towel on a sheet pan and generously dust it with flour. Heavily flour a section of the countertop and turn the dough out. Fold the top edge of the dough down a third of the way, then fold the bottom edge up a third, like folding a letter into a rectangle. Pat it out gently to a rectangle about 12 by 8 inches, then use a bench knife to divide the dough in half, making two rectangles, each about 6 by 8 inches. Coat the rectangles all over with flour. Gently lift each loaf onto the couche, leaving about 3 inches between the loaves. Lift the fabric in between the loaves to support their shape against one another, then fold the ends of the fabric loosely over the loaves. Leave to

ferment until the loaves are puffy and significantly risen, about 1 hour and 45 minutes.

BAKE. Place a large baking stone and hotel pan (see page 62) on the highest rack in your oven they will fit on. Preheat the oven to 450°F. Cut a sheet of parchment paper that will fit over the back side of a half sheet pan to use as a peel. Have two towels or hot pads and a spray bottle of water within reach, too.

Gently roll a loaf onto your hand, then transfer it to the parchment paper. If the dough is really loose, just roll it from the couche. The top can be the bottom or the bottom the top. Repeat with the second loaf, lining up both loaves evenly on the parchment.

Quickly but carefully open your oven, pull the rack that you are baking on partway out, and move the hot hotel pan to the stovetop. Slide the parchment paper and loaves onto the stone and cover with the hot hotel pan, spraying water into the pan before setting it onto the stone to trap steam. Close the oven and bake for 20 minutes. Then remove the hot hotel pan and bake, uncovered, for 10 minutes. Rotate the loaves, then bake until they are evenly browned, another 5 to 10 minutes. Remove to racks to cool.

This bread can be kept in a paper bag, bread box, or cupboard at room temperature for 5 to 6 days.

PAIN NORMAND

Day 1 → 10 minutes
active time over 1 hour
with overnight drying

Day 2 → 30 minutes
active time over 5 hours

My baking mentor, Nick Brannon, introduced me to this bread when I was just a baby baker. I was beyond impressed that he knew how to ferment his own cider, and the aromatic bread it produced stuck in my memory for a long time. I adapted this recipe from baking hero Jeffrey Hamelman. The bread originated in the apple region of Normandy, France. The apples are dried, which concentrates their sweetness and adds a pleasant chew to the bread. I recommend using whatever apples you have on hand and perhaps an affordable hard cider on the sweeter end of the spectrum. Then enjoy the bread with a cider that's more dry and funky. —CKM

DRIED APPLES

2 pounds apples, any type, unpeeled

STARTER

bolted hard wheat flour	166 g (1⅓ cups)	100%
water	100 g (7 tablespoons)	60%
ripe rye Sourdough Starter (page 147)	33 g (3 tablespoons)	20%
TOTAL	**299 g**	**180%**

DOUGH

bolted hard wheat flour	713 g (5⅔ cups)	100%
water	221 g (15 tablespoons)	31%
hard cider	292 g (1¼ cups)	41%
starter (from above)	250 g (1¼ cups)	35%
salt	17 g (2¾ teaspoons)	2.4%
dried apples (from above)	107 g (1¼ cups)	15%
TOTAL	**1,600 g**	**224.4%**

DAY 1: DRY APPLES. Preheat the oven to 250°F. Line a sheet pan with parchment paper. Core and dice the apples, then lay them out evenly on the prepared sheet pan. Bake for about 1 hour, then turn the oven off and leave the apples inside to continue drying overnight.

BUILD STARTER. Measure the flour and set aside. Combine the water, starter, and flour in a container with a tight-fitting lid. Cover and leave at room temperature (65° to 75°F) for

about 8 hours. Depending on your baking schedule, you could go as short as 7 hours, in which case, you may get a slightly stiff dough. You could also go as long as 12 hours, in which case, you may get a more extensible dough due to the extra fermentation and enzyme activity.

DAY 2: MIX DOUGH. Measure the flour and set aside. Combine the water, cider, starter, flour, and salt in the bowl of a stand mixer. Mix with the dough hook on low speed for 3 minutes. Switch to medium speed and mix for another 2 minutes. Add the apples and mix on the lowest speed, just until evenly incorporated, a minute or so (enjoy any extra dried apples as a snack). This dough is on the dry side compared to others, so it should feel only a bit sticky and stretchy; it will not look very shiny.

Transfer the dough to an oiled bowl and cover with a tea towel. Leave to rise at room temperature for 3 hours, giving the dough a four-fold (see page 28) after 1½ hours. After 3 hours, the dough should be puffy.

SHAPE. This dough needs only one round of shaping. Flour two large round bannetons or towel-lined bowls. Drizzle a little water on your countertop and spread it around so the surface is wet but not puddled. Turn the dough out onto the countertop and divide it into two pieces, each about 800 grams. For each piece, fold all four sides in toward the center, then roll the dough over so it is seam-side down. Tighten it into a boule (see page 49) by cupping your hands around the dough and rolling it in a circle, applying some pressure to create a nice taut ball. Flour the outside of each loaf and place them seam-side up in the floured bannetons. Cover with the tea towel and leave to rise at room temperature for 2 hours. The loaves should rise to about 1½ times their original size. Since this is not a very wet dough, they should be rising up more than they are relaxing out and have a nice tall dome.

BAKE. Place a large baking stone and hotel pan (see page 62) on the highest rack in the oven they will fit on. Preheat the oven to 450°F. Have two towels or hot pads, a spray bottle of water, and a razor within reach.

Quickly but carefully open your oven, pull the rack that you are baking on partway out, and move the hot hotel pan to the stovetop. Flip the loaves from the bannetons onto the stone, then quickly score a cross or X onto the top of each loaf. Cover the loaves with the hot hotel pan, spraying water into the pan before setting it onto the stone to trap steam.

Bake for 20 minutes. Then remove the hotel pan and bake for another 10 minutes. Rotate the loaves for even browning and bake until the crust is the color of kraft paper (a bit lighter than some of the other breads in this book), about 5 minutes more. Remove the loaves to racks to cool.

These boules can be kept in a paper bag, bread box, or cupboard at room temperature for 5 to 6 days.

FARRO MICHE WITH WHEY

MAKES 1 BOULE, ABOUT
12-INCH DIAMETER

Day 1 → 30 minutes
active time over 4½ hours
with an overnight rest

Day 2 → 10 minutes
active time over 1¾ hours

Whenever you make ricotta cheese, you get lots of leftover whey. There was a time at Vetri when we were making boatloads of ricotta, and this miche (a large round loaf) came from my unwillingness to see the salty dairy water just poured down the drain. This bread also includes a porridge made with cooked farro berries, a technique that gives bread a more moist crumb and an occasional crackle from the semi-intact grains on the crust. The farro I'm referring to here is emmer wheat, and that's supposedly what Italians mean when they talk about farro. But farro can also refer to einkorn or spelt. If you can't find emmer, you can use one of these two. —CKM

SOAKER

whole farro berries	100 g (½ cup)	100%
water	348 g (1½ cups)	350%
salt	2 g (⅓ teaspoon)	2%
TOTAL	**450 g**	**452%**

DOUGH

bolted hard wheat flour	375 g (3 cups)	70%
whole farro flour	161 g (1⅓ cups)	30%
water	193 g (¾ cup)	36%
whey, at room temperature (see Option)	193 g (¾ cup)	36%
ripe farro Sourdough Starter (page 147)	107 g (½ cup)	20%
salt	10 g (1¾ teaspoons)	2%
soaker (from above)	161 g (¾ cup)	30%
TOTAL	**1,200 g**	**224%**

DAY 1: MAKE SOAKER. Combine the farro berries, water, and salt in a small saucepan. Cover and bring to a boil over high heat, then turn the heat to low and simmer, covered, until tender, about 1 hour. Turn off the heat and leave the porridge to cool. You will have more porridge than you need for the recipe. Measure out 161 grams and eat the rest dressed up as if it were rice or oatmeal.

MIX. While the soaker cools, measure both flours and set aside. Combine the water, whey, starter, and flours in a large mixing bowl. With clean hands, mix until it comes together

in a shaggy mass, then mix it in the bowl for a few minutes more, alternately breaking the dough up and folding it back onto itself. The dough will be sticky and ragged, and that's okay. Get as much dough from your hands back into the bowl as possible, scraping down your hands and the bowl. Cover with a tea towel and let rest at room temperature (65° to 75°F) for 30 minutes. Add the salt and hand-mix again for 3 minutes. At this point, the dough should start to have some strength. Cover and rest again for 30 minutes. Add the soaker and hand-mix again, until the soaker is incorporated, about 3 minutes. Then cover and let rest for 1½ hours, giving the dough a four-fold (see page 28) every 30 minutes.

SHAPE. If you have a large round banneton, today's its day to shine. Flour it. Otherwise, line a large mixing bowl with a tea towel and dust it liberally with flour. Dampen your countertop with water, then turn the dough out onto it. This is the biggest loaf you get to shape in this book. Have fun. Stretch all four sides out and fold them over the center, then roll the loaf over, so it's seam-side down. Shape the loaf into a boule (see page 49): roll the dough in a circle on your countertop, cupping your hands around the dough to increase the surface tension all around it as you shape it into a nice taut ball. As you roll, the seam will seal and smooth out on the bottom. Dust the top of the loaf with flour, then slip your hand beneath the dough and invert it into the floured banneton, so the floured side is down, peeling your hand away from the loaf. Place the filled banneton in plastic grocery bags or loosely cover with plastic wrap or beeswax wrap and leave at room temperature for 1 hour, then move the covered banneton to the refrigerator to rest overnight.

DAY 2: BAKE. Place a large baking stone and hotel pan (see page 62) on the highest rack in the oven they will fit on. Preheat the oven to 450°F. Cut a sheet of parchment paper that will fit over the back side of a half sheet pan to use as a peel. Have two towels or hot pads, a spray bottle of water, and a razor within reach.

Pull the loaf from the fridge and dust it with flour or wheat bran. Turn the loaf out onto the parchment, then score the top with four slashes to make a square on top. Moving quickly but carefully, open the oven and pull the rack that you are baking on partway out and move the hot hotel pan to the stovetop or side of the oven. Slide the loaf and parchment paper onto the stone. Cover the loaf with the hot hotel pan, spraying water into the pan before setting it onto the stone to trap steam.

Bake for 20 minutes. Then, remove the hot hotel pan and rotate the loaf for even browning. Turn the oven temperature to 425°F and bake, uncovered, until the crust is browned and the raised edge along the score mark has scorched lightly, about 20 minutes more. Remove to a rack to cool completely before cutting.

This bread can be kept in a large paper bag, bread box, or cupboard at room temperature for 6 to 7 days.

OPTION

If you don't have leftover whey from making Homemade Ricotta (page 263), you can just use buttermilk.

BUCKWHEAT BUTTERMILK BREAD

MAKES 2 BOULES, ABOUT
10-INCH DIAMETER

Day 1 → 5 minutes
active time over 10 minutes
with an overnight soak

Day 2 → 30 minutes
active time over 5 hours
with an overnight rest

Day 3 → 10 minutes
active time over 1½ hours

In 2018, local buckwheat became available in Philadelphia, and that's when this bread came together. At the time, we were making a lot of butter at Vetri, so we had tons of buttermilk on hand. The flavors really worked. The buttermilk tang lifted and complemented the buckwheat's low tannic notes. This dough also feels really nice because the acid in the buttermilk helps tighten the gluten. We put this bread out with our entrees as a table bread, but it's hard to go wrong serving it any time of day. You'll need whole buckwheat groats to make the dough. If you can't find local whole buckwheat, check at the supermarket or online (Bob's Red Mill makes it). —CKM

SOAKER

whole buckwheat groats	82 g (½ cup)	100%
water	49 g (3⅓ tablespoons)	60%
TOTAL	**131 g**	**160%**

DOUGH

bolted hard wheat flour	726 g (5¾ cups)	100%
buttermilk	363 g (1½ cups)	50%
water	254 g (1⅛ cups)	35%
ripe whole-wheat Sourdough Starter (page 147)	109 g (½ cup)	15%
salt	17 g (2¾ teaspoons)	2.4%
soaker (from above)	131 g (¾ cup)	18%
TOTAL	**1,600 g**	**220.4%**

raw sunflower seeds for topping

wheat bran for dusting

DAY 1: MAKE SOAKER. In the evening, toast the buckwheat groats in a dry sauté pan over medium heat until fragrant, just a few minutes, shaking the pan for even browning. Transfer to a small container and let cool. Add the water and let soak overnight.

DAY 2: MIX. Measure the flour and set aside. Combine the buttermilk, water, and flour in a bowl (a stand mixer bowl is ideal), stirring just until incorporated. Cover with a tea towel and let rest at room temperature (65° to 75°F) for 2 hours.

Combine the buttermilk mixture, starter, and salt in the bowl of a stand mixer and mix with the dough hook on low speed for 4 minutes. Switch to medium speed and mix for 3 minutes. The dough will be somewhat loose, but it will come together when you fold it later. Add the soaker and mix just until incorporated, about a minute. Transfer the dough to an oiled bowl and allow it to rest at room temperature for 2½ hours, with a four-fold (see page 28) every 30 minutes.

CONTINUED

PRESHAPE. Drizzle a little water on your countertop and spread it around so the surface is wet but not puddled. Turn the dough out onto the countertop and divide it into two 800-gram pieces. Give each piece some shape by stretching up and folding all four edges in toward the center. Roll the dough onto its seam, cover with a tea towel, and let rest seam-side down on the countertop for 20 minutes.

SHAPE. Set up a wide shallow bowl of raw sunflower seeds to coat the tops of the loaves. Flour two large round bannetons or large towel-lined bowls. Dampen your countertop again, then shape each piece of dough into a ball by rolling the dough in a circle on the countertop, cupping your hands around the dough, and applying pressure all around it to increase the surface tension. This dough is loose but make the ball as taut as possible. To seed each loaf, spray it with water and slip your hand beneath the loaf, pick it up, and invert it into the seeds to coat the top, then transfer it to the floured banneton with the seeds down, peeling your hand from the dough. Repeat with the other loaf.

Place the filled bannetons in plastic grocery bags or loosely cover with plastic wrap or beeswax wrap, then move the covered loaves to the refrigerator to rest overnight.

DAY 3: BAKE. Place a large baking stone and hotel pan (see page 62) on the highest rack in the oven they will fit on. Preheat the oven to 450°F. Have two towels or hot pads, a spray bottle of water, and a razor within reach.

Dust the loaves with the wheat bran. Quickly but carefully open your oven, pull the rack that you are baking on partway out, and move the hot hotel pan to the stovetop. Gently invert the loaves onto the hot stone and quickly score each one (I like four slashes to make a square). Cover the loaves with the hot hotel pan, spraying water into the pan before setting it onto the stone to trap steam. These are larger loaves, and they will really fill the space. If you are worried about their touching each other or bumping the hotel pan,

they can also be baked one at a time. The upside of really filling the hotel pan is more humidity for better oven spring and crust formation.

Bake for 20 minutes, then remove the hot hotel pan and rotate the loaves for even browning. Bake, uncovered, until the crust is as dark as you can get it without the seeds burning, 15 to 20 minutes more. The crust itself should be medium brown. Remove the loaves to a rack to cool.

This bread will keep in a paper bag, bread box, or cupboard at room temperature for 5 to 6 days.

OMNI BREAD

MAKES 2 ROUNDISH
OVAL LOAVES, ABOUT
12-INCH DIAMETER

Day 1 → 30 minutes
active time over 5 hours
with an overnight rest

Day 2 → 10 minutes
active time over 1½ hours

This is my favorite bread that I produce for Ursa Bakery. It has everything: whole grains, seeds, crust, and tang. That's why I call it the Omni. With its moist crumb and toasty, nutty, wholesome flavor, this is the bread for people who want to bake bread and eat it throughout the week. It keeps well and can be used for sandwiches or toast, as an accompaniment to soups and stews, or for just about anything else you can think of. —CKM

SOAKER

pumpkin seeds and/or flax seeds	24 g (3 tablespoons)	50%
sunflower seeds and/or poppy or sesame seeds	24 g (3 tablespoons)	50%
polenta	20 g (1¾ tablespoons)	41%
water	73 g (5 tablespoons)	149%
TOTAL	**141 g**	**290%**

DOUGH

bolted hard wheat flour	605 g (4¾ cups)	90%
whole-grain spelt flour	67 g (9 tablespoons)	10%
water	538 g (2¼ cups)	80%
ripe rye Sourdough Starter (page 147)	134 g (¾ cup)	20%
salt	15 g (2½ teaspoons)	2%
soaker (from above)	141 g (⅞ cup)	21%
TOTAL	**1,500 g**	**223%**

1 cup pumpkin seeds (and/or flax seeds) for topping

1 cup sunflower seeds (and/or poppy or sesame seeds) for topping

wheat bran for dusting

DAY 1: MAKE SOAKER. In a medium skillet, toast all the seeds and the polenta over medium heat, until they smell nutty and fragrant, 2 to 3 minutes, shaking the pan to prevent burning. Pour the water into the pan while it's still hot and leave at room temperature (65° to 75°F) for about 3 hours.

MIX. Measure both flours and set aside. Combine the water, starter, and flours in a large mixing bowl. With clean hands, mix until it comes together in a shaggy mass, then mix it in

the bowl for a few minutes more, alternately breaking the dough up and folding it back onto itself. The dough will be sticky and ragged, and that's okay. Get as much dough from your hands back into the bowl as possible, scraping down your hands and the bowl. Cover with a tea towel and let rest at room temperature for 30 minutes. Add the salt and hand-mix again for 3 minutes. At this point, the dough

CONTINUED

should start to have some strength. Cover and let rest again for 30 minutes. Smear the soaker over the dough and give the dough a few folds to distribute the seeds, but don't worry about their being perfectly distributed. Cover and let rest for about 2 hours, giving the dough a four-fold (see page 28) during that time.

PRESHAPE. Drizzle a little water on your countertop and spread it around so the surface is wet but not puddled. Turn the dough out onto the counter and divide it into two 750-gram pieces. Give each piece some shape by gently pulling four sides of the dough up and outward and then folding in toward the center. Cover and let rest for 10 minutes.

SHAPE. Dampen your countertop again, then flip the loaves over onto the damp area. Shape the loaves into batards: fold in the left and right sides, then gently stretch and fold the bottom in toward the center and continue rolling the loaf toward the top, keeping pressure on the dough with your palms to create a taut oblong shape.

Lightly flour two medium oval bannetons or towel-lined bowls (obviously, you'll get a round loaf if using the latter). Pour all the seeds for the topping into a large shallow dish just larger than the loaves (or use a quarter sheet pan). To seed each loaf, slip your hand beneath it, pick it up, and roll the wet side in the seed mixture, coating it well. Then place each loaf seed-side down in the banneton, gently peeling your hand from the loaf. Place the bannetons in a covered container or loose plastic bag and move to the refrigerator to rest overnight.

DAY 2: BAKE. Place a large baking stone and hotel pan (see page 62) on the highest rack in the oven they will fit on. Preheat the oven to 500°F. Have two towels or hot pads, a spray bottle of water, and a razor within reach.

Dust the loaves with wheat bran. Quickly but carefully open your oven, pull the rack that you are baking on partway out, and move the hot hotel pan to the stovetop. Invert the loaves one at a time onto the stone and score each loaf with a diamond pattern about ½ to ¾ inch deep (see "Batard four score or diamond," page 60). Cover the loaves with the hotel pan, spraying water into the pan before setting it onto the stone to trap steam. Lower the oven temperature to 475°F and bake for 20 minutes.

Remove the hot hotel pan and rotate the loaves for even browning. Bake, uncovered, until the loaves are evenly browned and the raised edges along the score marks have scorched lightly, another 10 to 15 minutes. Remove to racks to cool. This bread will keep for 5 to 6 days at room temperature in a paper bag, bread box, or cupboard.

CIABATTA GRANO ARSO WITH EINKORN

MAKES 2 FREE-FORM
LOAVES, ABOUT
8 BY 10 INCHES

Day 1 → 15 minutes
active time with an
overnight rest

Day 2 → 30 minutes
active time over 4 hours

Everyone imagines ciabatta as the original Italian peasant bread. Well, it isn't. It was invented in 1982 by Arnaldo Cavallari, one of several Italian bakers concerned with the French baguette being overused to make sandwiches in Italy. Thanks to some clever marketing, ciabatta is now the go-to bread for Italian sandwiches around the world. This ciabatta recipe, however, is atypical, a crazy quilt of old and new. It's made with einkorn wheat, one of the first plants ever to be domesticated. And I burn some of the whole einkorn berries in a pan to make *grano arso* (burnt grain), a nod to the old Italian practice of torching the wheat fields after harvest to kill weeds and help fertilize the soil for the following year. *Grano arso* lends some bass notes to the flavor here. This is definitely not a white sandwich bread, and it doesn't have a giant open crumb structure like many ciabattas. Save this one for hearty sandwiches or to serve with long-simmered winter stews and braises. —CKM

STARTER

bolted hard wheat flour	108 g (¾ cup + 1¾ tablespoons)	100%
ripe rye Sourdough Starter (page 147)	22 g (1¾ tablespoons)	20%
water	70 g (4¾ tablespoons)	65%
TOTAL	**200 g**	**185%**

SOAKER

whole einkorn berries	37 g (¼ cup)	100%
water	32 g (2⅛ tablespoons)	87%
TOTAL	**69 g**	**187%**

DOUGH

bolted hard wheat flour	309 g (2½ cups)	50%
whole-grain einkorn flour	309 g (2½ cups)	50%
water	501 g (2⅛ cups)	81%
starter (from above)	155 g (¾ cup)	25%
soaker (from above)	69 g (⅔ cup)	11%
salt	17 g (2¾ teaspoons)	2.8%
TOTAL	**1,360 g**	**219.8%**

CONTINUED

DAY 1: BUILD STARTER. In the evening, measure the flour and set aside. Combine the starter, water, and flour in a small bowl. Cover and leave at cool room temperature (50° to 65°F) to rise overnight.

DAY 2: MAKE SOAKER. In the morning, toast the einkorn berries in a dry pan over high heat until burnt, shaking the pan for even burning. Yes, you want the grains totally burnt. Spread them on a sheet pan to cool. When cooled, crack the burnt grain in a flour mill set very coarsely or with a few pulses of a coffee or spice grinder. Pour the burnt flour into a small bowl, and mix in the water. Set aside for 1 hour.

MIX DOUGH. Measure both flours and set aside. Combine the water and starter in a large mixing bowl. Then add the flours. With clean hands, mix until the dough comes together in a shaggy mass, then mix it in the bowl for a few minutes more, alternately breaking the dough up and folding it back onto itself. At this point, the dough will still look shaggy and feel sticky and weak. Get as much dough from your hands back into the bowl as possible, scraping down your hands and the bowl. Cover the bowl with a tea towel and leave to rise at room temperature (65° to 75°F) for 1 hour.

After an hour, add the soaker and salt to the dough. Mix them in thoroughly with several rounds of folding the dough and then breaking it up by hand. Cover and leave to rise for 1 hour.

Give the dough a gentle four-fold (see page 28). By now, you should be seeing some signs of fermentation activity such as small bubbles at the surface of the dough. The dough should also be smooth and quite extensible. Cover and leave to rise again for about 1 hour. By then, the dough should show signs of moderate fermentation, such as a small increase in volume and some bubbles under the surface. To check, you could slash the edge of the dough with a sharp knife or razor to peek inside and look for bubbles.

SHAPE. Place a large baking stone and hotel pan (see page 62) on the highest rack in the oven they will fit on. Preheat the oven to 500°F. Have a couche or tea towel, flour for dusting, and a bench knife ready.

Liberally dust your countertop with flour. Turn the dough out, using a bowl scraper to get all of it. Fold in the left and right sides toward the center of the dough, so it is a rough rectangle on the counter. Then pat out the rectangle, so it's about 12 by 8 inches. Dust again liberally with flour and use a bench knife to divide the rectangle in half, making two rectangles, each about 6 by 8 inches. Toss a little more flour on the cut surfaces. The goal here is to evenly coat the entire outside of each ciabatta with flour. Unlike most breads, surface tension is not a crucial consideration here. Dust the couche with flour. Then, handling gently so you don't de-gas the dough, lift each ciabatta up by slipping your hands beneath the dough on either side as if you were scooping water into your hands and set the ciabatta onto the couche. (To get a pretty tiger-stripe pattern on the tops of the loaves, you've got to create wrinkles on the bottom. The scoop-and-lift maneuver should crumple the bottom of the loaf sufficiently so that it has the wrinkles when flipped to bake; all that extra flour will prevent the wrinkles from sealing and will create a slackness that will be filled up during the bake, creating the tiger stripes.) Support the sides of the ciabatta by folding ridges in the couche. Cover and let rest for 15 minutes.

BAKE. Cut a sheet of parchment paper that will fit over the back side of a half sheet pan to use as a peel. Have two towels or hot pads and a spray bottle of water within reach, too.

Pull the ends of the couche to spread it out and smooth out the support folds. You are going to invert and transfer the ciabatta, but the dough is very delicate. To do this properly, have your parchment-paper-and-sheet-pan setup nearby. Then lift up one side of the couche to roll the first ciabatta right-side up, put one hand beside the ciabatta, palm up (or use a narrow paddle), and roll the loaf into your hand. Quickly roll it off your hand onto one-half of the parchment paper on the sheet pan. Repeat with the second loaf. What was the bottom of the loaves on the couche should now be the top on the parchment paper. Quickly tuck any stretched-out edges back underneath to maintain the somewhat rectangular shape of the loaves.

Quickly but carefully open your oven, pull the rack that you are baking on partway out, and move the hot hotel pan to the stovetop. Slide the parchment paper and ciabatta onto the stone and cover with the hot hotel pan, spraying water into the pan before setting it onto the stone to trap steam. Close the oven and bake for 12 minutes. Then remove the hot hotel pan and rotate the loaves for even browning. Bake, uncovered, for about another 12 minutes. These ciabatta are very floury, but the crust peeking through should have a tortoiseshell mottling from tan to dark brown. Remove the loaves to racks to cool.

The ciabatta can be kept in a paper bag, bread box, or cupboard at room temperature for 4 to 5 days.

SOURDOUGH BAGUETTE

MAKES 4 BAGUETTES,
16 TO 18 INCHES LONG

Day 1 → 15 minutes
active time over 1½ hours
with an overnight rest

Day 2 → 30 minutes
active time over 3½ hours

Traditional baguettes are yeast breads, a product of the Industrial Revolution that made everything in life faster and more technologically advanced. But now, many bakers like to make everything naturally leavened. For this recipe, I followed the advice of the excellent Tasmanian baker Ian Lowe. This is one of those instances where I blindly followed someone else's instructions and felt totally out of my comfort zone. But it worked super well. The bread opens up enormously in the oven with a beautiful crust, crumb, texture, and flavor. Keep in mind that sourdough crusts tend to be chewier, and you're more likely to get a complex, tangy flavor rather than a traditional yeast baguette flavor. —CKM

bolted hard wheat flour	655 g (5¼ cups)	100%
water	462 g (2 cups)	70%
ripe bolted wheat Sourdough Starter (page 147)	67 g (⅓ cup)	10%
barley malt flour or powder (see Option, page 156)	3 g (1¼ teaspoons)	0.4%
salt	13 g (2⅛ teaspoons)	2%
TOTAL	**1,200 g**	**182.4%**

DAY 1: MIX. In the evening, measure the wheat flour and set aside. Combine the water, starter, reserved flour, malt flour or powder, and salt in the bowl of a stand mixer. Mix with the dough hook on low speed for 5 minutes. Make sure that no flour has clumped at the bottom of the bowl. If it has, manually scrape these clumps into the main dough mass, then mix for an additional 2 minutes. Transfer the dough to a lightly oiled container with a lid and leave to rest at warm room temperature (75° to 85°F) for 1 hour. During that time, give the dough a four-fold (see page 28) every 15 minutes. Then move the covered container to the fridge and retard overnight.

DAY 2: PRESHAPE. Pull the container from the fridge and allow to rest at room temperature (65° to 75°F) for 1 hour. Turn the dough out onto a lightly floured countertop and divide it into four 300-gram pieces. Give each piece some shape by loosely folding all four edges in toward the center, then rolling the dough over so it is seam-side down. Let rest for 15 minutes.

SHAPE. Set up a lightly floured couche or tea towel. Turn each loaf seam-side up and gently pat it down. Then roll it into a fat cylinder, stretching it out just a bit. Now, starting with one hand in the center of the cylinder, press lightly and begin rolling the baguette back and forth. Add your second hand and, pressing evenly, roll while stretching the baguette out. It will probably take a few passes to get the baguette to the right length of 16 to 18 inches. On the final pass from the center outward, press the tips out to a taper. Place each baguette seam-side up on the couche, pulling up a little ridge of fabric in between each baguette. Once all four baguettes are nestled in, fold the excess fabric over (or cover with a tea towel) to keep them from drying out. Leave to rest at room temperature for 45 minutes.

BAKE. Place a large baking stone and hotel pan (see page 62) on the highest rack in the oven they will fit on. Preheat the oven to 500°F. Cut a sheet of parchment paper that will fit over the back side of a half sheet pan to use as a peel (or line a large cutting board with parchment). Have a spray bottle of water, two towels or hot pads, and a razor within reach.

Gently lift and transfer two baguettes to the parchment paper, flipping them over so they are seam-side down. Adjust them so they are straight and evenly spaced from each other. To score, tilt the razor blade and hold it at an angle so that your cut will produce a flap instead of an open wound. Slash each baguette three to five times quickly in a few almost perfectly centered lines from end to end (see "Baguette scoring," page 60).

Now quickly but carefully open your oven, pull the rack that you are baking on partway out, and move the hot hotel pan to the stovetop or side of the oven. Slide the parchment paper onto the stone. Still working quickly, but without burning yourself or smooshing the baguettes, cover the baguettes with the hotel pan, spraying water into the pan before setting it onto the stone to trap steam. Close the oven and bake for 8 minutes. Then remove the hotel pan and rotate the loaves from side to side and front to back to ensure even color. Close the oven and bake until the predominant color all over the baguettes is a light terra-cotta, an additional 10 minutes or so. Remove the baguettes to a rack to cool. Repeat scoring and baking the remaining baguettes.

Try to eat the baguettes within 36 hours. You could also freeze them or use them to make Panzanella (page 246) or Ribollita (page 248).

9

——

ENRICHED SOURDOUGH BREADS

WHEN MOST PEOPLE THINK OF RYE BREAD, THEY PICTURE A LIGHT TAN LOAF WITH CARAWAY SEEDS IN IT. You know what I'm talking about: the typical Jewish deli bread used to make pastrami sandwiches. We make a great version of this bread called Deli Rye (page 199).

But the truth is, your typical deli rye, along with American pumpernickel and marbled rye (a combination of the two) actually contains very little rye flour. These breads are made mostly with refined white flour and just a small portion of rye flour along with sweeteners and coloring. Don't get me wrong. I enjoy this kind of bread, toasted with butter slathered all over it. But it's not real rye bread.

If there is one bread in this chapter that I recommend you make first, it's the All Rye (page 186). When Claire first came on board at Vetri, we started milling and making breads with 100% whole grain (no sifting), and the All Rye was the very first bread she made. It blew my mind. At the time, my wife was having a stomach issue and trying to figure out what to eat and what not to eat. This rye bread was the one thing that helped get her back on track. I started making four loaves a week at home and freezing it. With a little sour from the sourdough and a touch of sweet from the honey, this bread really shows off the flavor of rye itself.

So many people mistake the taste of caraway for the taste of rye because they're used to the kind of rye bread that has caraway seeds in it. I love the flavors of both, but it's important to know the difference. Rye differs quite a bit from wheat, too. Rye has a lot more chutzpah than wheat . . . less sweet, more sharp and spicy, with deep, earthy flavors that resonate like the stand-up bass in a jazz trio. But caraway has the distinctive aroma of anise and none of the deep bass notes. Make our All Rye and taste it. Then make the Deli Rye, which has caraway, and taste that. You'll see what I mean.

As we got more into milling, the second 100% whole-grain bread that Claire made was Seeded Schwarzbrot (page 183). This German "black bread" (the literal translation of *Schwarzbrot*) is half whole-grain rye, half whole wheat, with some pumpkin seeds and sunflower seeds mixed in. After you mix it up, it doesn't even look like bread dough. It looks like a paste that could never become a bread. But like the All Rye, the Schwarzbrot bakes into a dense, moist, delicious loaf with a super-tight crumb. Just lightly toasted and slathered in butter, with all of its vitamins and minerals, this whole-grain bread could serve as a small meal. It really fills you up and makes you feel so good and healthy.

These two rye breads shattered all of my misconceptions about rye bread in general. There's this notion that in order to make good bread with rye flour, you have to add other flours that form a better gluten structure so the bread will rise higher. Who says? Germans and Eastern Europeans have been making incredibly delicious 100% rye breads for centuries. Especially sourdoughs. Even so, sourdough rye breads don't tend to rise super high like those made with wheat flour.

So what? Rye tastes amazing! When you learn about different grains and flours, you start to appreciate each one for its own unique qualities. So rye doesn't make light, airy breads. Who cares? If you embrace its deep, complex flavors, you can make magnificent breads with it. If you are only going for crusty loaves with huge fermentation pockets, then you're missing the point. Different grains have different characteristics, and even different varieties of single grains like wheat have different flavor and texture characteristics. Celebrate each one for what it is instead of trying to make it like something else.

If you're new to baking rye breads, especially sourdough rye, the All Rye and Seeded Schwarzbrot are great places to start. They're both baked in loaf pans and among the easiest recipes in this chapter. If you already love baking rye breads, try the Pumpernickel (page 197), Horse Bread (page 194), and Chocolate Rye Sourdough (page 189), each great in its own way. My kids absolutely love the Chocolate Rye. It's got chocolate chips, cocoa powder, honey, and vanilla in it. Need I say more?

Each of the breads in this chapter is unique. In some ways, this is the weirdo chapter of the book. If you love weirdos in everyday life, you'll love these breads. They run the gamut from surprisingly idiot-proof (like the All Rye and Seeded Schwarzbrot) to the pretty technical and hard to explain. For example, Malted Grain Sourdough (page 204) and Sourdough Brioche (page 207) may seem simple, but are actually some of the more challenging breads in this book.

In the Malted Grain Sourdough, the malted grain (malted barley, rye, or even wheat) adds such a big enzyme load to the dough that you have a pretty narrow window when the dough is viable for baking. It's an amazing bread: the malted grain adds a fatty, nutty texture to the crust and a toasted caramel flavor to the crumb. But making it tests your powers of observation. Malted grains complicate the whole fermentation process. This dough pushes the usual thresholds of timing and temperature to the max. How do you know if the dough is ready to bake? Sometimes the only way is to overshoot the mark, to reach that moment when the dough puffs up so big that it starts to go the other way, and it starts breaking down. Then you know to dial back the fermentation for the next batch. But hopefully you're paying attention, and you can bake the loaves just before they go over the brink. Either way, take mental notes for next time or make literal notes by jotting down your observations in a baking log or right on the recipe page itself!

The Sourdough Brioche is another oddball. It's a pan loaf, which seems easy enough, but even if you are experienced with both yeast brioche and sourdough, this dough intro-duces new rules to the game. First off, it's a really intense mix that feels somewhat unnatural. During mixing, you're think-ing: "Shouldn't I stop now?" Just go with it. Follow the recipe and trust the process. Plus, since it's naturally leavened and super-enriched, the dough takes forever to ferment. The gen-erous amounts of butter, eggs, and sugar really slow down the rise, multiplying the total fermentation time exponen-tially. Again, just follow the recipe directions and you'll be fine. Everything just takes longer.

If you've been baking your way through this book, you should now recognize that you have waded into the deep end. There are some oddities here. Swim at your own risk! Keep your wits about you and follow the signs. You may be adrift in the water longer than you're used to, but work with the currents instead of against them, stay engaged and present, and everything will be okay. When you get back to shore, your reward will be some exceptional, one-of-a-kind breads! **—MV**

HAROLD WILKEN AND JILL BROCKMAN-CUMMINGS

Janie's Farm and Janie's Mill
East-Central Illinois

———

Harold Wilken is the owner-farmer at Janie's Farm, and Jill Brockman-Cummings is the head miller at Janie's Mill, both in east-central Illinois. Janie's Farm is a certified organic fifth-generation family farm, and Janie's Mill is its natural extension. The name comes from Harold's daughter Janie, who passed away in a car accident in 2001 at the age of fifteen. In Janie's honor, after twenty-three years of conventional farming, Harold transitioned to organic farming with one 30-acre field. Janie's Farm now grows more than 2,000 acres of certified organic wheat, rye, corn, and soybeans. Janie's Mill stone-mills the grains into a variety of flours for local and regional bakeries, restaurants, retailers, and home cooks.

 Our basic rotation is wheat, cover crop, corn, cover crop, and soybeans. Within that, we raise different wheat varieties, like white wheat, soft red winter wheat, Turkey Red, and another hard red called Warthog. Our neighbors call it Hogwarts. We have a few Harry Potter fans around here.

A lot of things are changing in grain farming. There's this awareness, and it's growing. Bakeries, craft brewers, distillers . . . they're all asking for these local high-quality grains.

Most of us grew up on roller-milled, sifted, bleached, bromated, enriched flour. But it was only 'enriched' because all the nutrients had been removed during these industrial processes. When you smell and taste freshly milled flour you realize just how rich, varied, and wholesome flour can be.

We built the mill to grind our grains and provide organic stone-ground flours to people in our community. We're now milling about 74,000 pounds of fresh flour a day, both for regional bakers and home bakers across the country. "

SEEDED SCHWARZBROT

MAKES 1 PAN LOAF,
9 BY 5 INCHES

Day 1 → 5 minutes
active time with an
overnight rest

Day 2 → 10 minutes
active time over 2 hours

Here is a Vetri Grain Project original. The formula came from a friend of a chef at Vetri who texted us a photo of a recipe handwritten in German. The recipe was her grandmother's. Many of the measurements were in handfuls, so we imagined what a German grandmother's handful measured, then weighed the ingredients and baked the bread in a plain old loaf pan. It was incredible and different and delicious . . . dense, moist, and a little sweet. This bread also uses 100% whole-grain flour. Slice it thin and serve it with cheese or simply enjoy it toasted and buttered for breakfast. This bread keeps exceptionally well. —CKM

STARTER

whole-grain hard wheat flour	113 g (1 cup)	50%
whole-grain rye flour	113 g (1 cup)	50%
water	226 g (1 cup)	100%
ripe rye Sourdough Starter (page 147)	10 g (1 tablespoon)	4%
TOTAL	**462 g**	**204%**

DOUGH

whole-grain hard wheat flour	113 g (1 cup)	50%
whole-grain rye flour	113 g (1 cup)	50%
sunflower seeds	113 g (¾ cup)	50%
pumpkin seeds	113 g (¾ cup)	50%
water	226 g (1 cup)	100%
salt	12 g (2 teaspoons)	5%
honey	68 g (3¼ tablespoons)	30%
starter (from above)	462 g (2⅓ cups)	204%
TOTAL	**1,220 g**	**539%**

DAY 1: BUILD STARTER. Measure both flours and set aside. Combine the water, starter, and flours in a container large enough to allow the mixture to double in volume. Stir, cover, and set aside at cool room temperature (50° to 65°F) to rest overnight.

DAY 2: MIX DOUGH. Measure both flours and set aside. Toast the sunflower seeds and pumpkin seeds in a large dry skillet over medium heat until fragrant, 1 to 2 minutes, shaking the pan a few times to prevent burning. Spread out on a sheet pan to cool. Preheat the oven to 450°F. Add the water, flours, salt, honey, and seeds to the starter. Stir well and leave to rest at room temperature (65° to 75°F) for 30 minutes. This is a very wet, weak dough. It should feel somewhat like wet cement.

BAKE. Butter a 9 by 5-inch loaf pan. Pour the batter into the pan, then smooth the top with a wet spatula. Generously

CONTINUED

dust the top with flour and leave to rest at warm room temperature (75° to 85°F) for 30 minutes.

Use a wet blade to score the top with a Z-pattern, then bake for 25 minutes. Rotate for even browning and bake for 25 minutes more. The crust should be quite dark, almost charred, and dry looking; if it's not there yet, bake for an additional 10 minutes. Remove the loaf from the oven, depan, and cool on a rack. Let the bread cool completely, for at least 6 hours, before eating because the interior of this bread needs time to firm up.

The bread will keep in a paper bag, bread box, or cupboard at room temperature for 5 to 6 days.

ALL RYE

MAKES 1 PAN LOAF,
12 BY 4 INCHES

Day 1 → 5 minutes
active time with an
overnight rest

Day 2 → 10 minutes
active time over 3 hours

This bread is a great example of pure rye flavor (100% whole rye, no caraway, no wheat). It's dense and moist, and really shows off the grain's deep, dark flavors. A little honey makes the perfect complement, balancing the sour taste in the bread. Try not to slice it on the first day. Let it sit for a day so the crumb can firm up a bit. You often see these rectangular pan loaves sliced super thin into small squares and topped with crème fraîche and smoked fish or pickles. —CKM

whole-grain rye flour	558 g (5½ cups)	100%
water	469 g (2 cups)	84%
ripe rye Sourdough Starter (page 147)	134 g (⅔ cup)	24%
salt	11 g (1¾ teaspoons)	2%
honey	28 g (1⅓ tablespoons)	5%
TOTAL	**1,200 g**	**215%**

DAY 1: MIX. In the evening, measure the flour and set aside. Stir together the water, starter, flour, salt, and honey in a large mixing bowl. Make sure everything is thoroughly mixed. The dough should be sticky and thick like cement. Cover with a tea towel and leave at cool room temperature (50° to 65°F) to rest overnight.

DAY 2: BAKE. In the morning, the dough should be aerated and looser. Give it a stir and leave it covered at room temperature (65° to 75°F) for 1 hour.

Butter a 12 by 4-inch loaf pan and scrape the dough into the pan. Smooth the surface down with a damp hand, generously dust the top with flour, and let rest at room temperature for 1 hour.

Preheat the oven to 450°F. Score the loaf with a wet blade in a double *X* pattern (one *X* on top of the other), then load into the oven and cover it with a sheet pan.

Bake for 30 minutes. Remove the sheet pan, rotate the loaf for even browning, and bake until it is nicely singed along the raised edges, about 30 minutes more. Remove the loaf from the oven and depan it immediately onto a rack to cool. Leave to rest for at least 12 hours to give the crumb time to firm up. Do not cut the loaf until the next day.

Once cut, this bread will keep in a paper bag, bread box, or cupboard at room temperature for 5 to 6 days.

OPTION

You could use a regular 9 by 5-inch loaf pan here if you like. Or, if you have a lidded pain de mie or Pullman pan, you can bake the loaf in that pan with the lid in place and skip the sheet pan cover.

CHOCOLATE RYE SOURDOUGH

MAKES 2 SMALL BOULES, ABOUT 6-INCH DIAMETER

Day 1 → 45 minutes active time over 2½ hours with an overnight rest

Day 2 → 10 minutes active time over 1½ hours

This recipe is adapted from my dear friend Chris DiPiazza's version. Chris let me rent out his Philadelphia bakery, Mighty Bread Company, during my first market season. Ursa never would have gotten going without him. Good man, good bread. —CKM

bolted hard wheat flour	305 g (2¼ cups)	75%
whole-grain rye flour	41 g (⅓ cup)	10%
whole-grain hard wheat flour	61 g (¾ cup)	15%
water	313 g (1⅓ cups)	77%
ripe rye Sourdough Starter (page 147)	88 g (⅓ cup)	22%
chocolate chips, semisweet or dark	81 g (½ cup)	20%
natural cocoa powder	16 g (2¾ tablespoons)	4%
honey	81 g (3½ tablespoons)	20%
vanilla extract	4 g (1 teaspoon)	1%
salt	10 g (1½ teaspoons)	2.5%
TOTAL	**1,000 g**	**246.5%**

DAY 1: MIX. Measure all the flours and set aside. Combine the water, starter, and flours in a large mixing bowl. Mix with clean hands just until it comes together in a shaggy mass. Cover with a tea towel and let rest at room temperature (65° to 75°F) for 20 minutes.

Meanwhile, combine the chocolate chips, cocoa powder, honey, and vanilla in a small bowl and stir into a thick paste.

After the 20-minute rest, add the salt to the dough and mix by hand in the bowl for a few minutes, alternately breaking the dough up and folding it back onto itself. At this point, the dough will still look shaggy and feel sticky and weak. Get as much dough from your hands back into the bowl as possible, scraping down your hands and the bowl. Cover the bowl with a tea towel and leave to rest for another 20 minutes. After this rest, mix in the cocoa powder mixture until all the dough is brown with no lighter streaks. It will take a few minutes of hand mixing to get everything evenly combined. When everything is incorporated, cover again and rest for 20 minutes. Give the dough a four-fold (see page 28), then let rest

for 90 minutes more, giving the dough two more four-folds at 30-minute intervals.

SHAPE. Drizzle a little water on your countertop and spread it around so the surface is wet but not puddled. Flour two medium round bannetons or bowls lined with tea towels. Turn the dough out onto the damp countertop and divide it in half. Shape the dough into boules (see page 49): for each piece, lift and fold all four sides in toward the center, then roll the dough over so it is seam-side down. Now, roll the dough in a circle on your countertop, cupping your hands around the dough and applying some pressure to increase the surface tension all around it as you shape it into a nice taut ball.

Flour the outside of the loaves, slip your hand beneath each loaf, then lift it up and invert it seam-side-up in the floured banneton, peeling your hand from the dough. Place the filled bannetons in plastic grocery bags or loosely cover with plastic

CONTINUED

wrap or beeswax wrap, then move the covered loaves to the refrigerator to rest overnight.

DAY 2: BAKE. The next morning, place a large baking stone and hotel pan (see page 62) on the highest rack in the oven they will fit on. Preheat the oven to 425°F. Check the loaves. They should have risen somewhat, about 50% larger than their size right after shaping. If they have not, pull them to room temperature and let them rise before baking. If they have risen nicely, leave them in the fridge until the oven is ready.

When ready to bake, cut a sheet of parchment paper that will fit over the back side of a half sheet pan to use as a peel. Have two towels or hot pads, a spray bottle of water, and a razor within reach.

Turn the loaves out onto the parchment paper, then quickly score each one with a cross or *X* all the way across the dough, cutting about ½ inch deep. Quickly but carefully open your oven, pull the rack that you are baking on partway out, and move the hot hotel pan to the stovetop. Slide the loaves and parchment paper onto the stone and cover with the hotel pan, spraying water into the pan before setting it onto the stone to trap steam.

Bake for 15 minutes. Then remove the hot hotel pan and rotate the loaves for even browning. Bake, uncovered, until the raised edges along the score marks are dark brown, another 10 to 15 minutes. Remove to racks to cool. Try not to dig into the bread until it is cool.

Wrap the loaves in paper bags or keep in a bread box, cupboard, or other cool, draft-free place. These loaves are best eaten within about 4 days.

APRICOT PECAN COURONNE

MAKES 4 RING-SHAPED
LOAVES, ABOUT
7-INCH DIAMETER

30 minutes active time
over 9 hours

People go apeshit for a fruit-and-nut loaf. Trust me. I used to make an apricot pecan demi-baguette that was great, but I thought it was ugly. Then at Bellegarde Bakery in New Orleans, I noticed a similar fruit-and-nut loaf on their shelves. But theirs was shaped in a ring and was called a couronne, from the French word that means "crown." I stole that idea and started shaping my apricot pan bread in a couronne. It's a better shape because this bread is dense and flavorful, and the ring allows you to cut tiny slices, perfect for shingling on a cheeseboard or snacking on with a swipe of butter and a drizzle of honey. This bread also makes great energy food to pack on a hike. It has sweetness, nuttiness, and some extra protein. For this dough, I like to use a 50/50 blend of bolted Redeemer flour (a hard red winter wheat) and whole-grain red spring wheat. The spring wheat has good protein, but it takes some time to hydrate, so I mix it with water and let it hydrate before mixing it into the rest of the dough. —CKM

whole-grain hard wheat flour	317 g (2⅔ cups)	50%
bolted hard wheat flour	317 g (2½ cups)	50%
water 1	317 g (1⅓ cups)	50%
water 2	247 g (1 cup)	39%
ripe whole-wheat Sourdough Starter (page 147)	127 g (⅔ cup)	20%
salt	17 g (2¾ teaspoons)	2.7%
pecan pieces	114 g (1 cup)	18%
whole dried apricots	114 g (¾ cup)	18%
canola oil	32 g (2⅓ tablespoons)	5%
TOTAL	**1,602 g**	**252.7%**

MIX. Measure both flours separately and set aside. Mix the whole-grain wheat flour with water 1 in a large mixing bowl in the morning when you build your starter. Cover and let sit for about 3 hours.

To the whole-grain mixture, add water 2, the starter, bolted wheat flour, and salt. With clean hands, mix until it comes together in a shaggy mass, then mix it in the bowl for a few minutes more, alternately breaking the dough up and folding it back onto itself. At this point, the dough will look shaggy and feel sticky and weak. Get as much dough from your hands back into the bowl as possible, scraping down your

hands and the bowl. Cover the bowl with a tea towel and leave to rise at room temperature (65° to 75°F) for 1½ hours, giving the dough a four-fold (see page 28) every 30 minutes.

Meanwhile, toast the pecan pieces in a dry sauté pan over medium heat until lightly browned and fragrant, 3 to 4 minutes, shaking the pan now and then for even browning. Remove to a bowl and let cool. Dice the apricots into ½-inch pieces. Before the third and final fold of the dough, add the pecans, apricots, and oil and mix by hand until evenly distributed. Cover and leave to rest for a final 45 minutes.

CONTINUED

PRESHAPE. Drizzle a little water on your countertop and spread it around so the surface is wet but not puddled. Turn the dough out onto the countertop and divide into four 400-gram pieces. Give each piece some shape by loosely rolling the dough over. Cover and let rest for 10 minutes.

SHAPE. Wet your hands, then shape each piece into a rough ball. To create the couronne shape, dig your fingers into the center of a ball and make a hole in the center. Then enlarge the hole with your hands all around the center circle to make a giant ring about 7 inches in diameter with a 3-inch ring in the center. Repeat with the remaining dough.

Cut two sheets of parchment paper that will fit over the back sides of two half sheet pans to use as peels. Transfer two loaves to each parchment–paper-lined peel, cover with tea towels, and leave to rise at room temperature for 3 hours. Alternatively, you can wrap the dough loosely in plastic wrap and refrigerate it for up to 18 hours. In that case, remove it from the fridge about an hour before baking.

BAKE. When ready to bake, place a large baking stone and hotel pan (see page 62) on the highest rack in the oven they will fit on. Preheat the oven to 450°F. Have two towels or hot pads, a spray bottle of water, and a razor within reach.

Quickly but carefully open your oven, pull the rack that you are baking on partway out, and move the hot hotel pan to the stovetop. Score one set of loaves with four quick slashes on top of the ring to make a disconnected square (leave the remaining loaves in the fridge). Then slide that set of loaves and parchment paper onto the stone, and cover with the hotel pan, spraying water into the pan before setting it onto the stone to trap steam.

Bake for 15 minutes. Then remove the hot hotel pan and rotate the loaves for even browning. Bake, uncovered, until the raised edges along the score marks are dark brown, another 10 to 15 minutes. Remove to racks to cool. Return the hotel pan to the oven and let the oven recover its heat for 10 minutes. Then repeat scoring and baking the remaining loaves.

Store in a paper bag, bread box, or cupboard at room temperature for up to 5 days. Freezing will prolong shelf life up to 1 month.

HORSE BREAD

MAKES 1 PAN LOAF,
9 BY 5 INCHES

Day 1 → 10 minutes
active time over 1 hour
with an overnight cooling

Day 2 → 15 minutes
active time over 8 hours

Seldom talked about these days, horse bread used to be common enough food for peasants and horses alike. It's a hearty bread, often including legumes, but here I've opted for malted barley to mimic that pop of flavor while adding some mellow sweetness along with it. If you don't know malted barley, it's used all the time in the brewing industry, and you can buy it at brewery supply shops or online. I've also chosen to put this dough into a pan rather than bake the bread in its traditional free-form format. —CKM

SOAKER

malted barley	92 g (⅔ cup)	100%
water	710 g (3 cups)	772%
TOTAL	**802 g**	**872%**

DOUGH

whole-grain hard wheat flour	514 g (4¼ cups)	70%
whole-grain rye flour	154 g (1½ cups)	30%
water	411 g (1¾ cups)	62%
ripe rye Sourdough Starter (page 147)	103 g (½ cup)	15%
cornmeal	41 g (¼ cup)	2%
soaker (from above)	190 g (1¼ cups)	28%
molasses	26 g (1¼ tablespoons)	4%
salt	13 g (2⅛ teaspoons)	2%
TOTAL	**1,452 g**	**213%**

DAY 1: MAKE SOAKER. Combine the malted barley and water in a medium saucepan. Bring to a boil over high heat, then remove from the heat and leave to cool overnight.

DAY 2: MIX DOUGH. Measure both flours and set aside. Combine the water, starter, and flours in a large mixing bowl. With clean hands, mix until it comes together in a shaggy mass, then mix it in the bowl for 3 to 5 minutes more, alternately breaking the dough up and folding it back onto itself. At this point, the dough will still look shaggy and feel sticky and weak. Get as much dough from your hands back into the bowl as possible, scraping down your hands and the bowl. Cover with a tea towel and leave at room temperature (65° to 75°F) to rest for 30 minutes.

Toast the cornmeal in a dry sauté pan over medium heat until lightly browned and fragrant, 1 to 2 minutes, shaking the pan to prevent scorching. Remove from the heat and leave to cool.

Drain off the liquid from the soaker. Add the toasted cornmeal, soaker, molasses, and salt to the dough and mix again by hand, breaking up the dough and folding it onto itself a few times. Cover and leave to rest for 1½ hours, giving the dough a four-fold (see page 28) every 30 minutes. The dough will be stiff. Just get in there and stretch and fold it.

SHAPE. Grease a 9 by 5-inch loaf pan and scrape in the dough. Smooth the top with a wet hand. Place the filled loaf pan in a plastic grocery bag or loosely cover with plastic wrap or beeswax wrap and leave at room temperature for 5 hours.

BAKE. Preheat the oven to 450°F with a rack positioned in the middle and a metal bowl or pan on a bottom rack (you'll add water to it later).

Score the top of the loaf in a sort of diamond-shaped tic-tac-toe pattern: twice across at a 45-degree angle, then twice more perpendicular to the first cuts (see "Batard four score or diamond," page 60).

Pour water into the hot metal bowl to presteam the oven. Load the pan into the oven and bake for 30 minutes, then rotate the pan for even browning, and bake until the bread is nicely browned and singed along the score marks, an additional 20 minutes. Remove from the oven and depan immediately onto a rack to cool. Let this bread cool completely or overnight before cutting. The crumb will still be setting up while it's warm.

The bread will keep in a paper bag, bread box, or cupboard at room temperature for 5 to 6 days.

OPTION

If you like, you can use some of the liquid from the malted barley soaker to replace up to 50% of the water called for in the dough. If you use more than that, the dough's enzymatic activity will be off the charts.

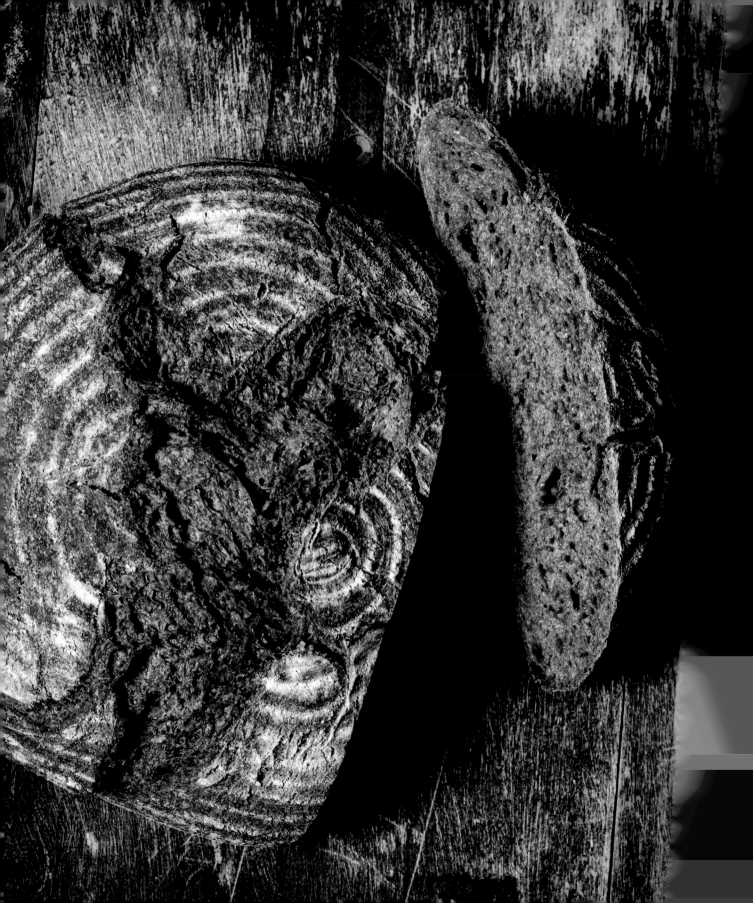

PUMPERNICKEL

MAKES 2 BOULES, ABOUT
6-INCH DIAMETER

30 minutes active time
over 5½ hours

In serious baking circles, American-style pumpernickel is not held in very high regard. Traditional pumpernickel from northern and central Europe is a high-percentage rye bread baked low and slow so the sugars caramelize all the way through the bread. But the American version often includes less rye flour and a host of hacks like coffee, cocoa, and/or caramel coloring to shortcut the low and slow baking while approximating the traditional color and flavor. Unfortunately, those flavors are now what most Americans associate with pumpernickel bread. This recipe is a modern artisan take on American pumpernickel. It's got a fair amount of rye, and we included a little bit of cocoa powder and molasses to tag the flavors that Americans are used to. —CKM

bolted hard wheat flour	463 g (3⅔ cups)	70%
whole-grain rye flour	198 g (2 cups)	30%
water	476 g (2 cups)	72%
ripe rye Sourdough Starter (page 147)	264 g (1⅓ cups)	40%
molasses	46 g (2⅛ tablespoons)	7%
natural cocoa powder	26 g (⅓ cup)	4%
salt	15 g (2½ teaspoons)	2.3%
caraway seeds	11 g (3¾ teaspoons)	1.7%
TOTAL	**1,499 g**	**227%**

MIX. Measure both flours and set aside. Combine the water, starter, flours, molasses, and cocoa powder in the bowl of a stand mixer. Mix with the dough hook on low speed until everything is incorporated, 1 to 2 minutes. Cover with a tea towel and let rest for 15 minutes. Then add the salt and caraway seeds and mix on low speed for 3 minutes. Switch to medium speed and mix until the dough clings to the hook and clears the sides of the bowl, another 3 minutes or so.

Transfer the dough to an oiled container, cover, and leave to rest at room temperature (65° to 75°F) for 1½ hours, giving the dough a four-fold (see page 28) halfway through that time.

SHAPE. Generously flour two medium round bannetons or bowls lined with tea towels. Drizzle a little water on your countertop and spread it around so the surface is wet but not puddled. Then turn the dough out and use a bench knife to cut it into two 750-gram pieces. Shape the dough into two boules (see page 49): for each piece, lift and fold all four sides in toward the center, then roll the dough over so it is seam-side down. Now, roll the dough in a circle on your countertop, cupping your hands around the dough and applying some pressure to increase the surface tension all around it as you shape it into a nice taut ball. Flour the seam side of the loaves generously, then place them seam-side down in the floured bannetons. The seam will become a natural opening on the top of the loaf when baked. Place the filled bannetons in plastic grocery bags or loosely cover with plastic wrap or beeswax wrap and leave at room temperature for 2 hours.

CONTINUED

BAKE. Place a large baking stone and hotel pan (see page 62) on the highest rack in the oven they will fit on. Preheat the oven to 475°F. Have two towels or hot pads and a spray bottle of water within reach.

Quickly but carefully open your oven, pull the rack that you are baking on partway out, and move the hot hotel pan to the stovetop. Invert the loaves onto the stone and cover with the hotel pan, spraying water into the pan before setting it onto the stone to trap steam. Close the oven and bake for 20 minutes. Then remove the hot hotel pan and rotate the loaves for even browning. Bake, uncovered, until the raised edges on top of the loaves are dark brown to black, another 10 minutes or so. Remove to a rack to cool.

Pumpernickel can be kept in a paper bag, bread box, or cupboard at room temperature for 5 to 6 days.

DELI RYE

Here's another American-style bread but with an artisan baker's touch. You have to understand that rye breads have long, deep roots in Europe, and when European bakers brought their breads to America, the breads changed over time. The rye breads were made with less and less rye and more and more wheat because lighter, whiter breads made with wheat flour were more in vogue then. This recipe will give you what most Americans think of when they think of rye bread, the sandwich staple of Jewish delicatessens all over the country. It's soft yet firm enough to hold up to juicy sandwich fillings. And you'll taste the unmistakable flavor of caraway. This bread is the reason people think the flavor of caraway is the flavor of rye. For a real taste of rye itself, try the All Rye (page 186). —CKM

bolted hard wheat flour	554 g (4½ cups)	70%
bolted rye flour	238 g (2⅓ cups)	30%
water	554 g (2⅓ cups)	70%
ripe rye Sourdough Starter (page 147)	63 g (⅓ cup)	8%
dry yeast	6 g (2 teaspoons)	0.75%
honey	55 g (2⅔ tablespoons)	7%
salt	17 g (2¾ teaspoons)	2.2%
caraway seeds	12 g (4¼ teaspoons)	1.5%
TOTAL	**1,499 g**	**189.45%**

MIX. Measure both flours and set aside. Combine the water, starter, yeast, flours, and honey in the bowl of a stand mixer. Mix with the dough hook on low speed for 3 minutes. Cover with a tea towel and let rest at room temperature (65° to 75°F) for 15 minutes. Add the salt and caraway seeds and mix on low speed for 3 minutes. Switch to medium speed and mix until the dough clings to the hook and clears the sides of the bowl, about 3 minutes more. Cover and leave to rest at room temperature for 1½ hours, giving the dough two four-folds (see page 28) at 30-minute intervals. This dough behaves more like a yeast bread than a sourdough: it rises fairly quickly because of the dry yeast in the mix.

SHAPE. Place a large baking stone and hotel pan (see page 62) on the highest rack in the oven they will fit on. Preheat the oven to 425°F. Cut a sheet of parchment paper that will fit over the back side of a half sheet pan to use as a peel.

Drizzle a little water on your countertop and spread it around so the surface is wet but not puddled. Turn the dough out onto the countertop and divide it into two 750-gram pieces. Shape the pieces into batards (see page 50): for each piece, position the loaf like a rectangle with sides left and right. Gently stretch and fold the left and right sides in toward the

CONTINUED

center. Then lift and fold the bottom side up, pressing it in about a third of the way up the loaf, and continue rolling away from you, tucking the dough into itself as you roll, increasing the surface tension on the dough as you shape it into a taut blunt log. Seal the seam, pressing along it, and smooth the ends as necessary. Place the loaves on the parchment paper, cover with a tea towel, and leave to rise for 30 minutes.

BAKE. Have two towels or hot pads, a spray bottle of water, and a razor within reach.

Dust the tops of the loaves with flour and brush off any excess. Score the loaves (I like four or five parallel lines on a slight angle across the loaves). Then quickly but carefully

open your oven, pull the rack that you are baking on partway out, and move the hot hotel pan to the stovetop. Slide the scored loaves and parchment paper onto the stone. Cover with the hotel pan, spraying water into the pan before setting it onto the stone to trap steam.

Bake for 20 minutes. Then remove the hot hotel pan, rotate the loaves for even browning, and bake until the crust is medium brown, another 10 minutes. Remove the loaves to racks to cool.

This bread will keep in a paper bag, bread box, or cupboard at room temperature for about 5 days. You can also freeze it for up to 2 months

HUNDO PAN LOAF

Day 1 → 20 minutes
active time over 3½ hours
with an overnight rest

Day 2 → 10 minutes
active time over 1½ hours

Hundo is baker lingo for breads made with 100% whole-grain flour. We have a handful of hundos in this book, including the Seeded Schwarzbrot (page 183), All Rye (page 186), and 100% Sonora Slab (page 161). This one is a spelt pan loaf that gets some tang from the sourdough but is still tender and structured enough to make great toast and sandwiches. Spelt embodies the greatest things about whole-wheat flour: it has sweet and bright flavors with just a little spicy edge. Some wheats have bran that becomes texturally unpleasant or too sharp tasting when you use the whole grain. But spelt bran is tender and agreeable. When you get a grain that smells particularly good (which you can observe if you mill the grain yourself), you just want to showcase it by using 100% of that flour in the bread. —CKM

whole-grain spelt flour	382 g (3⅛ cups)	100%
water	310 g (1⅓ cups)	81%
ripe spelt Sourdough Starter (page 147)	76 g (⅓ cup)	20%
salt	9 g (1½ teaspoons)	2.4%
canola oil (see Options)	11 g (2½ teaspoons)	3%
honey	11 g (1½ teaspoons)	3%
TOTAL	**799 g**	**209.4%**

DAY 1: MIX. Combine the flour and water by hand in a large mixing bowl, then cover with a tea towel and leave to rest at room temperature (65° to 75°F) for 30 minutes. Add the starter, salt, oil, and honey to the bowl and hand-mix for about 3 minutes, alternately breaking the dough up and folding it back onto itself. At this point, the dough will look loose and feel sticky and weak. Get as much dough from your hands back into the bowl as possible, scraping down your hands and the bowl. Cover and leave to rest for 30 minutes. Hand-mix again, this time for about 2 minutes. By now, the dough should feel more taut. Then cover and leave to rise at room temperature for 2 hours, giving the dough a four-fold (see page 28) every 30 minutes.

SHAPE. By now, the dough should show some signs of fermentation (such as a slight increase in volume), but it won't be fully aerated. Grease a 9 by 5-inch loaf pan, then drizzle a little water on your countertop and spread it around so the

surface is wet but not puddled. Turn the dough out onto the countertop and press the dough out gently. Fold the left and right sides in toward the center, then fold the bottom side up, and continue rolling the loaf up to the top. Set the loaf seam-side down in the pan. Place the pan in a plastic grocery bag or loosely cover with plastic wrap or beeswax wrap and leave at cool room temperature (50° to 65°F) for 30 minutes. After 30 minutes, move the covered loaf to the refrigerator to rest overnight.

DAY 2: BAKE. Preheat the oven to 400°F with a rack positioned in the middle and no rack directly above it, so there is space for the risen loaf. Place a metal bowl or pan on a lower rack (you'll add water to it later). Once the oven is ready, pull the loaf from the fridge. Now, depending on some factors, like the health of your starter and the temperature of your fridge, your loaf could be tall and puffy or pretty close to its original size. Either one can work, but if your loaf is still pretty small, I would score the top to give it a better chance to spring fully, whereas I would leave a puffy loaf alone. You make the call, based on what you observe in your dough.

Pour water into the metal bowl on the lower rack to humidify the oven. Load the pan onto the middle rack, bake for 20 minutes, then rotate the pan for even browning. At this point, the loaf should be fully sprung and the crust set, but it will probably be light in color. If it has already taken on quite a bit of color, tent it with aluminum foil. Otherwise, leave it uncovered, and bake until the crust is deep brown, an additional 20 minutes or so.

Pull the loaf from the oven, depan it immediately, and set it on a rack to cool. Brush the top of the loaf with oil or butter to soften the crust, then allow it to cool completely before cutting. If cut warm, the crumb of this bread will still be pasty.

The bread will keep in a paper bag, bread box, or cupboard at room temperature for 5 to 6 days.

OPTIONS

For the fat here (in the dough, for greasing pans, for brushing the crust), we use local expeller-pressed, non-GMO canola oil. Almost any neutral-tasting oil would work. Another good choice would be melted butter. A super-peppery olive oil would not be a good choice.

If you want to try a different flour other than spelt, Rouge de Bordeaux is a beautiful, flavorful heirloom wheat. The aroma is amazing.

You could make this a free-form loaf instead of baking it in a pan. In that case, roll a nice tight batard (see page 50) and proof it in a medium oval banneton instead of in a loaf pan. Turn the loaf out onto the hot stone, score it twice down the center, then bake it under a hotel pan with some steam. This is the same baking method described in the Pane di Genzano (page 155).

MALTED GRAIN SOURDOUGH

MAKES 2 BATARDS,
ABOUT 9 BY 5 INCHES

Day 1 → 10 minutes
active time with an
overnight rest

Day 2 → 45 minutes
active time over 8 hours

This bread includes soaked malted grains, which add soft, plump pops of sweet flavor as you chew. On the crust, the malted grains dry and crisp, a nice contrast to the moist, tender crumb. Be aware that this bread is never going to have a crazy-strong gluten structure because there is so much enzymatic activity from the malted grains that weakens the dough. When you mix and ferment the dough, you're trying to develop the gluten to its maximum without going so far that it weakens and fails to trap the expanding gases during the bake. —CKM

STARTER

bolted hard wheat flour	50 g (6½ tablespoons)	100%
water	33 g (2¼ tablespoons)	66%
ripe rye Sourdough Starter (page 147)	17 g (1⅓ tablespoons)	33%
TOTAL	**100 g**	**199%**

SOAKER

water	1,000 g (4¼ cups)	400%
malted wheat, rye, or hull-less barley (see Option)	250 g (1⅓ cups)	100%
TOTAL	**1,250 g**	**500%**

DOUGH

bolted hard wheat flour	633 g (5⅛ cups)	100%
soaker (from above)	443 g (2 cups)	70%
water	285 g (1¼ cups)	45%
malt liquid (from soaker, above)	127 g (½ cup)	20%
starter (from above)	63 g (⅓ cup)	10%
salt	17 g (2¾ teaspoons)	2.7%
barley malt syrup	32 g (1½ tablespoons)	5%
TOTAL	**1,600 g**	**252.7%**

wheat bran, cornmeal, or semolina for dusting

DAY 1: BUILD STARTER. In the evening, measure the flour and set aside. Combine the water, starter, and flour in a bowl, then cover and leave at cool room temperature (50° to 65°F) to rest overnight. This dough uses a small amount of starter.

That's because the high amount of malted grain triggers a ton of enzymatic activity in the dough, giving the sourdough yeast plenty of food and raising the dough more quickly.

MAKE SOAKER. In the evening, bring the water to a boil in a medium saucepan. Stir in the malted grain and remove from the heat. Partially cover and leave at room temperature (65° to 75°F) to rest overnight.

DAY 2: MIX DOUGH. In the morning, measure the flour and set aside. Drain off the liquid from the soaker, reserving 127 grams of the malt liquid for the dough.

Combine the water, reserved malt liquid, starter, flour, salt, malt syrup, and soaker in a large mixing bowl. With clean hands, mix until it comes together in a shaggy mass, then continue to mix it in the bowl for a few minutes more, alternately breaking the dough up and folding it back onto itself. At this point, the dough will still look shaggy and feel sticky and weak. Get as much dough from your hands back into the bowl as possible, scraping down your hands and the bowl. Cover the bowl with a tea towel and leave to rise at warm room temperature (75° to 85°F) for 1 hour.

Notice that the inclusions (the soaked malted grains) are added early rather than later in the mix. That's because the malted grain pieces are small, hydrated, and fermentable, so they don't get in the way of developing your gluten structure.

Hand-mix again for a few minutes, this time pinching the dough into small pieces, then folding the pieces back into the mass of dough. The gluten should have tightened and developed significantly from the hour's rest. Repeat the pinching and folding step. After that, you should see additional tightening of the gluten, although the dough will still be weak, sticky, and prone to tearing. Cover the bowl and leave to rest for 1 hour more.

By this point, the dough should be inflating with fermentation gases. Give it a less aggressive four-fold (see page 28), then cover and let rest for 3 hours, giving it increasingly gentle four-folds every hour. After the fourth and final fold, cover and leave the dough to rest for 30 minutes. At that point, the dough should be well risen and elastic.

SHAPE. Drizzle a little water on your countertop and spread it around so the surface is wet but not puddled. Turn the dough out onto the countertop. It will still be somewhat delicate. Divide the dough in half and gently shape into batards (see page 50).

Flour two medium oval bannetons or bowls lined with tea towels (you'll get round loaves if using the latter). Thoroughly flour the top of each loaf, then slip your hand beneath a loaf and invert it into the banneton, peeling your hand from the loaf. Cover the bannetons with a tea towel and leave at warm room temperature until the loaves have risen to 30 to 40% of their original size, about 2 hours.

BAKE. Place a large baking stone and hotel pan (see page 62) on the highest rack in the oven they will fit on. Preheat the oven to 450°F. Have two towels or hot pads, a spray bottle of water, and a razor within reach.

Once the final rise is complete, dust the bottoms of the loaves with wheat bran to prevent sticking. Quickly but carefully open your oven, pull the rack that you are baking on partway out, and move the hot hotel pan to the stovetop. Swiftly turn each loaf out onto the stone and score the tops with a single slash from end to end. Cover with the hotel pan, spraying water into the pan before setting it onto the stone to trap steam.

Bake for 20 minutes. Then remove the hot hotel pan and rotate the loaves for even browning. Bake, uncovered, until the raised edges along the score marks are dark brown, another 10 minutes. Remove to a rack to cool. Avoid cutting into the loaves until completely cool. Overnight cooling is fine.

Store in a paper bag, bread box, or cupboard at room temperature, where it will keep for about 1 week.

OPTION

For the soaker, use any hull-less malted grain you like, such as wheat, rye, or hull-less barley. Check your local home brew supply shop or the Craft Maltsters Guild website for a directory of small-batch maltsters in your area.

SOURDOUGH BRIOCHE

MAKES 2 PAN LOAVES,
9 BY 5 INCHES

Day 1 → 20 minutes
active time over 6½ hours,
with an overnight rest

Day 2 → 10 minutes
active time over 1½ hours

When Jim Lahey of New York City's Sullivan Street Bakery came to Vetri for an event, I was taken by his oddball humor, especially paired with his exacting standards. It was a real treat to spend time with him, and see how he made his bread. For this brioche, I use freshly milled, high-extraction flour, but otherwise this is very close to Jim's recipe. Making this bread will give you a sense of the finicky, time-consuming nature of highly enriched, naturally leavened doughs. It's so enriched that the fermentation happens extremely slowly. The approximate fermentation time depends entirely on the temperature of your environment and your dough. When it comes out right, you'll know why it's so worthwhile. This brioche is lighter, tangier, and more complex tasting than traditional Brioche (page 115). Have fun. —CKM

bolted hard wheat flour	539 g (4⅓ cups)	100%
water	199 g (¾ cup)	37%
unsalted butter	226 g (1 cup)	42%
sugar	178 g (1 cup)	33%
ripe bolted wheat Sourdough Starter (page 147)	248 g (1¼ cups)	46%
salt	11 g (2 teaspoons)	2%
eggs	199 g (¾ cup, about 4 medium)	37%
TOTAL	**1,600 g**	**297%**

egg for egg wash	
pinch of salt for egg wash	

DAY 1: MIX. Start this one in the morning. This is one of the most intense mixes in the book. To prevent your stand mixer from scooting off the countertop, dampen a towel and put the mixer on top of it. Measure the flour and set aside. Then combine the water and butter in a medium saucepan and warm over low heat until the butter melts.

Meanwhile, put the sugar in the mixer bowl. Once the butter is melted, pour the buttery water into the mixer bowl and mix with the paddle attachment on low speed, until the sugar dissolves and the mixture cools down to just warmer than room temperature, 4 to 6 minutes. Check the temperature by touching the outside of the bowl near its base. When it feels just slightly warm, turn the mixer off and add the starter, flour, salt, and eggs. Resume mixing with the paddle on low speed until all of the ingredients are incorporated. Switch to medium speed and mix until the dough comes together and clears the sides of the bowl. Depending on your mixer, this could take anywhere from 10 to 25 minutes. At first, the dough will seem too wet, and it will remain weak and batterlike for quite some time. Keep mixing until

CONTINUED

the dough clings to the paddle instead of to the sides of the bowl. After 8 to 10 minutes, you will see the beginning of gluten development, as a small amount of dough starts holding on to the paddle. From then on, it should slowly and steadily start clinging more, until the dough is fully wrapped around the paddle. If some of the dough starts climbing too high on the paddle before the mix is finished, stop the mixer, scrape down the bowl and paddle, and resume mixing.

Once the mix is finished and the dough clings to the hook and clears the sides of the bowl, transfer the dough to an oiled container, cover tightly, and let rise at warm room temperature (75° to 85°F) until nearly doubled in size, 4 to 8 hours. Within reason, this is a warmer-is-better situation. With all of the enrichments in the dough, it will move very slowly, so observe the current state of the dough, particularly its size. If it's in a plastic-covered bowl, some people like to trace the outline of the dough ball onto the plastic as a reminder of its original size. Others use a clear container and mark the side.

SHAPE. Once the dough has approximately doubled in size, grease two 9 by 5-inch loaf pans. Turn the dough out onto a floured countertop and gently pat it down. Divide the dough in half, so you have two sorta-kinda rectangular pieces. Position the rectangles with the short sides left and right. For each loaf, gently stretch and fold the left and right sides in toward the center. Then pat the dough out a bit more and roll the loaf from the bottom side up, tucking the dough into itself as you roll, increasing the surface tension on the dough as you shape it into a blunt log. Avoid tearing the outside of the loaf, since that will lead to an irregular final shape. The loaf should now be approximately the length of the pan. Place the loaves seam-side down in the pans. Cover loosely with plastic wrap so that the final rise will not be constricted and set the covered pans in a cool (about 60°F) place. If you have a cool basement closet, that may be a good spot. Leave to rise overnight for 8 to 12 hours. The loaves are ready to bake when they are doming over the rim of the pan by 1 to 1½ inches.

DAY 2: BAKE. Preheat the oven to 350°F with a rack in the center and enough space for the loaves to rise significantly. Beat the egg with the salt and brush it over the tops of the loaves. Load the pans into the oven and bake for 30 minutes. Then rotate the loaves and tent with aluminum foil if the color is getting too dark. Bake until deep brown, an additional 5 to 10 minutes. Set the loaves in their pans on a rack for a few minutes to cool. Then depan to finish cooling completely. Store in a paper bag, bread box, or cupboard at room temperature for up to 1 week.

SCHIACCIATA CON L'UVA

MAKES 2 ROUNDISH
LOAVES, ABOUT
7-INCH DIAMETER

Day 1 → 5 minutes
active time with an
overnight rest

Day 2 → 40 minutes
active time over 3½ hours

A Tuscan variation on focaccia, schiacciata (ska-CHA-ta) is flatbread topped with flavorings. Here we use grapes (*uva*) as the topping. But grape yeast water is what makes this schiacciata really special. We create a unique starter for this recipe by using grapes to cultivate the yeast that leavens the dough. Just as you can capture yeast with water and flour in sourdough starter, you can capture yeast with water and almost any produce. See the Options for directions on how to make grape yeast water. Basically, you set out grapes and water, provide the yeast with regular feedings and moderately warm temperatures, and you can capture yeast in a jar. It's an amazing experience, and the yeast water allows you to make a naturally leavened bread that isn't super sour. As with a flour-based starter, just give yourself about 10 days to get the grape yeast water going before you begin this recipe. —CKM

STARTER

whole-grain einkorn flour	129 g (1⅛ cups)	75%
bolted hard wheat flour	43 g (⅓ cup)	25%
grape yeast water (see Options)	172 g (¾ cup)	100%
TOTAL	**344 g**	**200%**

DOUGH

bolted hard wheat flour	688 g (5½ cups)	100%
water	344 g (1½ cups)	50%
grape yeast water (see Options)	172 g (¾ cup)	25%
starter (from above)	344 g (1¾ cups)	50%
salt	17 g (2¾ teaspoons)	2.5%
extra-virgin olive oil	34 g (2½ tablespoons)	5%
TOTAL	**1,599 g**	**232.5%**

TOPPINGS

1½ cups grapes, any variety or mix

2 tablespoons fresh thyme leaves

¾ cup extra-virgin olive oil

Maldon sea salt for sprinkling

DAY 1: BUILD STARTER. In the evening, mix both flours and the grape yeast water in a bowl or lidded container with some room for the starter to expand. Cover and leave at room temperature (65° to 75°F) to rest overnight.

DAY 2: MIX DOUGH. In the morning, measure the flour and set aside. Combine the water, grape yeast water, starter, flour, salt, and oil in the bowl of a stand mixer. Mix with the paddle

CONTINUED

attachment on low speed for 3 minutes. Switch to medium speed and mix until the dough clings to the paddle and clears the sides of the bowl, another 5 minutes or so. Transfer the dough to an oiled bowl, cover with a tea towel, and leave to rest at room temperature for 2 hours, giving it a four-fold (see page 28) after 1 hour.

PREP TOPPING. Meanwhile, halve the grapes and toss with the thyme and oil in a bowl. Leave to marinate at room temperature until you bake the schiacciata.

SHAPE. After 2 hours rest, the dough should be very active. Turn it out onto a well-floured countertop and divide into two pieces. Gently pat and stretch each piece into a rough circle or oval about 6 inches in diameter, with an even thickness of about ¾ inch. Carefully transfer the dough to a large sheet of parchment paper and reshape if necessary. Cover with a tea towel and let rest for about 20 minutes.

BAKE. Place a large baking stone on the middle rack of the oven, and preheat the oven to 500°F. Transfer the loaves and parchment to the back side of a half sheet pan to use as a peel. Pull the grapes from the oil and lay them over the loaves, then press them deep into the dough. As the bread rises in the oven, it will push the toppings up, so you want your toppings well planted. Drizzle with some of the thyme oil and sprinkle with Maldon salt.

Load the schiacciata into the oven by sliding the loaves and parchment paper onto the stone. Bake for 12 minutes, then rotate the loaves for even browning and bake until the crust is medium tan, another 3 to 5 minutes. Transfer to a rack to cool.

Schiacciata is best enjoyed the same day, but it can be kept in a paper bag, bread box, or cupboard at room temperature for a couple days.

OPTIONS

You can make **Yeast Water** from almost any produce. The water will capture the yeast as well as the essence of the produce. You can use the yeast water to leaven the dough and the fresh produce to top your schiacciata. Try blueberries, plums, or tomatoes. Either way, you'll want to use organic produce because fungicides kill yeast. To make grape yeast water for this recipe, put 1 cup of organic grapes into a clear container with a lid, such as a quart Mason jar. Add about 1½ cups of water to the jar and leave it, uncovered, at warm room temperature (75° to 85°F) for 3 days. Then feed it by discarding the grapes and draining off most of the water, leaving about ½ cup, which should have some invisible yeast in it. Add new grapes (about 1 cup) and new water (about 1½ cups) to the saved water. Let the water and grapes sit for another 3 to 4 days. After a week, you should see some bubbles, but the yeast water probably won't be strong enough to bake with yet. After the first week, feed as described every day for another week. After 2 weeks total, you may want to close the lid of the container to avoid attracting flies. By this point, the water should be very fizzy—like soda, and the grapes should start to float, a sign that fermentation has kicked off. The grapes will also be fizzy inside and you can snack on them. Once the water is active and fizzy, you can use the fermented grape yeast water for both the leaven and the dough. The amounts here make 1½ to 2 cups. To keep some of your yeast water going, save a little and feed it every few days with slightly fewer grapes. It is essentially the same process as keeping Sourdough Starter (page 147) but with water and fresh produce instead of water and flour.

If you don't have a baking stone, you can use a cast-iron pan instead, as shown in the photo. Preheat the pan in the oven as directed for the stone, then slide a loaf and parchment paper onto the hot pan. Bake in batches.

10

PASTRY

IT'S NOT EVERY DAY THAT YOU GET AN HONORARY DOCTORATE, ESPECIALLY WHEN YOU ARE NOT MUCH OF AN ACADEMIC. In 1985, I enrolled in Drexel University to major in marketing and finance. Five years later (not four), I graduated with an unimpressive 2.7 GPA. Then I took a left turn into the culinary world, and twenty-four years after that, I got a letter from John Fry, the president of the university, telling me that I was going to be the recipient of an honorary doctorate degree from Drexel.

During a phone call with John, I said, "You do know that I was a less-than-stellar student, right? Are you looking at the right transcripts?!" He chuckled and assured me that this doctorate was not based on grades but rather on the merit of what I had done with my degree since I had graduated. After a very humbling conversation, I was overwhelmed and honored to accept what is truly one of the greatest accomplishments of my life.

213

After receiving the degree and talking with other professors and administrators at Drexel, I got so inspired that I decided it was time to give back to the university. It was time to teach. I resurrected a Master Chef course in the school's Food and Hospitality Management program that had been abandoned years earlier. My first course happened in 2015, and I taught a ten-week winter semester with a four-hour class that met once a week. In class, we covered everything from butchering animals and making beautiful plates of food to culinary history and hosting guest chefs with their cookbooks.

This was right around the time that I had written my first book in the Mastering series, *Mastering Pasta*. At the restaurant, we had just plunged headfirst into buying and milling wheat, and I wanted to feature fresh milling in the class. So, I incorporated a couple weeks of pasta-making instruction and discussed how important it is to use freshly milled flour for the best flavor. The students loved it.

For the following year's course, I decided to take the fresh milling conversation one step further. I asked Drexel to buy a mill. And they did! Claire had just started working with us at Vetri, and with her help, we re-jiggered the entire course and called it the Wheat Lab. We invited guest lecturers like Dr. Stephen Jones (see page 13), the legendary wheat breeder from Washington, and Mark Fischer (see page 30), the owner of Castle Valley Mill, the historic grain mill just outside Philadelphia. Claire taught some classes on bread made with freshly milled flours, and I led some on pasta made with fresh flour. We even made a whole-grain Lemon Durum Cake (facing page) that everyone absolutely loved. After all, a well-rounded chef should be a good pastry chef, too.

By the end of that semester, the Wheat Lab helped send us even deeper into our local grain system. With the help of Castle Valley Mill, we partnered with Whole Foods Market in Philadelphia to produce a local baguette made with freshly milled grains. We also started buying more grains from Castle Valley Mill to use in the Vetri family of restaurants. And eventually, Claire started her own bakery, Ursa. The whole idea of supporting our local grain farmers and mills was catching on, and other Philly restaurateurs and bakeries started buying more local grains and flours.

It's super gratifying to see our culinary community support local farmers, millers, and bakeries. But one thing still nags at me: most pastry chefs still seem to work with refined white flour and nothing else. It's such a shame! There are so many applications where fresh flour really helps pastries taste better. With bread, you're so focused on gluten development to help the bread rise. But with pastry, you don't often need that to happen. You can get the right crumbliness of a cookie or the flakiness of pastry crust using freshly milled and even whole-grain flour. And you get much better flavor! You might think some trickier pastries, like puff pastry, have to be made with white flour, but even our Whole-Grain Rough Puff Pastry (page 229) tastes fantastic made with 100% whole-grain flour.

If there's one message we really want to get across to pastry chefs and home bakers, it's this: try using freshly milled whole-grain flour! Your pastries will taste so much better. Almost all of the recipes in this chapter are made with 100% freshly milled whole-grain flour, from Sonora Graham Crackers (page 216) and Hazelbutter Cookies (page 224) to Taralli (page 233); there's even Whole-Grain Pâte à Choux (page 226).

Here and there we call for some specific wheat flours like durum and spelt, but pastries don't generally require a strong gluten structure, so in most recipes, almost any soft wheat flour will work. If you're a baker who normally works with hard wheats or medium-protein wheats, like spelt or Sonora, work with what you have.

Either way, these doughs come together much more quickly and easily than those in the other chapters. There's no yeast or sourdough, so the leavening comes from baking powder, baking soda, butter, or beaten eggs. There's also no baker's math (percentages) to deal with because pastry chefs don't usually need it for cookies and other pastries. And since they have no fermentation flavors, these pastries really showcase the taste of the flour itself. Pizzelle (page 220) are the perfect vehicle for the sweet and lightly spicy flavors of spelt, while Fried Rye Crackers (page 234) give you a taste of rye's deep notes of caramel and earth. Don't be afraid to take a leap of faith. Using freshly milled flour—especially whole-grain soft wheat flour—is a simple way to improve the taste of every pastry you make. —MV

LEMON DURUM CAKE

MAKES 1 HALF SHEET CAKE,
18 BY 13 INCHES

15 minutes active time
over 1½ hours

I like cake. A lot. The simpler, the better. When we started baking with freshly milled flour, this is one of the first cakes we made. It was the "aha" moment for me. I wasn't convinced that freshly milled whole-grain flour would work well in pastries, but this cake totally rocks (see the photo on page 212). We go back to it all the time because it makes a great base for rustic desserts. Serve it with gelato or whipped cream and fresh berries marinated in some great red wine vinegar such as Barolo wine vinegar. Or go extra-simple with just a dusting of confectioners' sugar. —MV

eggs	300 g (1⅛ cups, about 6 medium)
extra-virgin olive oil	200 g (¾ cup + 2¾ tablespoons)
lemon juice	46 g (3 tablespoons, from 1 large lemon)
sugar	400 g (2 cups)
whole-grain durum flour	282 g (2⅓ cups)
almond flour	60 g (⅔ cup)
baking powder	6 g (1⅓ teaspoons)
salt	4 g (⅔ teaspoon)
black poppy seeds	16 g (5½ teaspoons)
lemon zest	8 g (4 teaspoons, from 1 to 2 medium lemons)
TOTAL	**1,322 g**

MIX. In a large mixing bowl, whisk the eggs, oil, and lemon juice until combined.

In a medium mixing bowl, combine the sugar, durum flour, almond flour, baking powder, salt, poppy seeds, and lemon zest. Add the dry mixture to the wet mixture and stir until thoroughly combined. This cake is whole grain, so it's best to let the batter rest at room temperature (65° to 75°F) for 1 hour to fully hydrate the flour.

BAKE. Meanwhile, preheat the oven to 350°F. Line a half sheet pan with parchment paper and grease the parchment. Pour in the batter, spreading it evenly to the edges with a spatula. Bake for 12 minutes, then rotate the pan and bake for an additional 6 minutes. The cake should be set but very moist.

Cool in the pan, then cut into squares, punch out circles, or cut whatever shapes you like. If you have any left, this cake can be kept in an airtight container at room temperature for 2 to 3 days.

OPTION

The almond flour in this recipe adds moisture to the crumb, but it can be replaced with durum flour in case of nut allergies.

SONORA GRAHAM CRACKERS

**MAKES ABOUT
30 CRACKERS**

**20 minutes active time
over 2¾ hours**

My peak graham-cracker years were the early 1990s in Seattle. My mom worked at a food co-op, and she would give us light lunches consisting of sliced apples, a dollop of peanut butter, and a couple graham crackers. When I developed this recipe, I thought I'd have to qualify things by explaining that this is "my version" of a graham cracker. Then, they came out exactly like commercial graham crackers—but better for you. These are great snacking crackers, perfect for those times when you want a cookie but also want to feel virtuous. They would also be right at home on a cheese board with a well-chosen Cheddar and some crisp apples. —CKM

unsalted butter	113 g (½ cup)
whole-grain Sonora wheat flour	400 g (3⅓ cups)
baking powder	4 g (¾ teaspoon)
baking soda	2 g (½ teaspoon)
salt	10 g (1⅔ teaspoons)
brown sugar	115 g (½ cup)
honey	40 g (2 tablespoons)
whole milk	125 g (½ cup)
TOTAL	**809 g**

MIX. Cube the butter and let it soften in the bowl of a stand mixer for about 30 minutes. In a separate bowl, combine the flour, baking powder, baking soda, and salt.

Add the sugar and honey to the butter and beat on medium-high speed with the paddle attachment until fluffy, 2 to 3 minutes. Switch to medium-low speed and add the dry ingredients alternately with the milk in three additions, mixing just until the dough comes together. Cover and chill the dough thoroughly, about 2 hours.

SHAPE. Preheat the oven to 350°F. Place a Silpat or sheet of parchment paper on a countertop and place the dough on top. Cover with another sheet of parchment paper and roll the dough out to an even ⅛ inch thickness. As necessary, reposition bits of dough and reroll, then square up the edges

with a knife so you have a perfect rectangle of dough. Peel off the top parchment paper, dock the dough all over with a fork or dough docker, then cut/score into 3-inch squares or other shapes, leaving all the dough in place (you bake the entire sheet of dough).

BAKE. Carefully slide the Silpat with the dough onto a half sheet pan and bake just until the crackers lose their sheen and firm up, browning ever so slightly at the edges, 13 to 15 minutes. Cool on the pan. When completely cool, cut the crackers along the score marks.

Remove and store the crackers in an airtight container at room temperature for 4 to 5 days or freeze them for 3 to 4 weeks.

PRUNE SCONES

MAKES 16 SMALL SCONES

30 minutes active time
over 1½ hours

Prunes get a bad rap, but they are delicious. I like to use whole-grain soft wheat flour here, but if you want fluffier scones, sift the flour instead of using whole-grain or use a combination. Scones don't need much gluten strength. If you have some uncommon grains or flours to use up, mix them in. A little barley malt flour adds to the flavor here, but if you don't have any, you could replace it with the same amount of whole-grain soft wheat flour. —CKM

whole-grain soft wheat flour	383 g (3¼ cups)
baking powder	8 g (1¾ teaspoons)
baking soda	4 g (¾ teaspoon)
salt	12 g (2 teaspoons)
granulated sugar	40 g (¼ cup)
barley malt flour or powder (see Option, page 156)	37 g (5 tablespoons)
cold unsalted butter	153 g (⅔ cup)
whole milk	205 g (¾ cup)
full-fat plain yogurt	100 g (6½ tablespoons)
pitted chopped prunes	175 g (1 cup)
TOTAL	**1,117 g**

egg for egg wash
pinch of salt for egg wash
turbinado sugar for sprinkling

MIX. Combine the flour, baking powder, baking soda, salt, granulated sugar, and malt flour or powder in the bowl of a stand mixer. Cut the butter into ¼-inch cubes, then mix into the dry ingredients by hand, just to break up the cubes and coat them in flour. Add the milk, yogurt, and prunes and mix with the paddle attachment on low speed until nearly blended, 1 to 2 minutes. If any dry ingredients remain on the bottom of the bowl, mix them in using your hands.

SHAPE. Line an 8-inch square, 2-inch deep baking dish with parchment paper and press the dough in. Move to the freezer to set up for 1 hour. Turn the dough out onto a countertop and cut the square into four smaller squares, then cut each smaller square diagonally to get eight large triangles. Cut these in

half again to get sixteen small triangular scones. (At this point, you can wrap them in plastic wrap and freeze in a sealed bag for a week or two. Unwrap and bake them straight from the freezer, adding 2 to 4 minutes to the bake time.)

BAKE. Preheat the oven to 325°F and line a half sheet pan with parchment paper. Separate the scones and spread them out on the parchment. Beat together the egg and salt, brush the egg wash all over the scones, then sprinkle generously with the turbinado sugar. Bake until puffed and golden (dark gold on the edges), about 25 minutes, rotating the pan once to ensure even browning. Enjoy these while still warm or store for a few days in an airtight container at room temperature. Refresh them in a 350°F oven for 10 minutes.

PIZZELLE

MAKES 20 TO 24 PIZZELLE

30 minutes, all active

Kitchen tools that only do one job may be hard to justify, but a pizzelle press is one that I will endorse. Pizzelle are perfect cookies: they're easy, quick, and impressive looking. Plus, they're not overly sweet. I like spelt in these cookies because it's naturally spicy, which complements the cinnamon. But this dough doesn't rely much on gluten, so your options are wide open. Rye flour would be a great substitution, or even buckwheat. —CKM

whole-grain spelt flour	150 g (1¼ cups)
ground cinnamon	2 g (¾ teaspoon)
baking powder	2 g (½ teaspoon)
salt	2 g (⅓ teaspoon)
sugar	120 g (⅔ cup)
eggs	100 g (6 tablespoons, about 2 medium)
egg whites	70 g (4 tablespoons, from 2 medium eggs)
melted unsalted butter	60 g (¼ cup)
TOTAL	**506 g**

MIX. Whisk the flour, cinnamon, baking powder, salt, and sugar in a medium bowl. Whisk the eggs, egg whites, and butter in a large bowl. Add the dry ingredients to the wet ingredients and whisk everything together. The batter should be sticky and smooth. Let it sit for a few minutes while you heat up the pizzelle press.

BAKE. Turn on the pizzelle press. If your press has a temperature control, set it to medium. Have tongs and a cooling rack handy. Modern presses have nonstick coatings, so you shouldn't need to grease between rounds. When the press is hot, use a spoon to scoop up about 2 teaspoons of batter. With a second spoon, scrape the batter onto the center of the pizzelle mold. Quickly repeat with the second pizzelle mold. Close the press gently and leave until golden brown, 30 to 50 seconds, depending on your press temperature. Open the press and, using tongs, transfer the finished pizzelle to the cooling rack. Repeat with the remaining batter, adjusting the temperature, time, and batter amount if necessary to get lightly browned cookies that fill the mold without spilling out. The cookies get more crisp as they

cool, so space them apart on the rack when they first come out. Once cooled, they can be stacked.

Once fully cooled, they can be stored in an airtight container for up to 2 weeks. They can also be frozen for about 1 month.

OPTIONS

To make **Cannoli Shells**, after you take the pizzelle from the mold, roll them around thick wooden dowels or a wooden spoon handle, and let cool into a tube shape. Fill with your favorite cannoli filling.

For taco shell shapes, you could drape them over a wooden dowel or spoon handle suspended over your countertop and let cool.

Or for cone shapes (for, say, ice cream waffle cones), roll them around a cone: a paper snow-cone cup wrapped in aluminum foil works well, or fashion one out of cardboard and a stapler.

FENNEL ORANGE BISCOTTI

MAKES ABOUT
36 BISCOTTI

30 minutes active time
over 2½ hours

Fennel and orange is always a slam-dunk combo . . . a little sweet, a little savory, and full of an anise and orange aroma. Pair these cookies with an espresso, and your day can only get better. —MV

fennel seeds	4 g (2 teaspoons)
bolted soft wheat flour	250 g (2 cups)
bolted spelt flour	250 g (2 cups)
sugar	350 g (1¾ cups)
baking powder	5 g (1 teaspoon)
salt	3 g (½ teaspoon)
extra-virgin olive oil	27 g (2 tablespoons)
eggs	200 g (¾ cup, about 4 medium)
grated orange zest	12 g (2 tablespoons, from 1 medium orange)
TOTAL	**1,101 g**

MIX. Toast the fennel seeds in a dry sauté pan over medium heat until fragrant, about 2 minutes, shaking the pan to prevent scorching. Let cool.

Combine both flours, the sugar, baking powder, salt, oil, eggs, orange zest, and fennel seeds in the bowl of a stand mixer. Mix with the paddle attachment on medium-low speed, until the dough comes together, 3 to 4 minutes. This dough will be dry, but it will come together.

SHAPE. Turn the dough out onto a floured countertop and divide it in half. Wet your hands to prevent sticking, then pat the pieces into long ovals and roll them into logs about 2½ inches in diameter and 12 inches long. Wrap in plastic wrap and refrigerate until firm, about 1 hour or up to 2 days. The dough is somewhat loose, so the logs will flatten a bit, which is fine.

BAKE. Preheat the oven to 350°F. Line a half sheet pan with parchment paper. Unwrap and transfer the logs to the sheet pan. Bake until the logs are lightly browned, firm to the touch, and slightly cracked on the surface, about 20 minutes. Remove the sheet pan and let the logs cool on the pan for

a few minutes. Then use a long spatula to carefully transfer the logs to a rack and cool until just barely warm, about 30 minutes.

BAKE AGAIN. Lower the oven temperature to 300°F. Cut the cooled logs crosswise on a steep angle into cookies about ½ inch thick (they'll resemble a finger shape). Lay the cookies flat (even the stubby end pieces) on sheet pans and bake until they are dry, another 20 minutes, turning the cookies over once for even cooking. Remove and transfer the cookies to racks to cool completely. They will crisp up as they cool.

These cookies taste best after they sit for 24 hours, and they will keep for up to 2 weeks in a cookie jar.

OPTION

To make **Chocolate Chunk Biscotti**, skip the fennel seeds and orange zest, and fold 340 grams (12 ounces/2 cups) of chocolate chunks into the dough toward the end of the mixing.

HAZELBUTTER COOKIES

MAKES ABOUT
24 LARGE COOKIES

45 minutes active time
over 1½ hours

So many customers have bought one of these cookies at my farmers' market stand, then looped back a few minutes later to buy another. I might just start selling them as a two-pack! The temperature of the butter is pretty important for this cookie. It should be cool yet pliable when you cream it with the sugar. —CKM

whole hazelnuts	229 g (1⅔ cups)
granulated sugar	204 g (1 cup)
vanilla extract	10 g (2⅓ teaspoons)
whole-grain spelt flour	407 g (3⅓ cups)
baking powder	2 g (½ teaspoon)
salt	3 g (½ teaspoon)
unsalted butter	344 g (1½ cups)
TOTAL	**1,199 g**

turbinado sugar for coating	

MIX. Preheat the oven to 325°F. Spread the hazelnuts out on a sheet pan and toast them in the oven until tan and aromatic, about 8 minutes. Pull them out to cool slightly (leave the oven on) and rub off the skins if they have not yet been skinned.

Meanwhile, combine the granulated sugar and vanilla in the bowl of a stand mixer. In a separate bowl, combine the flour, baking powder, and salt.

Grind the nuts in a food processor, until they are mostly fine with a few lentil-size pieces, about 20 seconds.

Add the butter to the sugar and vanilla and cream with the paddle attachment on medium-high speed, until the butter has lightened, gained a little volume, and taken on a light sheen, about 3 minutes. Scrape the bottom and sides of the bowl with a spatula and add the dry ingredients, including the nuts. Mix on low speed until evenly incorporated.

Cover the dough with a plastic grocery bag, plastic wrap, or beeswax wrap and chill in the refrigerator for at least 30 minutes or up to 3 days. You can also freeze it in an airtight container for up to 2 months (thaw in the fridge before using).

SHAPE. Line a cookie sheet with parchment paper. When ready to bake, fill a small bowl with the turbinado sugar. Portion the dough into 50-gram pieces. You can use a heaping tablespoon scoop if you have one. Roll each piece into a ball, depress the center slightly with your thumb, and dip the top in the turbinado sugar to coat the outer ring. Set the pieces sugared-side up on the cookie sheet with about 1 inch of space between each.

BAKE. Bake for 18 minutes. The cookies will puff and spread slightly, turn one shade darker, and have a nice ring of sparkly raw sugar. Pull from the oven and set aside to cool on the cookie sheet.

These cookies are best eaten within 48 hours, but they will keep for up to 5 days in an airtight container at room temperature. Over time, they will lose their crunch.

SPELT COCOA COOKIES

MAKES ABOUT
40 SMALL COOKIES

20 minutes active time
over 2¾ hours

Cocoa noir (black cocoa powder) is really low in acid, so the flavor is super mellow, very unlike the in-your-face flavor of Hershey's. Look for it at baking supply stores or online. This cocoa is what makes Oreo cookies look so dark. So that's what I went for here: a crispy cookie shell, something like a homemade Oreo, but made with better-tasting flour. To sandwich them with creamy filling and make tiny homemade Oreos, see the Option.

unsalted butter	227 g (1 cup)
bolted spelt flour	300 g (2⅓ cups)
black cocoa powder	30 g (⅓ cup)
salt	1 g (⅛ teaspoon)
sugar	191 g (1 cup)
vanilla seeds	1 g (⅛ teaspoon, scraped from 1 large vanilla bean)
egg yolks	45 g (3 tablespoons, from 3 medium eggs)
TOTAL	**795 g**

MIX. Cube the butter and leave it in the bowl of a stand mixer at room temperature for 30 minutes to soften up. In a separate bowl, combine the flour, cocoa powder, and salt.

Add the sugar and vanilla seeds to the softened butter and mix with the paddle attachment on medium speed until the mixture has lightened in color, gained volume, and taken on a slight sheen, 3 to 4 minutes. One by one, add the egg yolks, mixing until each has been incorporated. Once incorporated, switch to medium-low speed, add the dry ingredients all at once, and mix until everything is incorporated and the dough forms. Mix for 1 minute more. Chill the dough in the refrigerator until cold, about 2 hours.

SHAPE. Preheat the oven to 350°F. Turn the dough out onto a Silpat or large sheet of parchment paper and cover with a second sheet of parchment. Pat the dough into a rectangle, then roll it out with a rolling pin to an even ¼ inch thickness. If the dough is stiff, let it rest at room temperature for a few minutes to take the chill off, then roll it out. Use a medium (1½-inch) scalloped cutter to punch out cookies, leaving nearly an inch between each. Use a thin spatula to pull away the dough scraps, leaving the cookies on the Silpat. The

dough scraps can be rerolled right away on another Silpat to bake two sheets of cookies at once. Or, if you're baking in separate batches, push the scraps into a ball and refrigerate to keep it chilled between batches.

BAKE. Transfer the Silpats to cookie sheets and bake until the cookies just lose their sheen and firm up, about 8 minutes. They may spread a bit. Cool them on the pans for 15 minutes, then transfer to cooling racks. The cookies can be kept in an airtight container at room temperature for 5 to 6 days.

OPTION

For **Homemade Oreos**, make the filling by combining 115 grams (½ cup) of softened butter, 160 grams (1⅓ cups) of confectioners' sugar, and 2 grams (½ teaspoon) of peppermint extract in the bowl of a stand mixer. Mix with the paddle attachment on low speed until most of the sugar is incorporated, a minute or two. Then switch to medium-high speed and beat until fluffy, about 6 minutes. Spread a thick layer on half the cookies and top with the remaining cookies. These are best enjoyed immediately but will keep in an airtight container at room temperature for a couple days.

WHOLE-GRAIN PÂTÉ À CHOUX

MAKES ABOUT 36 PUFFS

30 minutes active time
over 1 hour

The Bicycle Coalition of Greater Philadelphia hosts an annual scavenger hunt called the ProfiteRoll. Cyclists ride through the city to find pastries at designated bakeries and restaurants. It was started in honor of a young pastry chef named Emily Fredricks, who was killed while biking to work. It's a very meaningful event, harnessing the overlap of Philly's restaurant and bike scenes. There are a ton of sweets, though, so one year I thought folks might like a break from all the sugar. I made a savory profiterole with light, whipped veggie cream cheese as the filling. Choux pastry (the English translation of the French *pâté à choux*) is super easy to whip up and it never fails to impress. You can even portion and freeze it to bake at a later date. Pull this dough out for any special event and check out some of the filling options. —CKM

unsalted butter	115 g (½ cup)
whole milk	160 g (⅔ cup)
salt	3 g (½ teaspoon)
whole-grain flour (wheat, spelt, or rye)	110 g (1 cup)
eggs	200 g (¾ cup, about 4 medium)
TOTAL	**588 g**

egg for egg wash
pinch of salt for egg wash

MIX. Preheat the oven to 400°F. Line two half sheet pans with parchment paper.

Cube the butter and place it in a medium saucepan. Add the milk and salt and bring to a boil over high heat. As soon as it boils, turn the heat to low and add the flour all at once. Stir with a wooden spoon until you have a cohesive mass of batter, then keep cooking and stirring for 2 minutes.

Take the pan off the heat and transfer the batter to the bowl of a stand mixer. Mix with the paddle attachment on medium speed for about 2 minutes to cool the batter down a bit. Then begin gradually adding the eggs, about one at a time, and mix thoroughly between each addition. Err on the side of mixing for an extra-long time between additions. The batter should look smooth and shiny.

SHAPE. Line a sheet pan with parchment paper. Use a rubber spatula to clean the sides of the bowl and transfer the batter to a piping bag or zipper-lock bag. Cut the tip of the bag and pipe 1-inch mounds onto the prepared sheet pan. Or just scoop out neat mounds with a spoon. Leave about ¾ inch between the mounds to accommodate puffing.

BAKE. If baking immediately, beat together the egg and salt, and paint each mound with the egg wash. Load into the oven and bake for 10 minutes. Rotate the pan and bake until golden and shiny, an additional 7 minutes.

Pâté à choux is best eaten fresh. But to bake it later, freeze the sheet pans until the mounds are solid. Then peel off the mounds and freeze them in a plastic bag or container with a lid. To bake, arrange the frozen mounds on parchment paper–lined sheet pans, paint with the egg wash while frozen, and leave for 15 minutes at room temperature to soften. Then bake as directed.

OPTIONS

To serve with loose or creamy fillings, use a pastry bag with a small tip to fill the cooked puffs, poking and piping it in. Otherwise, slice the puffs in half horizontally, add a layer of filling, then top with the other half.

To make **savory Pâté à Choux Hors d'Oeuvres**, fill with sliced cured meats and cheeses, smoked salmon whipped with herbs and mascarpone, Homemade Ricotta (page 263), Tomato Marmalade (page 245), or veggie cream cheese (beat cream cheese with a fork enough to soften it, then dice up and mix in whatever veg you want to get rid of, like red onion, bell pepper, spinach, or tomato).

To make a **sweet Pâté à Choux Dessert**, fill with pastry cream, whipped cream, chocolate ganache, jams, or Apple or Peach Butter (page 266). Once filled, top the puffs with chocolate glaze or a dusting of confectioners' sugar.

WHOLE-GRAIN ROUGH PUFF PASTRY

MAKES ABOUT 1¾ POUNDS
(ABOUT THIRTY-SIX
1-INCH SQUARES OR NINE
3-INCH SQUARES)

Day 1 → 30 minutes
active time over 5 hours
with an overnight chilling

Day 2 → 15 minutes
active time over 1½ hours

At Vetri, we serve *stuzzichini*, an Italian word that refers to an array of snacks to start the meal. The mix of nibbles changes all the time, and just in case we need it, I like having squares of puff dough in the freezer. It's so easy to bake them off and fill them with something like Taleggio cheese and strawberry jam for a nice, simple starter that's still impressive (see the Option on page 230). Traditional puff pastry is a fairly labor-intensive laminated dough, but rough puff is easier. It's hands-on but not nearly as fussy. —CKM

water	107 g (½ cup)
distilled white vinegar	5 g (1 teaspoon)
unsalted butter	363 g (1⅔ cups)
whole-grain soft wheat flour	303 g (2½ cups)
sugar	14 g (3½ teaspoons)
salt	8 g (1⅓ teaspoons)
TOTAL	**800 g**

DAY 1: MIX. Put the water and vinegar in the freezer to chill a bit while you measure the remaining ingredients. Cut the butter into ¾-inch cubes and transfer it to the freezer.

Combine the flour, sugar, and salt in the bowl of a stand mixer. Then, by hand, quickly mix the butter into the dry ingredients, just to break up the cubes and coat them with flour to keep them from sticking together. You're not trying to crush them or blend them in. Now, put the bowl on the mixer, attach the paddle, and set the mixer to low speed. Pour in the chilled water and vinegar and mix just until the dough sticks together but the butter is not yet blended in. It takes only a few seconds. The whole principle with rough puff is to have hunks of butter that get rolled out with the dough, then folded over and over, so that they become layers. When mixing, you do not want a homogenous mass with all the butter blended into the dough.

LAMINATE. Have a bit of flour for dusting, a rolling pin, and a bench knife on hand. Turn the blotchy dough and any loose flour out onto the countertop. At this point, the dough will be very unevenly mixed, with lots of nearly dry flour. Just scoop any loose flour onto the dough as you work so it will eventually be incorporated and hydrated. Smush the dough into a flat rectangle, about 4 by 6 by 1 inch. Then roll it out lengthwise to a longer rectangle about 6 by 24 inches, dusting it with flour as necessary. If the dough sticks to the countertop, loosen it with the bench knife. Fold the short edges in so they nearly meet in the center but leave about a ½-inch gap. Brush off any excess flour from the folded sides. Now fold the dough in half in the same direction over the gap in the center. This is called a book fold. At this point, the big butter pieces should be large, flattened blotches. Wrap the book in plastic or beeswax wrap and refrigerate for 30 minutes.

Let the dough rest at room temperature (65° to 75°F) for 5 to 10 minutes to take the chill off. Unwrap the dough, saving the wrap to reuse. For the next roll, you want to roll the dough in the opposite direction from the last roll. Alternating directions works the dough evenly; if you continually laminate in the same direction, the dough will bake unevenly, and you will get irregular shrinkage. To alternate directions, position the book so the sides that have four layers showing are the short sides, and the sides with one and

CONTINUED

two layers showing are the long sides. Then roll the dough again to a 6 by 24-inch rectangle. Fold in the short sides twice as before to make a book. Rewrap the book of dough and refrigerate for 90 minutes. The rests between rolling and folding help to minimize shrinkage overall, although you should still expect some shrinkage.

Let the dough rest at room temperature for 5 to 10 minutes to take the chill off. Reverse the orientation of the dough and again roll it out, this time to 8 by 24 inches. Fold one short side in toward the center, leaving the opposite one-third uncovered, then fold that side over like a letter. Rewrap and chill for 90 minutes.

Let the dough rest at room temperature for 5 to 10 minutes to take the chill off. Reverse the orientation and roll out to 8 by 24 inches again and do another letter fold. Rewrap and chill overnight.

DAY 2: SHAPE. Roll out the dough to ⅜ inch thick, maintaining a rectangle. Make sure you don't roll it too thin or you'll flatten out all the layers you created. Your puff is now ready to be cut and baked as is, topped or filled before baking, or frozen for use anytime in the next month. You can cut the dough to whatever sizes you like, such as thirty-six 1-inch squares or nine 3-inch squares (see also the Option). Puff pastry can be baked from frozen; just add a few minutes to the bake time.

BAKE. Preheat the oven to 375°F. Assemble small-cut pieces on a sheet pan and bake until puffed and deep golden brown, about 15 minutes. Bake larger pieces for about 20 minutes, or filled items such as turnovers for 30 to 40 minutes.

After baking, puff pastry should be eaten the same day.

OPTION

To make **Taleggio and Strawberry Stuzzichini** (shown in the photo on page 228), once the pastry is rolled, cut it into 1½-inch squares and freeze the squares. Preheat the oven to 375°F and pull your Taleggio cheese from the fridge to take the chill off. Bake the pastry squares on sheet pans for 12 minutes, then rotate the trays, and bake for another 3 to 5 minutes, until it has puffed dramatically and is lightly browned and slightly shrunken. Split each square in half like a bun, then spoon a bit of strawberry jam on the bottoms and top with a slice of Taleggio. Put the tops on, let them sit for a minute, and serve.

TARALLI

MAKES ABOUT 60 TARALLI

45 minutes active time
over 1½ hours

Italy's answer to hard pretzels, Taralli are especially popular in Puglia. They're boiled before baking, similar to the process for making bagels, which sets the crust before these crunchy snacks even hit the oven. The loop shape makes it easy to pick them up and dunk them in chilled wine. —CKM

fennel seeds	4 g (2 teaspoons)
sesame seeds	30 g (3½ tablespoons)
whole-grain durum flour	130 g (1⅛ cups)
whole-grain hard wheat flour	130 g (1⅛ cups)
salt	8 g (1⅓ teaspoons)
extra-virgin olive oil	60 g (4½ tablespoons)
white wine	110 g (½ cup)
honey	10 g (1½ teaspoons)
TOTAL	**482 g**

MIX. Toast the fennel seeds in a dry sauté pan over medium heat until fragrant, 2 to 3 minutes, shaking the pan to prevent scorching. Remove to a bowl and toast the sesame seeds in the same pan in the same way. Buzz up the toasted fennel seeds with a spice grinder or break them up with a mortar and pestle (or leave the fennel seeds whole if that's your style).

Combine both flours, the seeds, and salt in a medium mixing bowl. Add the oil, wine, and honey and mix by hand until everything is incorporated. Turn the dough out onto a dry countertop and hand-mix until smooth, 3 to 4 minutes. You can also mix the dough in a stand mixer with the dough hook for 6 minutes instead. Cover the dough with a tea towel and let rest for 30 minutes.

SHAPE. Preheat the oven to 325°F. Set up a half sheet pan or cutting board lined with a tea towel as well as two half sheet pans lined with parchment paper. Fill a large wide saucepan with water and bring to a boil over high heat.

Cut a strip off the dough ball and roll it into a rope about the diameter of a #2 pencil. Cut the rope into 4- to 6-inch segments and roll each rope segment smooth, tapering the ends. Curl each piece into a loop like a scarf, pinching the touch point to seal. Place each loop on the parchment paper–lined pan and repeat with the rest of the dough.

To boil, carefully drop about a dozen Taralli into the water. At first, they will sink, then after about a minute, they will float. At that point, use a slotted spoon to transfer the Taralli to the towel-lined tray. Boil another small batch. After a minute or so on the towel, the boiled Taralli will be dry enough to transfer to the parchment paper–lined sheet pan. Rotate through the process until all the Taralli are boiled, dried, and placed on sheet pans.

BAKE. Load the trays of Taralli into the oven and bake until they are lightly browned all over, about 25 minutes. They should be somewhat crisp and will continue to harden as they cool.

These puppies keep for a very long time, 2 or 3 weeks, in an airtight container at room temperature.

FRIED RYE CRACKERS

MAKES ABOUT
75 IRREGULAR
SHARD-STYLE CRACKERS

45 minutes active time
over 2 hours

Amanda Shulman, one of our sous chefs at Vetri Vegas, was on a *grano arso* kick for a while. *Grano arso* literally means "burnt grain" in Italian. She made some very good burnt-grain pastries, noodles, and breads. The *grano arso* also found its way into a cracker dough she was playing with, and she decided to fry the crackers instead of baking them. These were absolute keepers. Amanda gave the first batch to all the customers at the bar, along with a fat mound of whipped Homemade Ricotta (page 263). After a couple nibbles, the guinea pigs heartily approved! Enjoy these with a cold beer. —MV

BURNT RYE FLOUR

rye berries	23 g (2 tablespoons)

DOUGH

fennel seeds	15 g (2½ tablespoons)
coriander seeds	15 g (1½ tablespoons)
sesame seeds	15 g (1⅔ tablespoons)
water	100 g (½ cup)
dry yeast	3 g (1 teaspoon)
bolted soft wheat flour	150 g (1¼ cups)
whole-grain rye flour	40 g (⅓ cup)
burnt rye flour (from above)	10 g (1½ tablespoons)
salt	6 g (1 teaspoon)
extra-virgin olive oil	20 g (1½ tablespoons)
TOTAL	**374 g**

canola or safflower oil for frying
Maldon sea salt for sprinkling

BURN RYE. Toast the rye berries in a dry sauté pan over medium-high heat until burnt all over. Yes, you want them burnt. Set them aside to cool, then mill the burnt grains in a flour mill or pulse them to a powder in a coffee or spice grinder. You can also buy rye flour and burn it in a dry pan instead of milling the grain yourself.

MIX DOUGH. Toast the fennel, coriander, and sesame seeds in a dry sauté pan over medium heat until fragrant, 2 to 3 minutes, shaking the pan to prevent scorching (you don't want to burn these). Pour the seeds into a bowl to cool, and set aside.

Combine the water, yeast, all flours, salt, and oil in the bowl of a stand mixer. Mix with the dough hook on low speed for 5 minutes. Switch to medium speed and mix for another 3 minutes. Add the seeds and mix until they are incorporated. You could also mix this dough by hand for about 8 minutes. The dough will be stiff and somewhat dry.

Cover the bowl with a tea towel and leave the dough to rise until doubled in volume, about 1 hour.

SHAPE. Fill a wide heavy-bottomed pan with about 2 inches of canola oil. Preheat the oil to 350°F, checking the temperature with a frying thermometer.

While the oil heats, grab a rolling pin and some flour for dusting. Make yourself some space on the counter and lightly dust the countertop. Roll the dough super thin, about 1/16 inch thick. If the dough is too dry to roll, add a little water, pressing in the water until the dough becomes pliable. Once rolled thin, cut the dough into irregular triangles and rectangles, averaging about 1 by 3 inches.

FRY. Line a sheet pan or large tray with paper towels, and have a slotted spoon or spider strainer on hand. Carefully, one at a time, drop several crackers into the oil. Give them some space. The crackers should immediately puff with a thousand tiny bubbles, almost like pork rinds. Pull them out as soon as they start to change color from brown to golden brown and most of the bubbles subside, about 1½ minutes. Set on the paper towels to cool and immediately sprinkle with a little coarse salt. Repeat until all the remaining crackers are fried.

These crackers are best eaten within 24 hours of frying and best kept in an airtight container at room temperature.

OPTION

If you don't want to make a whole batch at once, you can place the rolled-out sheets of dough between sheets of parchment paper and freeze them. Once frozen, break the sheets into pieces and freeze the pieces in an airtight container for up to a few weeks. Fry the frozen pieces as directed, adding a few seconds to the cooking time.

11

EAT: FOODS MADE WITH BREAD

TWO YEARS INTO WORKING AT VETRI, I NOTICED THAT SOMETHING HAD CHANGED IN MY COOKING. As I got ready to head home one night, Jacob Rozenberg, one of the sous chefs, was in the basement, sorting through ingredients for a fall menu. He was staring at two scrawny lamb shanks, which were just not going to work for anything. Jacob usually finds a way to use every scrap of food we have, but that night, just as I headed for the door, he handed me these shanks.

I took them home with no plan whatsoever. I had never cooked a shank in my life. But after being around chefs all day for many years, I had seen how you cook a tough piece of meat: brown it in a pan, add some flavorful stuff, like onions, throw in some wine or other liquid, maybe some fresh herbs, and toss the whole thing in the oven. I didn't think about it for long. I just looked in my fridge and pantry and put dinner together. I roasted some squash alongside the lamb, cut some good sourdough, and when the lamb was done, poured two glasses of Burgundy. Everything fell into place. I didn't reference any recipes. I didn't fuss. About an hour later, my boyfriend, Zach, and I shared one of our most memorable meals ever. As we sipped the last drops of wine, we both knew that, this time, dinner was just a little greater than usual.

I had to stop and think: was this a fluke? Was it the lamb? I cycled back through my steps of putting the meal on the table and realized something: I think I had finally gotten a handle on cooking. Vetri was making me a better cook.

I have always been more of a baker. The whole process of transforming flour into bread engages me on every level, body and soul. Not so much with cooking. Cooking never came innately. Before Vetri, I had only three things I could make decently well: a green curry, a roast chicken, and a stir-fry. And I made the worst soups. Who makes bad soup?

Yes, I had been working in professional kitchens for years. But in most kitchens, the stations are pretty segmented with line cooks doing one job, sous chefs another, and bakers doing their own thing, often somewhere else. There isn't a ton of interaction between the chefs and bakers. Plus, the chef tends to only order food that is on the menu. And the sous chefs only cook menu items that have been tested many times over and approved by the head chef.

Vetri isn't like that. It's run like an old-school kitchen, where you buy whatever is seasonal and fresh at the market and keep a well-stocked pantry. There is much more cross-pollination among the chefs and between the chefs and the bakers. Chef Marc sets a collaborative tone. Everyone in the kitchen puts their creativity, passion, and skills into coming up with a great menu, and that kind of approach provides a lot of opportunity for growth among cooks.

I spent most of my days working near Matt Buehler, Vetri's executive chef. We would do our thing side by side and talk the way co-workers do—some trash talking and some complaining. We didn't talk about food. I'd be shaping boules and laminating cornetti dough, and he'd be cleaning rib-eye steaks and grinding romesco sauces. I didn't take notes or stare at what he was doing. But when you spend the whole day working next to a chef, you pick up on the little adjustments they make to the dishes: you see the entire meal coming together, and over time, you absorb an approach and an attitude.

I learned that having good ingredients around makes a huge difference. With a few great ingredients and some basic techniques, you can put together a fantastic meal. Some of our go-to ingredients got used so often, they turned into a joke: like colatura, the Italian fish sauce. It's made from fermented anchovies. We called it fish butts. We'd laugh about how disgusting it was. But, really, it is so good that the chefs put it on everything. They'd say, "Oh, you're sautéing mushrooms in butter? Put some colatura in there. Oh, you're searing a steak? Pour some colatura on top." It's like the Italian MSG.

Some chefs are very exacting in the kitchen. Others are more relaxed. And then there's Chef Marc, who is extremely relaxed when he cooks. It's funny to watch a cook get assigned to one of his special dinners in the upstairs dining room of the restaurant. He gives very little instruction, and that makes the cooks even more anxious about getting it right. But he doesn't think it's worth the time to tell them how to shop or how to cook a particular dish. Just buy good ingredients. Prep a good pantry. Use all your skills. He doesn't teach recipes. He demonstrates the correct attitude of a good cook: buy the best you can, understand the core principles of making food taste good—freshness, flavor, balance, texture, good technique, blending some things that are classic with some that are new—and just make reasonable decisions. Make whatever you want: but make it nice.

In a professional kitchen, that overall approach can be alarming for a new kid trying to do a good job. But it does make you a better cook.

That's essentially what we're trying to get across in this chapter. Even if you're more of a baker than a cook, you can become a better cook. Start by incorporating your best bread into your cooking. I mean, if you're going to make artisan bread, you might as well honor it with well-crafted toppings, like homemade Eggplant Caponata (page 267), Fava Bean Salad with Mint (page 244), or really good Apple Butter (page 266).

And you should, at least once in your life, make your own Cultured Butter (page 264). Bread and butter are married to each other. Why dedicate years of your life to perfecting a bread such as Simple Sourdough Table Bread (page 149), only to spread it with cheap grocery-store butter?

A lot of these recipes are just jumping-off points. In the Panzanella (page 246), a bread salad, there are an infinite number of vegetables you could use. Choose what you like. And the Bruschetta with Butter and Anchovies (page 243) can be topped with almost anything soft and flavorful, from Homemade Ricotta (page 263) to Tomato Marmalade (page 245).

On a more practical note, there is always leftover bread, and finding ways to not be wasteful should become second nature. If a bread just will not work for anything else, rip it into pieces, put it into the oven to dry out, then grind it into Bread Crumbs (page 240). Keep the crumbs in your pantry, and you can whip up something like Caciocavallo Agnolotti with Brioche Crumbs (page 258). Or turn leftover bread into every salad's best friend, Croutons (page 241). Use those uneaten ends to make a classic Tuscan soup, Ribollita (page 248). Build these little habits into your life in the kitchen, and none of your efforts to bake world-class breads will ever go to waste. —CKM

BREAD CRUMBS

MAKES ABOUT 3 CUPS

5 minutes active time
over 12 hours

I'll be honest: I like store-bought bread crumbs—the 4C brand to be precise. And if you're using them for a stuffing or a meatball, I still would go with the store bought. But for coatings where you'll taste it on the surface, these bread crumbs will give you a more flavorful, crusty bite. For this recipe, use any leftover or stale bread. It could be just a day old and still soft, or several days old and dried out. Either way, there's no reason to waste it. —MV

8 to 10 cups (500 g) leftover
bread, cut in ¾-inch cubes

Spread the leftover bread in a single layer on a sheet pan.

Let the pieces dry in a warm, dry place until the bread is entirely dry throughout. A good spot is near your oven or on a windowsill or radiator. The bread should dry out in 8 to 12 hours (or overnight), but it might take a little longer if your spot is cooler or more humid. After the bread is dried out, if it still feels warm, let it cool to room temperature.

Then transfer the pieces to a food processor and grind them to whatever consistency you like. For coatings, we like bread crumbs to have a rustic consistency similar to polenta, maybe ¹⁄₁₆- to ⅛-inch pieces. For a more consistent grind and to separate large pieces from small, pass the crumbs through a coarse or medium sieve.

Store in an airtight container in a cool, dry spot for up to 3 weeks.

CROUTONS

MAKES 8 TO 10 CUPS

10 minutes active time
over 2 hours

I have never known anyone who actually buys croutons from the market. But they are always so nice to have on a salad or soup. Making them is the perfect way to get a little more life from leftover bread odds and ends that are a few days old. Different breads make different croutons, so try out a few to find what you like best. —MV

8 to 10 cups (500 g) leftover bread, cut in ½-inch cubes or rustic, irregular shapes	¼ cup extra-virgin olive oil	1½ teaspoons fine sea salt

Preheat the oven to 350°F. Line two half-sheet pans with parchment paper.

Drizzle the oil all around the inside edge of a large mixing bowl, then sprinkle in the salt the same way. Add the cut bread and toss quickly because the oil will soak in fast. Mix with your hands to make sure the bread is evenly coated with the seasoned oil. Lay the oiled bread out in a single layer on the sheet pans.

Bake until the croutons are golden brown and crispy all over, 10 to 12 minutes total, stirring once or twice for even browning. If in doubt, err on the side of undercooking, because the croutons will crisp up and dry out a bit more while out of the oven. You don't want to make them too hard. Let the croutons cool completely on the pan before storing; if you cover them when they are warm, they will steam and soften.

Store, covered, or in a closed bag at room temperature for a few days. If they soften, recrisp them in a 350°F oven for 3 to 5 minutes.

OPTION

To make **Crostini**, just slice an Ursa Baguette (page 81) on a bias to get ¼- to ½-inch-thick crostini and brush the slices all over with the seasoned oil. Bake, cool, and store as directed.

BRUSCHETTA WITH BUTTER AND ANCHOVIES

MAKES 8 TO 10 SERVINGS

10 minutes, all active

A good marriage can last forever, like butter and anchovies or fava beans and mint. You can put almost anything on bruschetta, but the combinations should strike a balance. This isn't so much a recipe as it is a springboard for you to find out which combos you prefer. If you can think it, and it makes sense, just put it on some bruschetta. For bruschetta with big slices, try Simple Sourdough Table Bread (page 149), or for small slices, use the Ursa Baguette (page 81). —MV

1 loaf bread, about 500 g	1 cup Cultured Butter (page 264)	1½ cups best-quality canned anchovies in olive oil
About ¾ cup extra-virgin olive oil for toasting		

Slice the bread ¼ to ½ inch thick, on an angle if you like. In a large pan over medium heat, toast the bread in the olive oil (plus some extra butter if you like) until golden brown on both sides, 1 to 2 minutes per side. In a pinch, you could also brush olive oil all over the bread, then toast it on a hot grill or under the broiler.

Cool the toasts a bit, then arrange them around the cultured butter and anchovies on a platter and allow guests to make their own bruschetta by spreading on the butter and laying on the anchovies.

OPTIONS

For different bruschetta, set out other toppings such as Fava Bean Salad with Mint (page 244), Eggplant Caponata (page 267), Poached Artichoke Hearts (page 256), Tomato Marmalade (page 245), Homemade Ricotta (page 263), and Apple or Peach Butter (page 266).

FAVA BEAN SALAD WITH MINT

MAKES ABOUT 3 CUPS

30 minutes active time
over 1 hour

I have been making this little salad for years. Favas and mint are a classic combo, which tastes great on its own or spooned onto some crusty bread and topped with a few shavings of sharp Pecorino cheese. —MV

2 pounds fava beans in the pod

1 tablespoon red wine vinegar

¼ cup extra-virgin olive oil

½ small red onion, very thinly sliced

2 teaspoons chopped fresh mint leaves

2 teaspoons chopped fresh parsley leaves

Pinch of red chile flakes

salt and freshly ground black pepper

¾ cup shaved or grated Pecorino cheese

Bring a large pot of salted water to a boil. Remove the fava beans from the pods by breaking off an end and peeling the strings from the pods. Then wedge your fingertip into the seam and split the pod, removing the beans. Discard the pods. Add the fava beans to the water and blanch for 1½ minutes, then transfer to ice water to cool. Once cool, use your fingers to slip the tender, dark green beans from their tougher, light green skins. You should have about 2 cups. You can keep the peeled favas in the fridge for a day or two.

Put the vinegar in a medium serving bowl and slowly whisk in the oil in a steady stream until incorporated and thickened. Add the favas, onion, mint, parsley, and chile flakes and let marinate at room temperature for 10 to 20 minutes. Taste and season with salt and pepper. Just before serving, top with the Pecorino.

TOMATO MARMALADE

MAKES ABOUT ½ CUP

10 minutes active time
with an 8-hour rest

For years, I served oven-dried tomatoes on our vegetable antipasto plates at Vetri and Osteria. They were so delicious that we made them almost every night. Some nights, we had leftovers and would just snack on them. I thought we should use the leftovers somehow, so I pureed them with a little oil and vinegar into a marmalade. Then I put the tomato marmalade in the fridge and forgot about it for a while. A month later, I found it and tasted it. It was even better after aging for a bit. Serve this marmalade as a dip for Grissini (page 113) or a spread with almost any other bread in the book. —MV

10 Roma tomatoes

1 teaspoon sugar

1 teaspoon fine sea salt

½ teaspoon freshly ground black pepper

8 sprigs fresh thyme

¼ cup extra-virgin olive oil

1 teaspoon red wine vinegar

Set the oven to 500°F and let it heat for 15 minutes. Meanwhile, cut the tomatoes in half lengthwise, remove the cores and seeds, and lay the tomatoes cut-side up in a single layer on a sheet pan. Season with the sugar, salt, and pepper and break up the thyme sprigs, dividing them among the cavities. Place in the oven and turn off the heat, and let dry for 8 hours or overnight.

Remove the thyme sprigs, then use a food processor to puree the dried tomatoes with the oil and vinegar, adjusting the amount of oil as necessary. The mixture should be slightly thicker than ketchup, so it's spreadable. You can use this right away, but it tastes even better after a week or two (or four!) in the fridge. Keep it in an airtight container.

PANZANELLA

MAKES 4 TO 6 SERVINGS

20 minutes active time
over 30 minutes

Some people like to toast bread for this dish, but I find that frying the bread in olive oil makes it crispier, so it doesn't get soggy after soaking up the tomato liquid. It's one of my favorite things to do with leftover Simple Sourdough Table Bread (page 149). Red Onion Focaccia (page 84) works well, too. However, if you don't have one of these on hand, almost any bread will work. If something went wrong—but not too wrong—in one of your breads, you will be able to salvage it here. —MV

4 cups bite-size
bread cubes

extra-virgin olive oil
for frying, plus ⅓ cup

2 cups mixed small
tomatoes

1 medium, slender zucchini

¼ medium red onion

1½ tablespoons red wine
vinegar

salt and freshly ground
black pepper

¼ cup small fresh basil
leaves

In a very large pan (or two) over medium heat, fry the bread cubes in a thin layer of olive oil until golden brown all over, 5 to 8 minutes, tossing a few times. Transfer them to a bowl and let cool.

Cut the tomatoes into bite-size pieces, shave the zucchini lengthwise on a mandoline (or slice super thin with a knife), and thinly slice the red onion. Add them to the bowl with the bread and drizzle the ⅓ cup oil and the vinegar over everything. Season with salt and pepper and toss to coat. Taste it and adjust the seasoning, oil, and/or vinegar until it tastes good to you. Let the salad sit for 10 to 15 minutes, then toss gently with the basil before serving.

OPTIONS

If you have time, you could marinate the cut tomatoes in the oil and vinegar to draw out some of their juices before tossing everything together. You could also cut the zucchini a little thicker and grill it if you like. A few pieces of fresh mozzarella are always welcome in a salad like this, too.

RIBOLLITA

MAKES 8 TO 10 SERVINGS

Day 1 → 5 minutes
active time with an
overnight rest

Day 2 → 30 minutes
active time over 3 hours

When you go to Tuscany, you will most certainly eat this soup. There are lots of variations, because there is always leftover bread. It's essentially a vegetable stew and a great way to utilize bread scraps or those ends that the kids won't eat. Go ahead and use whatever leftover bread and whatever seasonal vegetables you like. —MV

4 cups dried cannellini beans

1 gallon water, plus enough to cover the stew

1 medium leek

1½ pounds (3 bunches) lacinato kale

1 large onion

2 medium carrots

1 medium bulb fennel, white part only

4 cloves garlic

2½ cups chanterelle mushrooms (optional)

15 small creamer potatoes (about 1 pound)

½ cup extra-virgin olive oil

1 teaspoon chile flakes

salt

1 cup white wine (optional)

4 to 5 medium peeled tomatoes, fresh or canned

freshly ground black pepper

1 large Parmesan rind

2 sprigs rosemary

½ large loaf day-old bread

1 cup grated Parmesan cheese

DAY 1: Combine the beans and 1 gallon water and let soak overnight.

DAY 2: Preheat the oven to 300°F.

Clean the leek by cutting it in half and rinsing between the layers to remove any sand or dirt. De-stem the kale and finely chop four or five of the stems. Discard the remaining stems. Wash the kale leaves in cold water and cut them into 2-inch pieces. Then medium-dice the leek, onion, carrots, and fennel. Mince the garlic. Slice the mushrooms, if using. Halve the potatoes if necessary (you want ½- to 1-inch pieces). Set aside.

In a large ovenproof soup pot or Dutch oven, warm the oil over medium heat. Add the kale stems and garlic, then shake the pan and cook until the stems and garlic are tender and aromatic but not browned, about 2 minutes. Add the chile flakes and cook in the oil until fragrant, about 1 minute. Before the chile turns dark and bitter, add the leek, onion, fennel, and carrots. If you are using mushrooms, add them

as well. Season the vegetables with a pinch of salt for flavor and also to draw out some moisture. Then stir and sweat the vegetables over medium heat until the onion is tender, 4 to 5 minutes. Stir in the kale leaves and cook until they wilt to about half the original volume, a few minutes. Stir in the wine, if using, and cook until the bottom of the pan is almost dry, 4 to 5 minutes. Then add the potatoes and tomatoes to the pot. Stir and cook until the tomatoes break down some and the bottom of the pan begins to dry out again. Season the stew with a healthy amount of black pepper. Drain the soaked beans and add them to the pot along with the Parmesan rind and rosemary sprigs. Add enough water to cover the stew, then put on the lid (or cover with aluminum foil) and place the pot in the oven. Cook for 2 to 3 hours. After 1 hour, check the ribollita by tasting a bean. (Some beans take longer to cook than others.) When the beans are tender and creamy in the middle, the ribollita is ready. If necessary, stir in a little water to maintain a thick consistency and to prevent the stew from drying out.

To finish the ribollita, remove the Parmesan rind and season the soup with salt. Portion into heatproof crocks or bowls, then rip the bread into large chunks and lay over the top of the stew. Sprinkle generous amounts of Parmesan on top of the bread and broil the ribollita or bake in a 400°F oven until the cheese is browned and the bread is soaking in the liquid. Serve immediately.

OPTIONS

You can use precooked or canned beans in place of dried beans. In that case, cook the stew in the oven just until the potatoes are tender, 45 minutes to 1 hour.

If you don't finish eating the whole dish in one seating, it makes a great pancake for breakfast! Simply mix in a few eggs to your leftover ribollita. Sauté the mixture in a nonstick pan like it's a pancake and top with a sunny-side up egg.

HERB TART (TORTA D'ERBE)

MAKES 8 TO 12 SERVINGS

35 minutes active time
over 70 minutes

When you go to the restaurant Osteria della Brughiera in Bergamo (and you definitely should), you are escorted into a small cave on the other side of the dining room before you sit down for dinner. There, you sip wine and snack on house-cured salumi and cheese that's sliced right in front of you along with little nibbles like *torta d'erbe*, or *errbazoni*, as it's also called. This torta has a super-thin dough made with polenta and different flours, all encasing seasonal vegetables that steam inside as the whole thing bakes in the oven. It is magical. One bite and you won't be able to stop eating. —MV

DOUGH	FILLING	
200 g (1⅔ cups) bolted hard wheat flour	1 large russet potato	¾ cup parsley leaves
80 g (⅔ cup) bolted durum flour	½ large red onion	1½ cups grated Parmesan cheese
30 g (3 tablespoons) coarsely ground polenta	1 large zucchini	fine sea salt
110 g (½ cup) water	3½ cups arugula leaves	freshly ground black pepper
	3½ cups Swiss chard, leaves only	extra-virgin olive oil for rubbing

MIX DOUGH. In a medium bowl, combine both flours, the polenta, and water and mix them together with your hands until a smooth, pliable dough forms. You may need to add a sprinkle more of flour or water to make the dough pliable yet firm. Cover the bowl with plastic wrap and set aside at room temperature while you make the filling.

MAKE FILLING. Peel the potato and onion, then chop the potato, onion, and zucchini. In a food processor, pulse the potato until it is minced. Then add the onion and zucchini and process until they are also minced. Transfer the mixture to a medium bowl. Pulse or hand-chop the arugula, Swiss chard, and parsley until they are minced as well but not pureed. Add everything to the bowl along with the Parmesan, 1 teaspoon salt, and ½ teaspoon pepper. Mix it all together; it should resemble tabbouleh salad and taste fresh and delicious. Taste it and add more salt and pepper as necessary. Transfer the filling to a colander and let it drain in the sink while you roll out the dough. (You don't want too much liquid in the filling or it could make the crust soggy.)

ROLL DOUGH. Preheat the oven to 350°F. Generously oil a quarter sheet pan or a shallow 13 by 9-inch baking dish. Divide the dough in half. On a lightly floured countertop, roll out half the dough into a thin rectangle, about ¹⁄₁₆ inch thick or less (just a little thicker than pasta), a bit larger than the pan. Transfer the sheet of dough to the pan. There should be some overhang. Roll out the other half of the dough the same way and leave it, covered, on the countertop. (If you want, you could use a pasta machine to roll out all the dough at once. In that case, roll it to the same thickness but cut the sheets as necessary to fit the pan, as shown in the photos on page 253.)

Pack the drained filling onto the bottom crust, forming a layer of filling that is ½ to ¾ inch thick. Lay the top crust over the filling and trim up the perimeter with a knife or pastry wheel all around the top edges of the pan, removing excess dough. Seal the edges all around the top of the pan

CONTINUED

by pressing them together with your fingers or the tines of a fork, as you would when forming the rim on a pie. The top of the torta should be roughly flush with the top of the quarter sheet pan. Use the fork or a knife to put some vents in the top crust, then rub the crust generously with olive oil.

BAKE. Bake until the tart is light golden brown all over, about 30 minutes, rotating the pan after 15 minutes. Let the tart cool down a bit before slicing.

Serve warm or at room temperature. It can be kept at room temperature for several hours.

OPTION

The most satisfying dishes are always made with fresh, seasonal ingredients. Put whatever is fresh into this simple torta. The filling contains a volume of roughly one-third potato and onion, one-third greens, and one-third vegetables like zucchini. Using these proportions, you can easily swap in other starchy vegetables, hearty greens, herbs, and soft fruit-like vegetables.

EGG AND ARTICHOKE TRAMEZZINI

MAKES 8 TO 10 SERVINGS

15 minutes, all active

I worked a ton of weddings when I lived in Italy. There was always a *stuzzichini* hour (snack time) with prosciutto, salumi, all kinds of vegetables, and these little *tramezzini* (triangular sandwiches). We often filled them with soft, semi-cured nduja sausage. When we started milling fresh flour and baking our own brioche at Vetri, I thought . . . what better way to highlight the suppleness of the bread than to make *tramezzini*? Here's the basic idea with egg salad and Poached Artichoke Hearts, plus a few options for serving these appetizers at your next party. —MV

EGG SALAD

4 medium hard-boiled eggs, peeled and finely chopped

3 tablespoons mayonnaise

2 tablespoons finely chopped cucumber pickles

1 tablespoon pickle brine

1 small shallot, minced

2 small celery stalks, finely chopped

1½ tablespoons chopped fresh chervil and/or parsley leaves

salt and freshly ground white pepper

Dijon mustard (optional)

½ loaf Brioche (page 115)

1½ cups Poached Artichoke Hearts (page 256)

MIX EGG SALAD. In a medium bowl, mix the eggs, mayonnaise, pickles, brine, shallot, celery, and herbs. Season with salt and white pepper and add a little mustard if you want some kick.

Cut the crusts off the bread and slice the bread about ¼ inch thick. Slice the artichokes about ¼ inch thick. Spread the egg salad on half the brioche, then layer on the sliced artichokes. You want the filling for these sandwiches to be fairly thin, maybe ½ inch thick at most. Top with the remaining brioche to make sandwiches, then cut them in half on the diagonal and serve within 1 hour.

OPTIONS

To make **Tramezzini with Smoked Salmon**, for each sandwich, spread some crème fraîche on a slice of brioche. Top with thinly sliced smoked salmon, chopped chives and/or dill, and thinly sliced cucumber.

Traditional tonnato is a creamy tuna sauce served over cold, sliced veal. **Tramezzini with Porchetta Tonnato** uses mortadella instead. To make the tonnato, start with 1 cup béchamel: melt 3 tablespoons of butter in a saucepan, add ¼ cup of minced onion and sweat until soft. Whisk in 5 tablespoons of bolted hard wheat or all-purpose flour to make a roux and cook for a minute or two. Then whisk in 4 cups of milk and simmer until thickened, whisking now and then. Season with salt and pepper. Now, measure out 1 cup of béchamel and blend it in a food processor with 4 cups of cubed mortadella. Weigh the mixture (it should be about 675 grams) and fold in one-half the weight in mayonnaise (about 336 grams). Then fold in about 3 cups of oil-packed tuna with a little of the packing oil and a couple teaspoons of drained capers. Spread on the brioche to make sandwiches. These are soooo good.

POACHED ARTICHOKE HEARTS

MAKES ABOUT 1½ CUPS
(306 G), PLUS 2 CUPS
POACHING LIQUID

20 minutes active time
over 1½ hours

These little gems can be used in a ravioli stuffing, tossed in a salad, mixed into bread dough such as Artichoke Fougasse (page 87), or layered into sandwiches such as Egg and Artichoke Tramezzini (page 254). The poaching method works with other tough vegetables, too—try turnips and celery root. The vegetables absorb the flavors in the poaching liquid, and the poaching liquid itself makes a great accompaniment to the vegetables. Add this simple technique to your vegetable repertoire. —MV

1 lemon	2 sprigs fresh mint	2 tablespoons salt
6 fresh medium artichokes	1 cup extra-virgin olive oil	1½ teaspoons freshly ground black pepper
4 cloves garlic	½ cup white wine	

Set up a bowl of lemon water: cut the lemon into slices ¼ inch thick. Then take two of the slices, squeeze them over a medium bowl and drop them in the bowl. Add cold water (2 to 3 cups). Clean the artichokes by removing the dark green outer leaves until you get down to the lighter green, tender leaves. Trim and peel the stems, then remove the fuzzy chokes in the centers with a small spoon or a melon baller. Drop the artichokes in the lemon water as you work to keep them from browning.

Lightly smash the garlic and drop into a medium saucepot. Pick the mint leaves from the stems, setting the leaves aside for garnish, and add the mint stems to the pot. Add 3 cups water, the oil, wine, and salt. Place the artichokes stems-up into the liquid. The stems will stick out of the liquid; this is fine. Cover the artichokes with a sheet of aluminum foil pressed onto the liquid and around the stems, and bring the liquid to a simmer over medium-high heat. Once it simmers, lower the heat to maintain a lazy simmer, about 200°F. Cook the artichokes until they are very tender, 45 minutes to 1 hour.

When the artichoke stems are tender, remove them from the heat and remove the foil cover. Add the rest of the lemon slices and the black pepper. Let rest for 20 minutes to steep the artichokes in the liquid. Remove the artichokes, then strain the poaching liquid, reserving the liquid. Discard the solids and serve the artichokes warm with some of the poaching liquid. Chop the reserved mint leaves and use them to garnish the artichokes.

The poached artichokes will keep refrigerated in the strained poaching liquid for a few days and can be served whole or quartered as chilled antipasti.

BREAD GNOCCHI

MAKES 4 TO 6 SERVINGS

20 minutes active time
over 45 minutes

These simple dumplings are like the Italian version of matzoh balls but better. They're often served for staff meals at restaurants in Italy. Try different breads to switch up the texture and flavor. You could serve these in chicken broth, but I like them better served with brown butter and a sprinkle of Parmesan and fresh herbs. Either way, they warm your heart on a cold day. —MV

GNOCCHI

300 g (½ loaf) Simple Sourdough Table Bread (page 149)

200 g (¾ cup) whole milk

50 g (3½ tablespoons) heavy cream

50 g (3½ tablespoons) extra-virgin olive oil

100 g (⅓ cup) eggs (about 2 medium)

50 g (½ cup) grated Parmesan cheese

18 g (1 tablespoon) fine sea salt

1 g (½ teaspoon) freshly ground black pepper

1 g (½ teaspoon) grated nutmeg

100 g (¾ cup) bolted soft wheat flour

1 cup flour for dusting

¼ cup unsalted butter

¼ cup grated Parmesan cheese

2 tablespoons chopped mixed fresh herbs (parsley, thyme, rosemary)

MAKE GNOCCHI. Remove the crust from the bread, then cube the bread. You should have about 250 grams (5 cups) total. In a large bowl, whisk together the milk, cream, oil, eggs, Parmesan, salt, pepper, and nutmeg. Stir in the bread and then the soft wheat flour and let stand for about 30 minutes.

Bring a large pot of salted water to a boil. Put the 1 cup flour in a wide shallow bowl, then scoop the bread-milk mixture into small balls about the size of a golf ball (an ice cream scoop works great) and drop them in the flour, rolling the balls gently until dusted with flour. Shake off the excess flour. The gnocchi will be loose and soft. Drop the dusted gnocchi in the boiling water, in batches if necessary to prevent overcrowding, and cook until they float, 3 to 4 minutes. Remove from the boiling water with a slotted spoon or spider strainer and transfer to a bowl or plate.

Heat the butter over medium heat until deep amber in color, about 5 minutes, swirling the pan for even browning. Don't let the solids burn on the bottom of the pan.

Divide the gnocchi among plates (three to four per serving) and sprinkle with the ¼ cup Parmesan. Drizzle with the browned butter and shower with the herbs. Serve immediately.

CACIOCAVALLO AGNOLOTTI WITH BRIOCHE CRUMBS

MAKES 6 SERVINGS

1 hour active time
over 1½ hours

The technique of soaking bread in milk and then mixing it into meatballs makes a nice, tender meatball. It also works in ravioli fillings, like this one. You can use almost any bread, but I really love the soft texture and richness of Brioche. Caciocavallo cheese tastes similar to aged provolone but is a bit creamier. Look for it in specialty cheese shops. Or adapt this recipe by using whatever bread or cheese you have on hand. You could also swap out the fresh lima beans for fresh fava beans. —MV

PASTA DOUGH	FILLING	
85 g (⅔ cup) bolted hard wheat flour	1 cup finely crumbled Brioche (page 115)	1½ pounds lima beans in the pod
28 g (¼ cup) bolted durum flour	½ cup whole milk	⅓ cup unsalted butter
75 g (⅓ cup) egg yolks (from 5 medium eggs)	1 medium egg	2 tablespoons chopped shallot
8 g (1¾ teaspoons) extra-virgin olive oil	1 cup grated caciocavallo cheese	½ cup grated Parmesan cheese, plus more for garnish
20 g (1½ tablespoons) water	salt and freshly ground black pepper	salt and freshly ground black pepper
		1 tablespoon chopped fresh oregano

MIX DOUGH. In the bowl of a stand mixer or other large bowl, combine both flours. Begin mixing with the paddle attachment on medium-low speed or with your hands, then gradually add the egg yolks, about one at a time, mixing until each is incorporated. Add the oil and then the water and mix just until the dough comes together, 2 to 3 minutes. If necessary, add a little more water, a tablespoon at a time, for the dough to come together. Turn the dough out onto a lightly floured countertop and hand-mix it until it feels silky and smooth, about 5 minutes, kneading in a little more flour if necessary to keep the dough from sticking. The dough is ready when it gently pulls back into place when stretched with your hands. Shape the dough into a disk, wrap it in plastic wrap, and set it aside for at least 30 minutes or refrigerate it for up to 3 days. You can also freeze the dough for up to 3 months. Thaw overnight in the refrigerator before using.

MAKE FILLING. In a medium bowl, combine the brioche crumbs and the milk and soak for 5 minutes. Drain, pressing gently on the bread to force out any excess moisture. Stir in the egg and caciocavallo cheese, then season with salt and pepper.

Divide the dough into two equal pieces—or, if you have a very long countertop, you can leave the dough in one piece for rolling. If the dough was chilled, let it sit, covered, at room temperature for 10 minutes. The dough should be cool but not cold. Shape one piece of the dough into an oblong disk that's wide enough to fit the width of your pasta roller. Lightly flour your countertop and a sheet pan and set the pasta roller to its widest setting. Lightly flour the disk of dough, pass it through the roller, and then lightly dust the rolled dough with flour, brushing off the excess.

Set the roller to the next narrowest setting and again pass the dough through, dusting again with flour and brushing off the excess. After going down two settings, fold the sheet of dough in half lengthwise over itself. At the point of the fold, cut about ¼ inch off the corners. This folding and cutting helps to create an evenly wide sheet of dough (if left on, the corners would get rolled out into long points). Continue passing the dough once or twice through each progressively narrower setting. Roll the dough to about ⅟₃₂ inch thick, about the 6 or 7 setting on a KitchenAid pasta attachment. The sheet of dough should be thin enough that you can read a newspaper through it. As you roll and as each sheet gets longer, drape the sheet over the backs of your hands to easily feed it through the roller. Repeat for the second piece of dough, if necessary.

Lay a pasta sheet on the lightly floured countertop. Cut the pasta sheet in half lengthwise to make two long sheets. Spoon ½-inch balls of filling along the length of each sheet, leaving a 1½-inch margin around each ball. Mist the dough with water to keep it from drying out and to create a good seal. On each sheet, fold the long edge of the dough over the filling, so it meets the other long edge, pressing gently to seal. Press out the air around each ball of filling, starting at one end and working your way to the other. Use a 2-inch round cutter to cut out half-moons by positioning the cutter halfway over the filling. Repeat with the remaining pasta dough and filling. You should have about 75 agnolotti. Place on the floured sheet pan, cover, and use them within an hour or refrigerate them for up to 8 hours. You can also freeze them in a single layer, transfer them to zipper-lock bags, and freeze them for up to 2 weeks. You can take the pasta right from the freezer to the pasta water.

Bring a pot of salted water to a boil. Remove the lima beans from the pods by breaking off an end and peeling the strings from the pods. Then wedge your fingertip into the seam and split the pod, removing the beans. Discard the pods. Add the lima beans to the water and blanch for 1½ minutes, then drain and transfer to ice water to cool. Once cool, use your fingers to slip the tender, dark green beans from their tougher, light green skins. You should have about 1 cup of limas.

Bring another large pot of salted water to a boil. Meanwhile, in a large deep sauté pan over medium heat, melt the butter. Add the shallot and sauté for about 1 minute. Add the limas and cook for 1 minute more. Keep warm.

When the pot of water boils, drop in the agnolotti in batches to prevent crowding and cover the pot to quickly return the water to a low boil. Gently cook the agnolotti until they are tender but still a little chewy when bitten into, 1 to 2 minutes.

Add 1 cup of the pasta water to the sauté pan. Then use a spider strainer or slotted spoon to drain and transfer the pasta directly to the pan of sauce. Stir gently or shake the pan like crazy until the liquid is blended and emulsified and the pasta and sauce become one thing in the pan, adding a little more pasta water if necessary to create a creamy sauce. Remove from the heat and add the ½ cup Parmesan, stirring gently or shaking the pan until it incorporates into the sauce. Season with salt and pepper.

Dish out pasta onto pasta plates and garnish with the oregano and a little more Parmesan if you like. Serve immediately.

FILONE SANDWICH WITH ROAST LAMB AND HORSERADISH

MAKES 1 LARGE
SANDWICH

40 minutes active time
over 2½ hours

Coffee company La Colombe opened in Philadelphia in the mid-1990s. The owners, Todd Carmichael and JP Iberti, became really good friends of mine, and when they opened a store in Fishtown that served sandwiches, I started popping by for lunch. I ate so many of their sandwiches, I started making them myself! Here's a basic sandwich template using Olive Filone. When you make the bread, just skip the olives and roll the tops of the loaves in sesame seeds instead. Then you can make almost any sandwich. Lamb and horseradish are an easy combo if you've already got some roast lamb on hand. Or check out another combo in the Options. The roast lamb recipe here makes about 5 pounds, and you only need 8 ounces for a filone sandwich. Keep the rest in the fridge. It handily feeds a crowd. —MV

ROASTED LEG OF LAMB	HORSERADISH SAUCE	
1 boneless leg of lamb (about 5 pounds), trimmed and tied	½ cup mayonnaise	1 loaf Olive Filone (page 100), made without olives
salt and freshly ground black pepper	1 tablespoon sour cream or crème fraîche	a few leaves butter lettuce
1 tablespoon canola oil	1½ teaspoons Dijon mustard	2 teaspoons extra-virgin olive oil
¼ cup unsalted butter	2 teaspoons grated pickled horseradish	1 teaspoon red wine vinegar
		salt and freshly ground black pepper

ROAST LAMB. Preheat the oven to 300°F. Let the meat sit at room temperature for 30 minutes to take the chill off. When ready to cook, season the meat liberally with salt and pepper. Turn on a fan or open a window because there will be some smoke. In a large heavy pan over medium-high heat, warm the oil until it is nearly smoking. Add the meat to the pan and sear, turning slightly every minute or so. Hold the meat with tongs to get it evenly browned all over. It will take a good 10 minutes. When nicely browned, add the butter and lower the heat to keep it from burning. Baste the roast by spooning the butter all over it, turning the meat every minute or so, and basting until the roast has an even, medium-dark sear all over, another 3 to 5 minutes. Transfer the lamb to a roasting rack set in a sheet pan. Put the pan in the oven and cook the lamb until a thermometer reads 115°F in the thickest part, 45 to 65 minutes. Let rest for 30 minutes before slicing. To use as a cold cut for sandwiches like this one, let the roast rest for 1 hour, then cover and transfer it to the fridge overnight. It will keep for several days refrigerated. Remove the string before slicing.

MAKE SAUCE. In a small bowl, mix together the mayonnaise, sour cream, mustard, and horseradish. You will only be using a portion of the sauce—the remainder can be kept in a covered container in the fridge for a week or so. Make more sandwiches with it or spread it on thin slices of All Rye (page 186) and top with smoked fish or pickles.

CONTINUED

Thinly slice about 8 ounces of the lamb. Split the filone loaf in half lengthwise but not all the way through, so the halves remain attached. Spread about ¼ cup of the sauce on the cut halves of the bread. Top with the lettuce and sliced lamb, then sprinkle with a little oil, vinegar, and salt and pepper. Serve immediately.

OPTIONS

We prepare our own horseradish at Vetri. It's so simple. Just peel fresh horseradish (most grocery stores stock it) and soak the pieces in distilled white vinegar at room temperature for 1 to 2 days. Then you can keep it in an airtight container in the fridge for weeks. Grate as much as you need. If using store-bought prepared horseradish, use a bit less because it has a sharper taste.

To make **Filone Sandwiches with Ham and Cultured Butter,** use really good ham like prosciutto cotto or even culatello. Slice it really thin. Then split the filone down the middle and spread with Cultured Butter (page 264), sprinkle with a little sea salt, and fold slices of the ham on top. So good.

HOMEMADE RICOTTA

MAKES ABOUT 1 POUND

5 minutes active time
over 45 minutes

Once you taste homemade ricotta, you'll never buy store-bought again. Use it wherever you normally use ricotta or serve it with Bruschetta with Butter and Anchovies (page 243) or Fried Rye Crackers (page 234). When you make this, you will get a bunch of leftover whey. Use it to bake the Farro Miche with Whey on page 164. Or toss it into a smoothie for a little extra protein. Just be sure to use raw or pasteurized milk and cream. Avoid ultra-pasteurized dairy because it doesn't form curds for cheesemaking. —MV

½ gallon whole milk

1 cup heavy cream
1½ tablespoons fine salt

¾ cup freshly squeezed and strained lemon juice

In a large pot, combine the milk, cream, and salt (you will want plenty of extra room to keep the mixture from boiling over). Warm over medium-high heat, stirring occasionally to avoid scorching the bottom of the pot. Bring just to a boil, then remove from the heat. Immediately add the lemon juice and stir gently. Then let stand until the white curd coagulates and separates from the watery, yellowish whey, 10 to 15 minutes.

Line a large strainer or perforated pan with several layers of cheesecloth and place over a pot or pan to catch the whey. Gently ladle the solid curd into the cheesecloth. Let it strain for 30 minutes for medium-wet ricotta or 60 minutes for drier, firmer ricotta. Gather the ricotta in the cheesecloth and gently squeeze out any remaining whey.

Save the whey in an airtight container in the fridge for 2 to 3 days. The ricotta will hold for up to 1 week in an airtight container in the fridge.

CULTURED BUTTER

MAKES ABOUT 1 POUND
(2 CUPS) BUTTER AND
2 CUPS BUTTERMILK

Day 1 → 5 minutes
active time with an
overnight rest

Day 2 → 2 minutes
active time with an
overnight chilling

Day 3 → 20 minutes
active time over 2 hours

For twenty years, we served extra-virgin olive oil and Gaeta olives with our bread at Vetri Cucina. Then our bread program grew, and we had so many different kinds of breads made with freshly milled flour. People asked for butter. Like everything else we serve, I didn't want to just buy it. I thought we should make our own butter. It's not hard. To make cultured or fermented butter, you first make crème fraîche and then make butter from that. Leaving a dairy product out to ferment on purpose seems scary at first, but you have to let go and trust the process. Fermenting the liquid mixture gives you cultured butter with a richer, tangier flavor than regular butter. So, no more olives and olive oil. Bread and butter are back! By the way, after making this butter, you can use the leftover buttermilk to make Buckwheat Buttermilk Bread (page 167) or English Muffins (page 125). —MV

4 cups heavy cream	¾ cup buttermilk	fine sea salt

DAY 1: MAKE CRÈME FRAÎCHE. First, mix the heavy cream and the buttermilk together in a large bowl, cover with cheesecloth, and let sit in a slightly-warmer-than-room-temperature (about 80°F) spot for 24 hours. (Above a stovetop or in a closet with a space heater is good.) If the ambient temperature is lower, the culture may take longer to develop.

DAY 2: CHILL IT. When the culture develops, you'll notice that the cream mixture is slightly thicker when stirred, similar to loose sour cream. At that point, chill the mixture in the fridge for another 24 hours. Then, you can make the cultured butter right away or store the chilled crème fraîche in the fridge for up to 2 weeks.

DAY 3: MAKE BUTTER. Chill the bowl and paddle attachment of a stand mixer until cold. Cut a large piece of cheesecloth and lay it in a separate medium bowl.

Pour the cold crème fraîche into the chilled mixer bowl. Do not fill the bowl more than halfway or you will end up with a buttermilk mess. Attach the paddle to the mixer. If you have a plastic shield for your mixer bowl, now is the time to use it—or tape a shield of plastic wrap around the front of the mixer and mixer bowl. Beat on medium-high speed. The

crème fraîche will loosen up at first and then firm back up into a whipped cream. This should take only a couple minutes. Keep mixing until the crème fraîche breaks: it will start to look grainy and curdled. At that point, switch to medium speed and watch it like a hawk. The solids and liquids will continue to separate from each other: the butter will start sticking to the paddle, and the buttermilk will spatter around the bowl. As soon as that happens, switch to low speed. Things could get a little messy. Keep mixing on low speed until the butter clings around the paddle and the buttermilk pools in the bottom of the bowl. This whole process should take only a few minutes more.

Strain the butter and buttermilk through the cheesecloth into the medium bowl. Reserve the butter. Cover the buttermilk and chill in the fridge for up to 1 week.

Weigh the butter in the cheesecloth or in a bowl. It should weigh about 1 pound. Calculate 2% of that weight for the salt. For instance, 2% of 454 grams (1 pound) is 9 grams, or about 1½ teaspoons fine sea salt. In the bowl of your stand mixer, combine the butter and the calculated amount of salt and mix it with the paddle attachment on medium-low speed until the salt is evenly incorporated.

Meanwhile, set up a large bowl of ice water and line a large strainer or perforated pan with a generous amount of cheesecloth. Once the salt is evenly incorporated into the butter, gather the butter in your hands and transfer it to the ice bath, swishing it around and squeezing firmly to remove excess buttermilk. Then transfer the butter to the cheesecloth, wrapping it in the cloth to cover completely. Put a heavy weight on top and press the butter to remove all excess liquid, 1 to 2 hours.

Remove the cheesecloth and make sure there are no residual pieces of cloth in the butter. Now you can shape the butter however you like by transferring it to any clean, dry 2-cup container. To make a traditional block, line a mini-loaf pan (5½ by 3 by 2½ inches) with a generous amount of parchment paper. Press the butter into the lined pan, cover with the excess parchment, and chill until firm, 2 to 3 hours. Once firm, you can remove the pan and keep the block of butter chilled in the parchment paper as you use it.

The butter will keep, covered, in the refrigerator for 1 to 2 months.

APPLE OR PEACH BUTTER

MAKES ABOUT 4 CUPS

20 minutes active time
over 2½ hours

Fruit butters are dead-easy to make, and it's fun coming up with your own flavors. Be creative! This cardamom-vanilla-bourbon combo is one of my favorites. But maybe you prefer cinnamon and rum. Or maybe you have pears instead of apples or peaches. Make this recipe your own. Then spread it on any of the breads in this book. —MV

10 medium ripe apples or peaches (about 4 pounds)	1 cardamom pod	¼ cup unsalted butter
4 cups sugar	1 cinnamon stick	¼ cup bourbon
1 cup water	1 vanilla bean, seeds scraped from pod	

Cut the apples or peaches into roughly 1-inch pieces. You can leave the peels and cores/stems/pits on the apples or peaches because the butter will be passed through a food mill later, removing the peels, cores, and seeds in the process.

In a large saucepan, combine the sugar, water, cardamom, cinnamon, and vanilla seeds. Cook the mixture over medium-high heat until it turns a medium-caramel color, 340°F on a frying thermometer, swirling the pan gently now and then. Avoid swirling too much on the sides of the pan or stirring with a spoon because the sugar will crystallize, creating a gritty texture. When the caramel reaches 340°F, remove it from the heat, stand back, and carefully stir in the butter. It might sputter a bit.

After the butter is melted, add the apples or peaches to the pan and return to medium-low heat. The mixture may seize, and the sugar may look a little solid, but as the fruit cooks, everything will melt together. Cook until the apples are falling apart and the mixture is dark brown in color, about 2 hours, stirring now and then.

Stir in the bourbon and cook for 5 minutes to cook out most of the alcohol. Then remove from the heat and pass the mixture through the fine holes of a food mill. If you don't have a food mill, you can use a fine-mesh strainer. Discard the solids and pack the butter into an airtight container. It will keep in the fridge for up to 3 months.

OPTION

If you don't have a food mill, use ground cinnamon, ground cardamom, and vanilla extract. After cooking, puree the mixture in a food processor.

EGGPLANT CAPONATA

MAKES ABOUT
2½ QUARTS

15 minutes active time
over 30 minutes

Eggplant is the most underrated vegetable. It's so versatile: you can roast it whole, make a puree, grill slabs, make *spiedini* (Italian for skewers), stuff it, fry it, bake it, even braise it. Or just dice it up and sauté it to make this caponata. This little spread has it all: sweet, savory, salty . . . everything! Change up the nuts and dried fruit to suit your taste. Try hazelnuts and currants. Or almonds and dried cherries. Spoon the caponata on bruschetta (see page 243) or serve it with Grissini (page 113). —MV

3 to 4 small eggplant (about 2 pounds)

1 medium bulb fennel, white part only

½ medium red onion

3 whole canned tomatoes (preferably San Marzano)

1 clove garlic

3 tablespoons pine nuts

6 tablespoons extra-virgin olive oil

⅓ cup golden raisins

2 teaspoons red wine vinegar, plus more as needed

salt and freshly ground black pepper

Trim the eggplant and fennel and cut them into bite-size pieces. Chop the onion and tomatoes and mince the garlic. Set aside.

In a large heavy frying pan over medium heat, toast the pine nuts until fragrant and lightly browned, 2 to 3 minutes. Shake the pan a few times for even browning. Remove to a plate, then heat 4 tablespoons of the oil in the pan over medium-high heat. Add the eggplant and sauté until the pieces are lightly browned, about 10 minutes, turning often. Remove with a slotted spoon and drain on paper towels.

Add the remaining 2 tablespoons oil to the pan and cook the fennel and onion over medium heat until they are lightly browned, about 5 minutes. Add the garlic and cook for 1 minute. Stir in the tomatoes, scraping up any brown bits from the bottom of the pan. Add the sautéed eggplant, pine nuts, and raisins and mix gently so you don't break up the eggplant. Add the vinegar, starting with 2 teaspoons, then taste and season with salt and pepper, adding more vinegar as needed (it should be just slightly tangy). Let cool to room temperature before serving.

The caponata keeps covered in the fridge for nearly 1 week. It tastes best at room temperature.

12

BONUS TRACK: PANETTONE ALLA VETRI

I'VE ALWAYS BEEN OBSESSED WITH PANETTONE, ITALY'S SWEET GIFT TO THE HOLIDAYS. Every autumn, when I go to bed at night, I start dreaming of those long fermentation bubbles that stretch when you hang the panettone upside down. An Italian friend of mine, Stefano Arrigoni, has a restaurant in Bergamo, called Osteria della Brughiera. He makes amazing panettone. Around the holidays, he hires extra hands to make this bread every day. People reserve theirs well in advance because they know it is hard to come by really good panettone.

I started making this yeasty cake-bread years ago, but it was never good enough for me. It wasn't until I learned the technique from Stefano that the whole process started to make sense. There are so many steps to getting it right. In 2013, we finally began making what I would call a worthy version. Mind you, ours has been tweaked every year since then, and it will be tweaked every year in the future. The panettone we make now is truly special, with our own signature flavor. It was so good in 2013 that I decided to send out panettone to forty chef friends as holiday gifts. We bought little hat boxes that fit them perfectly, and we made all forty panettone over the span of 48 hours, so they would arrive just in time for Christmas. It was an ideal gift to show my crazy community of cooks just how much I appreciate everything that they do.

But if that first year was any premonition of what was to come, I should have known the heartache that would befall me. Now, every year, the week before Christmas is a nail biter! You see, with panettone, things rarely go as planned. Adam Leonti was Vetri's chef de cuisine that first year, and he took it upon himself to mix, ferment, and bake them all. Each one was lovingly filled with dark chocolate and candied fruit, then glazed with a hazelnut topping and baked. They were glorious. Adam made the first batch, and we sent them out the next day. After baking the second batch, he hung them upside down to cool, the final step in the process, and he told one of the sous chefs to wait until they had completely cooled, then wrap them in plastic, and leave them for the reservationist to box up. But the sous was in a hurry, and he didn't wait until the panettone had cooled. He wrapped them while they were still a little warm. And they all sank. Good-bye long, beautiful fermentation bubbles. We needed to remake the entire second batch. Luckily, we had given ourselves an extra day, and the next batch went off without a hitch. After a few days, the texts and emails from many happy chefs eating their panettone started pouring in . . . and from that year forward, the frenzy of getting on the Vetri panettone list began. And, simultaneously, the recurring panettone nightmare was born!

When Claire came on board in 2015, she watched the whole process as we moved into Thanksgiving and the panettone shuffle went into full swing. First, there were the test batches. Then some tweaking. Then more tweaking, until we got it right. As the weeks went on, all the chefs gave a helping hand with mixing the first dough or the second dough, fermenting and checking it, moving the dough to a cooler spot or warmer spot so it would rise but not too much, baking the loaves, and hanging them upside down to cool. Every day, the panettone was a little different, depending on who was making it. Same recipe, same time in mixer, same process . . . but different panettone every time. That year was rough, but we got through it, and in the end, we sent out some gorgeous Christmas gifts.

As Claire watched the panettone process in her first year, I sensed that she wanted to take on the challenge. As expected, after the holidays, she came to me and said she'd like to take care of production the following season. I gladly left it in her capable hands. All year, she tweaked and tested, read, and tested some more. We tried different mix speeds and mix times, fermentation temperatures, and really pushed our panettone to another level of deliciousness. The test batches were amazing, and Claire was thrilled to be making the best panettone of her life. We thought we had the perfect recipe.

But panettone has a mind of its own. Right when you think you've got it, it changes the game. For instance, our test batches showed that after the first mix, our best option was to put the dough in a 90°F proofing box to bulk ferment it so it would rise well but not too fast. Then the weather changed, and the mill room where we kept the proofing box got much colder than usual. While we were in production, Claire came into the mill room the morning after the first mix, and the dough had barely moved. It was rising a little but not as much as it should have. The options were: throw away the whole batch, keep going, or course correct before moving on. She decided to course correct by giving the dough more time to ferment in the proofer. With most breads, that would be an easy decision to make, but with panettone you've already pushed everything to the limit with intense mixing and tons of enrichments. Plus, as this dough rises, it's also breaking down and constantly getting weaker, so longer fermentation brings a greater risk of failure.

Luckily, the correction seemed to work. The dough was looking good. But it still didn't feel quite right. The texture was off. Claire went into emergency mode and tweaked a bunch of other things that could have sunk us while mixing the second dough and folding in the inclusions. After that, things got better but the panettone was still not as good as the test batches. What was the problem? We didn't know. We carried on and, in the end, we sent out some beautiful panettone that year. Yet we knew, deep down, that they were not the best we had ever made.

Claire figured out that it must have been the flour because we had been using a new pallet of flour for this batch. That is the only variable that had changed . . . a new pallet of flour. You can do everything right with panettone, from mixing to fermentation to baking, then something unexpected can throw a wrench in the works. That's one reason why this bread is so crazy hard. There are many more reasons: it's a sourdough, which is a little harder than making a yeast dough. Plus, it's very enriched, which is harder than making a lean dough. Then the dough is extremely intensively mixed. And it's maximally fermented. Repeatedly. Some breads exaggerate one of the basic steps in the bread-making process, such as the mixing or the fermentation, but this recipe exaggerates every single step. And when you are pushing every step as far as it can go, even the slightest change in the weather or in the quality of an ingredient can throw things off. But when everything goes right, panettone is simply amazing.

Claire likens the whole process of making this bread to a bad relationship that you just can't walk away from because the sex is so good. A great description!

The recipe here is the culmination of many years of growth and development in panettone making. Please understand that you may think you've done everything perfectly, and it still may not work. I know this makes no sense at all, yet this is what you have to be ready for when making this bread. But when it's perfect, oh man, there is nothing more satisfying in the world than slicing into one and seeing those long, oval, fermentation holes, then tasting the rich, sweet, milky-sour, complex, caramelized flavors and the soft, airy, crunchy, crackling textures. From Thanksgiving to New Year's, I come in every morning and have a slice with my coffee. It is the most satisfying time of the year. —MV

Overview of the Panettone-Making Process

Here's what to expect and what to look for in the different stages of making this bread.

Two weeks before: Convert your starter to lievito madre (see Option, page 148).

Day 1: Feed the lievito madre every few hours throughout the day. Then, at night, mix impasto (dough) 1 and let it rest overnight.

Day 2: In the morning, the dough should have tripled in volume. Mix impasto (dough) 2, fold in the inclusions, and let the dough rest. Divide it into portions, shape, place in molds, and let it rise again. Bake the panettone in the evening, then hang it upside down and let it cool for 3 hours. Hanging the bread upside down during cooling keeps it from falling down on itself and compacting the texture, keeping the bread light and fluffy.

What you're looking for: With panettone, you always want to catch the fermentation momentum on the upswing. In other words, with both the starter and the dough, you want to move to the next step right when the fermentation is reaching its peak but before the starter or dough collapses.

To keep the lievito madre and the dough fermenting at a steady, gradual rate, keep them relatively warm (88° to 90°F). You also build and feed the lievito madre more frequently than you normally would a starter for another kind of bread. In other words, you interrupt the fermentation and feed it just before the starter has reached an acidified collapsing state.

The lievito madre is ready to be mixed into impasto 1 when it is supremely primed to do its leavening work but before it's on the brink of collapse. If it's not there yet and it's not aerated, it won't be robust enough to raise the dough.

Likewise, after mixing impasto 1, you want to ferment the dough to just shy of its peak before moving on to mixing impasto 2.

When to course correct: With the lievito madre, if you feel as if you've taken it too far and it has begun to sink and weaken, it's best to regroup and start over. Otherwise, you may just waste ingredients. Try making the lievito madre again and adjusting the times and temperatures. Maybe you didn't allow enough days to develop it and build its strength.

With the dough, if you've already mixed impasto 1 and you think it may be a bit overrisen, you might as well mix impasto 2. See if you can get the dough to be nice before you add the inclusions. Mix impasto 2 for far longer than you think could be right—there's nothing to lose in that. But if it's just not working, that's the moment to cut your losses. Inclusions can be pricey. For more details on how to tell if the dough is feeling right and whether things are going well during mixing and fermentation, see the recipe itself beginning on page 275.

PANETTONE ALLA VETRI

MAKES 2 LOAVES,
6-INCH DIAMETER

Day 1 → 45 minutes
active time over 10 hours
with an overnight rest

Day 2 → 45 minutes
active time over 6 hours,
plus at least 3 hours cooling

Panettone takes every step of the bread-making process to the extreme. But don't let that scare you. If you've baked a few loaves in your day and you're ready for a holiday project, panettone will reward you and some special friends with one of the richest, sweetest, most airy, tender, and crisp breads on the planet. We use King Arthur bread flour, at 12.7% protein, because it is more consistent than freshly milled flour. Another unbleached, unbromated flour with a similar protein percentage should also work. Pick up two 6 by 4-inch paper panettone molds and pearl sugar at a baking supply store or online. —CKM

LIEVITO MADRE, FIRST FEEDING

lievito madre (see Option, page 148)	75 g (¼ cup)	150%
bread flour	50 g (⅓ cup)	100%
warm water (100°F)	25 g (⅛ cup)	50%
TOTAL	**150 g**	**300%**

LIEVITO MADRE, SECOND FEEDING

old lievito madre	75 g (¼ cup)	150%
bread flour	50 g (⅓ cup)	100%
warm water (100°F)	25 g (⅛ cup)	50%
TOTAL	**150 g**	**300%**

LIEVITO MADRE, THIRD FEEDING

old lievito madre	150 g (½ cup)	150%
bread flour	100 g (¾ cup)	100%
warm water (100°F)	50 g (¼ cup)	50%
TOTAL	**300 g**	**300%**

IMPASTO 1

bread flour	400 g (3¼ cups)	100%
lievito madre (from above)	180 g (¾ cup)	45%
warm water (100°F)	160 g (⅔ cup)	40%
sugar	180 g (⅞ cup)	45%
egg yolks	240 g (1 cup, from 16 medium eggs)	60%
unsalted butter, at room temperature	260 g (1⅛ cups)	65%
TOTAL	**1,420 g**	**355%**

CONTINUED

IMPASTO 2

impasto 1 (from page 275)	1,420 g (7 cups)	1,420%
bread flour	100 g (¾ cup)	100%
vanilla seeds	1 g (¼ teaspoon scraped from 2 vanilla beans)	1%
sugar	40 g (¼ cup)	40%
honey	15 g (2⅛ teaspoons)	15%
egg yolks	60 g (¼ cup, from 4 medium eggs)	60%
salt	12 g (2 teaspoons)	12%
unsalted butter	60 g (4¼ tablespoons)	60%
water	10 g (2 teaspoons)	10%
inclusions (see Options, page 283)	450 g (2½ cups)	450%
TOTAL	**2,168 g**	**2,168%**

GLAZE

2½ tablespoons granulated sugar plus 2¾ cups

¼ cup raw skinned hazelnuts

2¼ tablespoons cornstarch

1¾ teaspoons natural cocoa powder

¼ cup egg whites (from 1½ medium eggs)

TOPPINGS

5 tablespoons pearl sugar

¼ cup raw skinned hazelnuts, crushed a bit

DAY 1: FEED LIEVITO MADRE. In the morning, put 75 grams of the lievito madre in a small mixing bowl. It will probably have thick skin, so just remove the skin and use the soft, sticky lievito madre inside. Using a spoon or your hands, mix in 50 grams bread flour and 25 grams warm water. Mix until the gluten develops enough to tighten it into a ball with no visible tearing on the ball, 3 to 4 minutes by hand. Hand-roll the dough into a smooth ball, then cut an X in the ball to loosen the structure and so you can monitor how the lievito madre has risen over time. Return the ball to the bowl, cover with plastic wrap, and let rest in a warm place (ideally, 90°F) for 3 to 4 hours. At the end of that time, you should see the X expand and nearly flatten out, good signs of fermentation (see first photo on page 279).

From here on out, the temperature of the spot you put the dough in is crucial. You want it consistently at 88° to 90°F. The dough just won't rise much in a cooler spot, and when it finally does, it will be too sour tasting. If you have a bread proofer with adjustable temperature, that's ideal (you can get one for home use online for about $150). Or, if your oven has a bread-proofing mode at 90°F, use that. You can also create a 90°F environment by putting a heating pad or a small electric buffet food warming tray in the bottom of a cooler and closing the lid. Put a digital thermometer in there to monitor the temperature and place a wire rack on the heating pad or tray to set the dough onto. You can even set up a space heater in a closet and dial in the temperature until it maintains a steady 90°F. Either way, set up some kind of 90°F box and plan to maintain it for the next 2 days. A bowl of water in the environment will help keep it from becoming too dry. Shoot for 40 to 50% humidity, which can also be monitored with an indoor digital thermometer/hygrometer, like the ones from Acurite and Thermopro.

For the second feeding, discard all but 75 grams of the lievito madre, leaving that amount in the same unwashed mixing bowl. Add 50 grams bread flour and 25 grams warm water. Mix again until the gluten develops enough to tighten it into a smooth ball, 3 to 4 minutes by hand or on low speed in a stand mixer. Cut another X in the ball, then cover and let rest again in the same warm place until risen, 3 to 4 hours.

Finally, for the third feeding, leave all 150 grams of the lievito madre in the bowl, and add 100 grams bread flour and 50 grams warm water. Again, mix until the gluten develops enough to tighten it into a nice, firm, smooth ball, 3 to 4 minutes by hand or on low speed in a stand mixer. Cut an X in the ball again, cover, and let rest again in a warm place until risen, 3 to 4 hours. By this time, it will be the evening. If the X hasn't flattened out much and the starter isn't at its peak, let it go until it is.

MIX IMPASTO 1. These instructions are for mixing with a stand mixer with at least a 5-quart capacity. The mixing speed is important: it should be medium to medium-low, which is speed 3 on most KitchenAid mixers. In the evening, measure the flour and set aside. Place 180 grams of the fully risen lievito madre into the mixing bowl. (Save the rest of the lievito madre just in case you have problems with this batch of panettone; feed it as described, and you can try another batch the next morning.) Add the water, flour, sugar, and egg yolks and manually mix using the unattached paddle to incorporate the flour and keep it from going airborne, just 10 seconds or so. Then attach the paddle and mix on medium speed for 5 to 6 minutes. Stop the machine, detach the paddle, and use the paddle to scrape the dough from all around the bottom of the bowl. You want to make sure no unmixed flour is hiding there. Scrape the dough from the paddle, then switch to the dough hook. Mix with the hook on medium speed for 25 to 30 minutes. At this point, the dough will have increased in strength and gathered around the hook. It should look shiny, smooth, and elastic. To check the dough, lift it from the bowl; most of the dough should lift out of the bowl and feel strong with some pullback as it stretches. It should stretch without ripping (see photo #6 on page 279). If it rips, mix longer until it doesn't. When it's ready, you should be able to stretch the dough into a thin window, almost like a piece of plastic wrap. It should feel moderately elastic and will get more extensible after you add the butter. This is the most important stage for developing the dough's strength. If it seems weak, you may want to mix it longer before adding the butter, or you may have overmixed it on too high a speed! Either way, once the butter is added, the gluten won't develop as much.

Break the butter into pieces and add it to the bowl. Continue mixing on medium speed until the butter is fully incorporated and the dough is again gathering around the hook, 6 to

CONTINUED

7 minutes. The butter will get stuck on the sides of the bowl, and you'll need to stop to scrape it down several times during mixing. Watch the dough as it mixes: most of the dough should clear the sides of the bowl and cling to the hook. At this point, the dough will have increased in strength, adhering less to the sides of the bowl and forming itself into a ball around the hook. Pull on a bit of the dough with your fingers. Compared to other bread doughs, this dough, when fully mixed, will have a bit more extensibility rather than elasticity, and it will be shiny, looking almost like taffy. Transfer the dough to a clear 4-quart container with a lid, so you can see how much the dough is rising. The dough will nearly triple as it rests, so make sure there is space in your container for the dough to expand (see last two photos on the facing page). Put on the lid or cover with plastic wrap and let the dough sit in a warm (88° to 90°F) spot to rest overnight. Again, the temperature of your rising spot is crucial.

DAY 2: MIX IMPASTO 2. After 8 hours, check the dough to see how it's rising. At that point, it may not have risen much. But after 10 hours, it starts to rise more. After a total of 16 hours, the dough should have risen to 2 to 3 times its original size. That's your end goal: two to three times the original volume. You want the top to be aerated, delicate, and slightly domed; that shows the dough is holding tension. If the dough shows some pockmarks, that means it's losing some bubbles, which may be okay. As long as the dough is rising, it should be fine. To see where the dough is at, jostle the container. The dough should jiggle but not collapse, a sign that it's holding air. If it doesn't jiggle much, it may need more rising time.

When the dough has risen 2 to 3 times its original size, transfer it back to the mixer bowl. Attach the dough hook and add the flour amount for impasto 2. Mix on medium speed until the dough has developed strength and elasticity again, 15 to 20 minutes. At first, the dough may look loose, then it will come together. It actually comes up and bunches around the hook and then releases a couple times before it comes together. Eventually, the dough should cling to the hook instead of to the bowl. It should look and feel somewhat like taffy but won't be super stretchy just yet. To test the dough, grab a piece and stretch it away from the rest. The stretched piece should not have tear marks in it. It should look smooth and shiny, feel silky, and not have a mottled texture (see photo #7 on page 280). Once the dough exhibits those signs, mix the vanilla seeds into the sugar in a bowl, then add the vanilla-sugar mixture to the dough. Add the honey as well and mix on medium speed until they are incorporated and the dough becomes strong, shiny, and elastic again, 3 to 4 minutes. Watch the dough as it mixes in the bowl. At this point, the dough may look paler and more matte in appearance (sort of like creamed butter) rather than deep yellow and shiny. Don't worry, it will look more yellow when you add the egg yolks and butter. Once the dough is strong again, add the yolks, and mix for another 3 minutes. Then add the salt and butter and mix for about 4 minutes. You will need to stop and scrape down the butter again from the sides of the bowl. Be sure to mix in each ingredient until it is fully incorporated and the dough regains its strength, clings to the hook, and clears the sides of the bowl. After mixing in the butter, the dough should be soft, shiny, and stretchy, very much like taffy. If you stretch a piece of dough with your fingers, it should make a thin film, like plastic wrap or like you could blow a balloon with it. Once the dough is soft, shiny, and stretchy, mix in the water. Some of the dough will stick to the sides of the bowl, and the water helps to incorporate all the dough together. When finished mixing in the water, 1 to 2 minutes, the dough should feel firm, but when you let it go, it should slowly spread, similar to the texture of Gak or Slime, those strange colloid compounds sold as a kid's toy. It should also have more cohesion than adhesion, meaning the dough holds on to the hook and itself more than it holds

CONTINUED

IMPASTO 1

1. Ingredients for impasto 1. Notice how the lievito madre has expanded and the *X* has nearly flattened out.

2. One minute after you start mixing with the paddle.

3. Five minutes after mixing with the paddle. Then switch to the dough hook.

4. Fifteen minutes after mixing with the hook. The dough gathers around the hook.

5. Twenty-five minutes after mixing with the hook. The dough gains more strength.

6. Thirty minutes after mixing with the hook. The dough feels strong with some pullback as it stretches.

7. Add the butter and scrape down the sides.

8. A few minutes after mixing in the butter, the dough becomes nice and smooth.

9. End of mixing impasto 1.

10. The dough is shiny and extensible.

11. Transfer impasto 1 to a clear, 4-quart container with a lid.

12. Impasto 1 after 14 hours in a very warm (88º to 90ºF) spot.

IMPASTO 2

1. Transfer impasto 1 back to the mixing bowl.

2. Ingredients for impasto 2.

3. Add the flour amount for impasto 2.

4. One minute after mixing. The dough looks loose, but it will come together with more mixing.

5. Five minutes after mixing, the dough gains some strength.

6. Ten minutes after mixing, the dough gains more strength but it still rips and has tear marks. At this point, it is not yet strong and smooth enough.

7. Twenty minutes after mixing, the dough is strong and shows no tear marks when stretched into a thin window.

8. Add the vanilla-sugar and honey. Mix until the dough regains its strength, 3 to 4 minutes.

9. Add the egg yolks and mix for 3 minutes.

10. Add the salt and butter, and mix for 4 minutes, scraping down the sides. After mixing, the dough should be smooth, soft, shiny, and stretchy.

11. Add the water and mix for 1 to 2 minutes. The dough should clean the sides of the bowl.

12. Add the inclusions.

13. Mix in the inclusions with gloved hands.

14. Pour the dough out onto a floured countertop.

15. The dough should still be shiny and extensible.

16. Preshape each piece by stretching one edge of the dough outward and folding it into the center.

17. Continue folding in all edges of the dough until there is some tension. Then flip it over on the countertop and let rest for 10 minutes.

18. Give the dough a final shape by tightening and rolling it around against the countertop.

19. The dough should be slightly domed, relatively taut, and evenly round.

20. Use a scraper if necessary to help pick up the dough and place it in the molds.

21. Line up the ball of dough seam-side down over the center of the mold, then gently lower it and place it in the center.

22. Cover the filled molds with plastic wrap and let rise in a warm spot for 5 to 7 hours.

23. Unwrap the molds and pipe the glaze in a spiral in an even layer over the tops of the loaves, not covering them completely.

24. Scatter the pearl sugar and hazelnuts over each loaf.

on to the sides of the bowl. When you transfer the dough, it should almost pour out of the bowl, cleaning the sides of the bowl as it goes.

Once the water is incorporated and the dough is fully mixed, add the inclusions and mix them in with gloved hands.

PREP THE MOLDS. Set up two 6 by 4-inch paper panettone molds with long wooden or metal skewers piercing the bottoms. For each mold, if using wooden skewers, use two parallel skewers and two more perpendicular to those to make a double cross. If using metal skewers, two parallel skewers per mold is sufficient (see photo on page 271). Place the prepared molds on a sheet pan.

PRESHAPE. Pour the dough out onto a lightly floured countertop, using a dough scraper to get it all. Let rest for 10 minutes; don't be alarmed if it spreads some. Divide the dough into two pieces, each about 1 kg, and preshape each piece by stretching one edge of the dough outward and folding it into the center. Repeat this action all around the dough, making a little packet. If it's sticky, use a scraper or a little more flour. Continue folding in the edges until there is some tension, then flip it over on the countertop and let rest for another 10 minutes.

SHAPE. Give the dough a final shape by tightening and rolling it around against the countertop. It should be slightly domed, relatively taut, and evenly round. Even if the inclusions protrude slightly, they should be held in tightly by the dough.

Use a scraper if necessary to help pick up the dough. To place each loaf in a mold, line up the ball of dough seam-side down over the center of the mold, then gently lower it and place it in the center. If any dough sticks to the side of the mold, let it be. It could be worse if you try to fix it. Cover the molds with plastic wrap and set the sheet pan

of filled and wrapped molds in your warm (88° to 90°F) spot. Leave the loaves to rise for 5 to 7 hours. They should rise 1½ to 2 times their original volume and come within 1½ inches of the top of the molds (see photos #22 and #23 on page 281).

MAKE GLAZE. Buzz the 2½ tablespoons granulated sugar and hazelnuts in a food processor until the hazelnuts are very finely chopped, like almond meal. You could also grind them in a coffee or spice grinder in a couple batches. When ground, transfer to a mixing bowl and stir in the remaining 2¾ cups granulated sugar, the cornstarch, cocoa powder, and egg whites. Mix well. Transfer the mixture to a piping bag (or a zipper-lock bag that you can cut a corner from), seal shut, and refrigerate until bake time or for up to 2 days. Remove the glaze from the refrigerator at least 1 hour before bake time to take the chill off.

Preheat the oven to 325°F.

Cut about a ⅜-inch opening at the top of your piping bag. The glaze will be thick and somewhat stiff. Pipe the glaze in a spiral in an even layer over the tops of the loaves, not covering them completely but making a sort of Jewish yarmulke on top. You want about a ⅜-inch-thick layer of glaze on top. Just let it run down the loaves for 10 to 15 minutes.

ADD TOPPINGS. Scatter the pearl sugar evenly over each loaf, then scatter the lightly crushed hazelnuts evenly over each loaf. Finally, the loaves are ready to bake!

BAKE. Load the loaves in the oven. No steam. No fan. Bake for 60 minutes. Do not rotate or otherwise move as they bake, even if your oven has hot spots. This dough is a very delicate foam, and you don't want it to collapse after all your hard work.

When this dough bakes perfectly, the oven spring will last a really long time: the loaves will be concave at first and then fill in vertically. The top of the dome will be the last bit to puff up. If you have too much glaze on top, the bread may rise around the center and a little bit of the dome may be bare: that's okay. If you absolutely must rotate the loaves for even browning, only do it during the last 10 minutes of baking. Don't dare move the loaves during the first 45 minutes. When done, the panettone glaze should be golden brown and crisp on top.

Before the loaves are finished baking, set up your panettone hanging station. Milk crates work well if the skewers are long enough because you can hang each panettone inside one. Or you can position two sturdy boxes or chairs near each other and hang the panettone between them. Whatever you're using, test it to make sure it works with your skewers, is sturdy, and is ready to go when the loaves are fully baked. As they come out of the oven, swiftly but gently invert each loaf and hang it by its skewers.

That's it! Leave the panettone alone for *at least* 3 hours. They've been through a lot. After that, you can take down the hanging station but still try not to cut into the panettone for a few more hours. The crumb is still setting up. But, at this point, you've been through a lot, too. Do what you want. The panettone will keep for a few weeks at room temperature wrapped tight in plastic wrap or a nice plastic bag. You can also freeze it in an airtight bag for a couple months. Thaw at room temperature. *HAPPY HOLIDAYS.*

OPTIONS

The temperature of the spot that the starter and dough rise in is critical. You want an environment that's 88° to 90°F. Any hotter than that and the dough may overproof and spill out of the container. Any cooler, and it may take so long to proof that the dough becomes too sour tasting. If your proofing temp is 85°F or cooler, add 30 grams honey instead of 15 grams honey to impasto 2 to counteract the sourness.

Our standard inclusions are chocolate and orange. We use a mix of 275 grams dark chocolate pistoles (or chunks) and 175 grams chopped candied orange peel, along with 10 grams orange blossom water in place of the 10 grams water in impasto 2. You could also use golden raisins, dried cherries, or chopped dried apricots for the fruit. Or use another type of chocolate or confection. For test batches, my standard inclusion is leftover Halloween candy such as chopped Snickers.

To make **Panettone with Zabaione**, combine 2 large egg yolks, 2 half-eggshells of sugar, and 2 half-eggshells of Marsala or Muscat wine (or use half alcohol and half orange juice) in a heatproof bowl. A copper bowl works best, but you can also use the top of a double boiler. Whisk vigorously until the mixture is thick and pale yellow, 2 to 3 minutes. Set the bowl over a saucepan of barely simmering water. Whisk constantly until the mixture takes on enough air to triple in volume, thicken slightly, and fall in sheets when the whisk is lifted. It should register 145° to 150°F on an instant-read thermometer and take about 5 minutes of whisking over the hot water. Serve with slices of the panettone.

NORTH AMERICAN REGIONAL SOURCES FOR GRAINS AND FLOURS

Some of these sources are farmers, some are millers, some are bakers. The Whole Grains Council website also has a local grains map for farms, mills, and malt houses. For other baking supplies, visit restaurant supply stores or websites like Breadtopia and King Arthur Flour.

Northeast

Beiler's Heritage Acres, Lebanon, PA
Castle Valley Mill, Doylestown, PA
Champlain Valley Milling Corporation, Westport, NY
Elmore Mountain Bread, Wolcott, VT
Farmer Ground Flour, Trumansburg, NY
Maine Grains, Skowhegan, ME
Nitty Gritty Grain Company, Charlotte, VT
Small Valley Milling, Halifax, PA
Weatherbury Farm, Avella, PA

Mid-Atlantic

Next Step Produce, Newburg, MD
Seylou, Washington, DC

Southeast

Anson Mills, Columbia, SC
Bellegarde Bakery, New Orleans, LA
Boulted Bread, Raleigh, NC
Carolina Ground, Asheville, NC
DaySpring Farms, Danielsville, GA
Independent Baking Company, Athens, GA
Louismill, Louisville, KY
The Comerian, Comer, GA
Weisenberger Mill, Midway, KY

Southwest

Barton Springs Mill, Dripping Springs, TX
BKW Farms, Marana, AZ
Blue Grouse Bread, Norwood, CO
Dry Storage, Boulder, CO
Grateful Bread, Golden, CO
Hayden Flour Mills, Queen Creek, AZ
Mountain Mama Milling, Monte Vista, CO

Midwest

Breadtopia, Fairfield, IA
Lonesome Stone Milling, Lone Rock, WI
The Mill at Janie's Farm, Ashkum, IL
Whole Grain Milling Company, Welcome, MN

Northwest

Bluebird Grain Farms, Winthrop, WA
Cairn Springs Mill, Burlington, WA
Camas Country Mill, Junction City, OR
Fairhaven Organic Flour Mill, Burlington, WA
Island Grist, Lopez Island, WA
Lonesome Whistle Farm, Junction City, OR
Nash's Organic Produce, Sequim, WA
Nootka Rose Milling, Metchosin, British Columbia, Canada
Northwest Mills, Skagit Valley, WA

West

Capay Mills, Rumsey, CA
Community Grains, Oakland, CA
Grist and Toll, Pasadena, CA
Hillside Grain, Bellevue, ID
The Mill, San Francisco, CA

SELECTED BIBLIOGRAPHY

Books

Basey, Marleeta F. *Flour Power*. Salem, OR: Jermar Press, 2004.

Beard, James. *Beard on Bread, Reprint Edition*. New York: Knopf, 1995.

Clayton, Bernard. *Bernard Clayton's New Complete Book of Breads*. New York: Simon & Schuster, 1987.

Corriher, Shirley. *BakeWise*. New York: Scribner, 2008.

Field, Carol. *The Italian Baker, First Revised Edition*. Berkeley, CA: Ten Speed Press, 2011.

Forkish, Ken. *Flour, Water, Salt, Yeast*. Berkeley, CA: Ten Speed Press, 2012.

Hamelman, Jeffrey. *Bread, Second Edition*. Hoboken, NJ: Wiley & Sons, 2012.

Joachim, David, and Andrew Schloss. *The Science of Good Food*. Toronto: Robert Rose, 2008.

Katz, Sandor Ellix. *The Art of Fermentation*. White River Junction, VT: Chelsea Green Publishing, 2012.

Lahey, Jim. *The Sullivan Street Bakery Cookbook*. New York: W. W. Norton & Company, 2017.

Leader, Daniel. *Living Bread*. New York: Avery Publishing, 2019.

McGee, Harold. *On Food and Cooking*. New York: Scribner, 2004.

Miscovich, Richard. *From the Wood-Fired Oven*. White River Junction, VT: Chelsea Green Publishing, 2013.

Myhrvold, Nathan, and Francisco Migoya. *Modernist Bread*. Bellevue, WA: The Cooking Lab, 2017.

Ortiz, Joe. *The Village Baker*. Berkeley, CA: Ten Speed Press, 1993.

Quinn, Bob, and Liz Carlisle. *Grain by Grain: A Quest to Revive Ancient Wheat, Rural Jobs, and Healthy Food*. Washington, DC: Island Press, 2019.

Reinhart, Peter. *Crust and Crumb*. Berkeley, CA: Ten Speed Press, 1998.

——. *The Bread Baker's Apprentice*. Berkeley, CA: Ten Speed Press, 2001.

Robertson, Chad. *Tartine Book No. 3*. San Francisco: Chronicle Books, 2013.

Rubel, William. *Bread: A Global History*. London: Reaktion Books, 2011.

Vetri, Marc. *Mastering Pasta*. Berkeley, CA: Ten Speed Press, 2015.

——. *Mastering Pizza*. Berkeley, CA: Ten Speed Press, 2018.

Articles

Adler, Jerry. "Artisanal Wheat on the Rise." *Smithsonian Magazine*. December 2011.

Barber, Dan. "Save Our Food. Free the Seed." *New York Times*. June 7, 2019.

Curtis, B. C., S. Rajaram, H. Gómez Macpherson. "Bread Wheat." *Food and Agriculture Organization of the United Nations*. Rome, 2002.

Czerny, Michael, and Peter Schieberle. "Important Aroma Compounds in Freshly Ground Wholemeal and White Wheat Flour—Identification and Quantitative Changes During Sourdough Fermentation." *Journal of Agricultural Food Chemistry* 50, no. 23 (October 2002).

Di Cagno, Raffaella, Maria De Angelis, Paola Lavermicocca, Massimo De Vincenzi, Claudio Giovannini, Michele Faccia, and Marco Gobbetti. "Proteolysis by Sourdough Lactic Acid Bacteria: Effects on Wheat Flour Protein Fractions and Gliadin Peptides Involved in Human Cereal Tolerance." *Applied and Environmental Microbiology* 68, no. 2 (February 2002).

Hartwig, Pam, and Mina R. McDaniel. "Flavor Characteristics of Lactic, Malic, Citric, and Acetic Acids at Various pH Levels." *Journal of Food Science* 60, no. 2 (March 1995).

Hrušková, Marie, and Dana Machová. "Changes of Wheat Flour Properties During Short Term Storage." *Czech Journal of Food Sciences* 20, no. 4 (2002).

Jones, Stephen. "Kicking the Commodity Habit." *Gastronomica: The Journal of Food and Culture* 12, no. 3 (Fall 2012).

McWilliams, Margaret, and Andrea C. Mackey. "Wheat Flavor Components." *Journal of Food Science* 34, no. 6 (November 1969).

Pico, Joana, José Bernal, and Manuel Gómez. "Wheat Bread Aroma Compounds in Crumb and Crust: A Review." *Food Research International* 75 (September 2015).

Robbins, Jim. "A Perennial Search for Perfect Wheat." *New York Times*. June 5, 2007.

Wink, Debra. "Lactic Acid Fermentation in Sourdough." *Bread Lines, a Publication of The Bread Bakers Guild of America* 15, no. 4 (December 2007).

ACKNOWLEDGMENTS

From Marc Vetri

We dedicated this book to our grain community around Philadelphia and around the country, and these tireless, passionate people are at the heart of it all. Among them, Josey Baker, Mark and Fran Fischer, Graison Gill, Steve Jones, Tom and David Kenyon, Steve Scott, Brett Stevenson, Harold Wilken and Jill Brockman-Cummings, Kelly Whitaker, Jim Williams, and so many others . . . thank you for telling us your stories. Your work in wheat breeding, grain farming, flour milling, bread baking, and community building has made better bread available to everyone . . . something we should all be thankful for.

Claire, when you walked into our lives here at Vetri, it changed us forever. We couldn't have found a better partner to help launch our grain program, and the evolution that unfolded while you were here still pushes us forward. I can't imagine having co-authored this book with anyone else.

Dave, you are my soul brother in music and in writing. You somehow transform my words into melodies, which help my ideas become realities. What should we write next?!

Ed, you managed to capture the beauty of tans and browns in a way that few photographers can, and you did it under pressure, with composure. Grazie!

Emma, Betsy, Kelly, Aaron and the rest of the team at Ten Speed Press, you guys are the best in the biz. Thanks again for keeping quality at the top of the priority list, especially during a tough time.

From Claire Kopp McWilliams

Thank you to my work dad, my mentor, Marc. You supported me from the minute we met—often with a confidence that I couldn't understand. It means the world to me.

Thank you to Dave, my unlicensed therapist and the man who really made the book work. I never would have tried to write a cookbook without the encouragement of both you and Marc, and in the end, I'm so grateful that we wrote it.

Thank you to all my Vetri coworkers and to my amazing Philly baker friends—especially Chris DiPiazza of Mighty Bread Company and Pete Merzbacher of Philly Bread—for sharing your bakeries with me, and to the wonderful supporters of Ursa Bakery—you all keep me inspired when the alarm clock is getting me down. For that matter, I am incredibly grateful for the camaraderie of bakers all over the country.

And thank you, I love you, to my support network—my partner Zach, my awesome family, and my community of brilliant friends. It's good to be together.

From David Joachim

Marc, it looks like the "dough trilogy" is complete. Thank you for walking me through the ins and outs of making amazing panettone.

Claire, you have the patience of a rock. For all the hours we spent analyzing the minutiae of stuff you do instinctively on a daily basis—I can't thank you enough. You've made me a better baker, and if I've done my job, that sentiment will be shared among everyone baking from this book.

Lisa and Sally Ekus, here's to the birth of yet another beautiful baby!

Thanks to those who offered feedback and insight during recipe testing and tasting, including Ariel Einhorn, Lauren Sylvester, Louis Manza, Jacob Rozenberg, Matt Buehler, Matt Rodrigue, Mike and Erica Yozell, Keith Plunkett, Christine Fennessy, Alec Ackerman, Andy Schloss, Christine Bucher, and August and Maddox Joachim. You last three: I don't know how you put up with umpteen bags of grains, starters on windowsills, flour everywhere, and doughs all over our house. You are saints, and I am grateful.

SPAGHETTI AGLIO E OLIO

MAKES 3 SERVINGS

**15 minutes active time
over 20 minutes**

I bet you're wondering what this pasta recipe is doing here. Simple. I've been waiting to put it into a book! At home, I make pasta *aglio e olio* more than any other dish, but the recipe never made it into one of my books. So here it is. Use any of the great crusty breads in this book to scoop up all that leftover sauce! —MV

8¾ ounces spaghetti

4 cloves garlic, finely chopped

½ cup extra-virgin olive oil

¼ cup chopped flat-leaf parsley

1 tablespoon colatura (Italian fish sauce)

Pinch of red chile flakes

Pinch of freshly ground black pepper

Cook the pasta in salted boiling water until it is still firm to the bite. Drain, reserving the pasta water.

Meanwhile, in a large deep sauté pan over medium-high heat, simmer the garlic in the oil until the garlic is soft and tan in color but not browned, just a minute or two. Add the parsley and fry it in the garlic and oil for about 20 seconds. Add the colatura, ¾ cup of the reserved pasta water, the chile flakes, and pepper. Continue simmering for 2 to 3 minutes to cook off some of the water.

Add the drained pasta and finish cooking it in the pan, stirring like mad to release some starch and blend it with the water in the pan. The goal is to marry the pasta and sauce in a bond of creaminess. If the pan looks dry, add a little pasta water and/or oil, so the bottom of the pan still has a thin layer of creamy sauce.

Twirl the pasta artfully onto the plate and serve.

INDEX

Library of Congress Cataloging-in-Publication Data
Names: Vetri, Marc, author. | McWilliams, Claire Kopp, 1985- author. |
        Joachim, David, author. | Anderson, Ed (Edward Charles), photographer.
Title: Mastering bread : the art and practice of handmade sourdough,
        yeasted bread, and pastry / Marc Vetri and Claire Kopp McWilliams with
        David Joachim ; photography by Ed Anderson.
Description: First edition. | Emeryville : Ten Speed Press, 2020. |
        Includes bibliographical references and index.
Identifiers: LCCN 2020013296 (print) | LCCN 2020013297 (ebook) |
        ISBN 9781984856982 (hardcover) | ISBN 9781984856999 (ebook)
Subjects: LCSH: Bread. | Cooking (Sourdough) | Pastry. | Cooking (Bread). |
        LCGFT: Cookbooks.
Classification: LCC TX769 .V47 2020 (print) | LCC TX769 (ebook) |
        DDC 641.81/5—dc23
LC record available at https://lccn.loc.gov/2020013296
LC ebook record available at https://lccn.loc.gov/2020013297

Hardcover ISBN: 978-1-9848-5698-2
eBook ISBN: 978-1-9848-5699-9

Printed in China

Photo on page 13 by Janine Johnson, The Bread Lab; page 30 by Liam Migdail,
Pennsylvania Farm Bureau; page 43 by Brett Stevenson; page 76 by Emily Kenyon;
page 109 by Catherine Scott; page 144 by Theo and Theresa Morrison; and
page 182 by John Merkle.

Design by Betsy Stromberg
Prop styling by Maeve Sheridan

10 9 8 7 6 5 4 3 2 1

First Edition